ASSOCIATE REFORMED PRESBYTERIAN

DEATH AND MARRIAGE NOTICES

FROM

The Christian Magazine of the South

The Erskine Miscellany AND

The Due West Telescope

1843–1863

COMPILED

BY

Lowry Ware

HERITAGE BOOKS
2021

HERITAGE BOOKS

AN IMPRINT OF HERITAGE BOOKS, INC.

Books, CDs, and more—Worldwide

For our listing of thousands of titles see our website
at
www.HeritageBooks.com

Published 2021 by
HERITAGE BOOKS, INC.
Publishing Division
5810 Ruatan Street
Berwyn Heights, Md. 20740

Heritage Books by the author:

Associate Reformed Presbyterian Death and Marriage Notices from The Christian Magazine
of the South, The Erskine Miscellany, *and* The Due West Telescope, *1843–1863*

Associate Reformed Presbyterian Death and Marriage Notices, Volume II: 1866–1888

Associate Reformed Presbyterian Death and Marriage Notices, Volume IV, 1897–1902

Chapters in the History of Abbeville County: The "Banner County" of South Carolina

Old Abbeville: Scenes of the Past of a Town Where Old Time Things Are Not Forgotten

International Standard Book Number
Paperbound: 978-0-7884-0975-2

Preface

The Associate Reformed Presbyterians of the South sponsored two periodicals before the Civil War. Although endorsed by the Associate Reformed Synod of the South, both were published by individual ministers without any financial support from the Synod. The earliest of these was *The Christian Magazine of the South*, a monthly founded and edited by the Rev. James Boyce in 1843. It was issued from his home in Winnsboro, S. C. until December, 1851.

The second publication, a weekly which enjoyed the blessing of the Synod of the South, was founded in Due West in 1851 by the Rev. J. I. Bonner and his brother-in-law, the Rev. J. O. Lindsay. It was first titled *The Erskine Miscellany,* but within a year the Rev. Lindsay withdrew from the venture, and the title was changed to *The Due West Telescope.*

These publications regularly carried death and marriage notices until the *Telescope* was suspended due to the pressures of the war in 1863. The style of the death notices was influenced by the Associate Reformed Synod's views on burial services. Its *Book of Worship* warned that the services were to be carried out "without unnecessary ceremony" and were to be "free from injudicious eulogies, and confined mainly to the improvement of the occasion and the providence of God to the living" (found in the *Minutes of Synod,* 1899, p. 393).

Sometimes there was unusual detail, and I have included some stories which have special human interest and others which were clearly intended as warning of how sudden and uncertain death may be. For example, see page 81.

The file of *The Christian Magazine of the South* is complete; unfortunately, that of *The Erskine Miscellany/ The Due West Telescope* is very incomplete. These files are located at Bowie Divinity Hall, Erskine Theological Seminary and McCain Library, Erskine College.

Lowry Ware

The Christian Magazine
of the South

I(January, 1843), 32.

Departed this life on Steel Creek, York District, S. C. on the morning of Sabbath, 11th December, Mrs. **Clementina Boyce**, wife of William Boyce.

Departed this life on Little River, Fairfield District, on the morning of Friday, the 13th instant, Mrs. **Margaret Brice**, wife of Robert Brice, in the 42nd year of her age. ... She left a husband and a large family of children.

I(February, 1843), 64.

Died at Chesterville, S. C. on the 15th day of November, 1842 of consumption, Dr. **Charles Strong Moffatt** in the 31st year of his age. ... He took his degree of A. B. at Jefferson College, Pa. with distinction in September, 1833 and in April, 1837, after completing his medical education, he located himself at Chesterville, where he continued to practice until a few weeks.

I(March, 1843), 96.

Departed this life on Coddle Creek, N. C. on the 12th of February, **Isaac Newton**, son of Rev. John G. and Martha H. **Witherspoon**, aged one year.

Died at his residence on Rocky Creek, Chester District, S. C. on the 14th of January, 1843, **Francis Wylie** in the 93d year of his age. He was a soldier in "the Revolutionary war," and had a share in most of the battles in South Carolina, especially in the backcountry. He has been an exemplary member of the Associate Reformed Church for more than half a century.

I(April, 1843), 128.

The subject of the following notice is Mrs. **Nancy Strong**, widow of the late Rev. Charles Strong and daughter of Capt. John Harris of York District, S. C., who departed this life on the 8th November last in the 48th year of her age at her residence in Mecklenburg, N. C.

I(June, 1843), 192.

Died at his residence in Chester District from the effect of measles, Major **John Moore**, on the evening of the 17th March in the 40th year of his age.

I(August, 1843), 255-256.

Departed this life on May 8th in Mecklenburg Co., N. C., Mrs. **Elizabeth**

Grier, wife of Arthur Grier and daughter of James Irvin, aged 30 years and 2 months. ... The deceased has left a husband and two small children.

Died at his residence near Portersville, Tenn. on the evening of the 30th May after a severe illness of six weeks, **William Simonton**, in the 53d year of his age. ... So far as lay influence was concerned, he exerted a more effective instrumentality, from first to last, in building up the Associate Reformed Church in this place, than perhaps any other individual. His efforts and prayers were crowned with success, in evidence of which it will suffice to say that a congregation, consisting of nearly one hundred and fifty members, with a settled minister, occupies the spot where the deceased, with three or four brethren, drew up the first petition for supplies from Synod only ten years ago.

At Clarke's Ford, York District, on the morning of 11th June, died **John McElwee**, in the 78th year of his age. ... member of Session.... Eight or ten years before his death, the congregation to which he was attached and several others of the same denomination, being dissatisfied with their existing ecclesiastical relations, were taken under the care of the 1st Associate Reformed Presbytery of the Carolinas.

I(November, 1843), 351-352.

Died at his residence in Cobb Co., Ga. on the 9th June, 1843, **Robert Meek**, aged seventy seven years, eight months and five days. He was the son of Adam and Elizabeth Meek of North Carolina. His father was an elder of Rev. Archibald's congregation at Poplar Tent meeting house [He and his parents left that church over the introduction of Watt's version of the Psalms and came under the pastoral care of Rev. James McNight, in the congregation of Gilead, in Mecklenburg County]. The subject of this memoir and his brother James were both elders in this pastoral charge of Rev. McNight, as well as their father. ... While living in Hall County, Georgia, which was his home from Jan. 17th, 1824, till about three years ago, when he removed to Cobb County, he had no association with brethren of his own branch of the church, only as he visited a congregation in Newton County about fifteen miles distant.

Died after a short illness at her own residence on King's Creek, Newberry District, S. C. in the month of August last, Mrs. **Margaret Erskine**, aged about seventy five. ... from early life a consistent member of the Associate Reformed Church.

Died in August last in Newberry District, S. C., Mrs. **Martha Clarey**, wife of Capt. James Clarey and daughter of Rev. John and Jane Renwick, in the 29th year of her age. She had for several years been a consistent member of the Associate Reformed Church.

Died in August last in Newberry District, S. C., Miss **Gracey Clarey**, daughter of John and Jane Clarey in the sixteenth year of her age.

Died at his residence in the town of Portersville, Tipton Co., Tenn. on the 18th of February last of a protracted illness, Mr. **Robert Hood** in the 56th year of his age.

II(January, 1844), 30-32.

Died at his residence in Lancaster District, S. C., on 8th September last, **David Lathen**[Lathan], Esq., in the 60th year of his age. ...For a long time previous to his death, he had acted a ruling elder in Tirzah congregation.

Died at his residence near Hopewell, Maury County, Tenn., on the 11th September, **Robert Matthews**, in the 68th year of his age. ... For 38 years he had been a member of the A. R. Church and had been a ruling elder 23 years... two surviving daughters.

Departed this life on 17th October near Due West Corner, Abbeville District, S. C., an **infant** son of Rev. David and Lethe Ann **Pressly**, aged about two weeks.

It becomes our duty to announce the death of the Rev. **Isaac Grier**, D. D., which occurred at his residence in Mecklenburg County, N. C., on the afternoon of the 2d of November. ... He was born in Greene Co., Georgia, in the eventful year of 1776, being the first Presbyterian minister born in that state, and was baptized by an itinerating Covenanter minister, the Rev. Mr. Martin, in Cabarrus Co., N. C., where his father had taken refuge from the more dangerous hostilities on the frontier. ...He received his academical education under the Rev. Messrs. Cunningham and Cummins, who conducted an academy in Georgia. He graduated in 1800 at Dickinson College, Carlisle, Pa., under the presidency of the distinguished Dr. Nesbit. In the absence of theological seminaries, there being none at that time in the United States, he prosecuted his theological studies under the Rev. Mr. Porter, the pastor of Long Cane, Abbeville District, S. C., and received license Sept. 2, 1802. In 1804, he was ordained at Sardis, Mecklenburg, N. C., and installed pastor of that congregation in connection with Providence and Waxhaus [sic], each place receiving one third of his labors, it being a provision in the meantime that the latter place, in consequence of the distance, should be stricken off as soon as another more convenient congregation should be substituted. Accordingly, in 1808, Steel Creek, having been demitted by Mr. Blackstocks, was taken under his pastoral superintendence in place of Waxhaw. In 1815, having resigned his charge at Providence, he divided his time equally between Sardis and Steel Creek, and so continued their pastor until resignation in 1842. ...It deserves to be recorded, not so much in praise of the deceased, as an example worthy of imitation by surviving ministers, that perhaps nowhere in the Southern Synod has there been so happy an influence exerted among the colored people, as put forth by him among those in the limits of his charge--many of whom are now professing Christians, claiming him as their spiritual father. . . . his ministry was blessed in another channel. . . . about two thirds of the ministers and probationeers now constituting the First Presbytery, were brought up under his ministerial charge....

Departed this life on the 7th November on Little River, Fairfield District, **Isabella Kilpatrick**, daughter of Thomas Kilpatrick, aged 23 years and 5 months.

II(February, 1844), 63-64.

Departed this life on the 7th of October, 1843, Mrs. **Mary Lowrey**, in the 67th year of her life, leaving an aged husband and numerous family and children and grandchildren to feel her loss. She was many years a member of the Church at Ebenezer, Jessamine Co, Ky.

On November 2d, Mrs. **Amelia Steele**, advanced in life and for many years a member in Ebenezer, where she has witnessed a good profession.

December 24th--Mrs. **Nancy C. Drake**, (a sister of Mrs. Lowrey) in the 64th year of her age. She too was long a member of Ebenezer congregation.... left early a widow, the care of a large family devolved upon her.

Died of congestive fever on Little Rocky Creek, Chester District, on the 13th October, 1843, **Hugh Henry**, in the 21st year of his age.

II(April, 1844), 128.

Departed this life on the 28th of February in Mecklenburg, N. C., **Elam B. Boyce**, aged twenty six years. His illness was of short duration, but 48 hours.

Also, on the 23d February, after a short illness, **Mary G. Boyce**, daughter of Wm. Boyce, in the 7th year of her age.

II(May, 1844), 160.

Departed this life on the 2nd of March, at the residence of Dr. George Pressly, Abbeville, Dr. **William A. Smith**. His disease was scarlet fever. He was a young gentleman of talents, of fine literary attainments, and an excellent physician.

Died at the residence of her mother near Lowndesville, Abbeville District,

S. C. on the 10th of October, 1843, Miss **Elvira Pressly**, in the 20th year of her age. ...member of the Associate Reformed Church at Generostee, Anderson District.

Departed this life on the 10th of March, near Moffattsville, Anderson District, an **infant** daughter of Rev. J. C. and M. L. S. **Chalmers**, aged two months.

Died on Coddle Creek, Cabarrus Co., N. C., on the 13th of February, **Caleb Ross**, aged about 5 years.

Also, on the 16th of February, **Isaac G.** and **Joseph Ross**; the former aged about seven years, the latter about eleven years; the children of Robert and Jane Ross. They all died of scarlet fever. In four days these parents buried three of their children. Two of them in one day.

Died at his residence in Cabarrus Co., N. C., on the 25th of January last, **Isaiah Dewese**, in the 80th year of his age. He left an aged widow and twelve children, all of whom were present to witness his departure, having previously buried two children. For more than fifty years he has been a consistent member of the Presbyterian Church.

Departed this life in Rowan Co., N. C., on the 28th of February last, Mr. **Wm. Hall**, in the 82d year of his age. He was a consistent member of the Associate Reformed Church for many years, though placed at a distance of twenty three miles from a church of that denomination.

Departed this life at her residence in Shelby Co., Tenn., on the 24th of January, Mrs. **Martha Thomas**, wife of John M. Thomas, after a protracted illness. The deceased was a native of Mecklenburg, N. C., but spent the last sixteen years of her life in the place where she died. ... She left a husband and six children.

II(June, 1844), 192.

Departed this life March 21st, 1844, Mrs. **Sarah Eliza Reid**, in the 27th year of her age. She and her husband, Shannon Reid, Esq., had united with the Associate Reformed Church in Shelbyville, Ky., at the last communion which was held there for some years, previous to the application for ordinances, which was made to the Synod of the South. ... She left three children behind her, too young to know their loss. Her two eldest had gone before her to the land of spirits. She was the last of her father's house.

Died near Portersville, Tenn., on the 23d of November, 1843, Mrs. **Margaret McCain**, in the 87th year of her age. The deceased had been an exemplary member of the Associate Reformed Church at Tirzah, in Waxhaw, from its first organization, whence she removed in 1839.

II(July, 1844), 224.

Died of scarlet fever at Lowndesville, Abbeville District, S. C. on the 4th April, **James Chalmers**, son of L. W. and Matilda L. **McAlister**, aged 2 years, 8 months and 6 days.

Died at Coddle Creek, N. C. on 6th April, Mrs. **Margaret Cochran**, wife of Robert Cochran, Jr., aged 35 years and 8 months. Mrs. Cochran was a daughter of Mr. **Adam Ross**, an elder in the church at Coddle Creek, who also died on the 4th November last.

Died in Maury Co., Tenn., April 5, 1844, Mrs. Jane R. Harris, wife of **Henry Harris,** and daughter of Alexander Baldridge, aged 30 years, 2 months and 7 days. ... She left a disconsolate husband and three small children.

II(September, 1844), 287-288.

Died at his residence in Chester District, S. C. on the 1st day of May, 1844, **William F. Moffatt**, in the 47th year of his age. The deceased had been in close communion with the Associate Reformed Church from early youth; and ten years since, he was elected to the office of ruling elder in the congregation of Hopewell. ... He left a wife and numerous family.

Departed this life, May 1st, in the 28th year of her age, **Nancy Louisa Hood**, only daughter of Wm. Reed, Esq. and Margaret Reed. She was married in her 14th year, soon after which, she was admitted to full communion in the Associate Church, Shiloh, Lancaster District, S. C. ..[at her death bed] five of them [her children] were brought to her bed-side where she addressed herself to each according to its age and capacity.

Died in Yorkville on the 24th May, **Eli Anderson McElwee**, in the 22d year of his age. His illness was protracted and severe--from childhood.

Died in Lancaster District, on Saturday, June 29th, in the 23d year of his age, of congestive fever, **William P. Craig**, eldest son of James D. and Elizabeth Craig.

II(October, 1844), 320.

Died on the 4th of July last at his late residence in Jefferson Co., Ga., **Thomas McBride**, in the 80th year of his age. The subject of the following notice was born in Ireland, whence his parents emigrated to this country, when he was about five years of age and settled in Jefferson County, Georgia, where he remained up to the day of his death. He was a member of the Associate Reformed Church.

Died in Holmes Co., Miss., on the 10th July, **Josiah**, son of Josiah and Martha **McCaw**, aged about seven years.

II(November, 1844), 352.

Died of congestive fever on the 31st of August, **Elizabeth Reid**, consort of Joseph Reid and daughter of John and Jane Clary. The subject of this notice has been for several years a member of the Associate Reformed Church at Head Spring, Newberry District, S. C. She left a husband and three children.

Died in Lancaster District, S. C. on September 1st in the 28th year of his age, **James Pringle Craig** of but little more than twelve hours of sickness. He left a disconsolate mother and only sister.

Departed this life in Lancaster District on the morning of September 20th in the 23d year of her age, **Jane Minerva**, wife of Capt. J. P. **Davis**, and eldest daughter of Col. J. W. and Martha L. Huey. She had a little brother and younger sisters.

II(December, 1844), 381-382.

It becomes our duty to announce the death of the Rev. **Joseph McCreary** of the Alabama Presbytery and **William Watt**, Esq. of Starkville, Miss., which occurred on the 23d of October on the Ohio River, a few miles below Portland. These brethren, in company with the Rev. James M. Young of Dallas County, Alabama; Rev. David Pressly of Starkville, Miss.; Rev. John Wilson and lady of Tipton, Tenn. and Wm. R. McCain, Elder of Mr. Wilson embarked on board the *Lucy Walker* on Wednesday afternoon, on their return from Synod, which had closed its session in Jessamine Co., Kentucky the Thursday preceding--and in less than an hour afterwards, the three boilers burst with horrific effect, dealing death and destruction around. ...From a letter of Mr. Wilson (who escaped unhurt), in the *Protestant and Herald*, written the 26th October, at New Albany, Indiana, we learn the result of this awful catastrophe to our friends was--the death of Mr. Watt and Mr. McCreary, the former being killed instantly, the latter dying shortly after he was taken to a house--the infliction of wounds upon Messrs. Young, McCain and Pressly--the two former being badly injured, the latter having his hands badly scalded. The wounded were taken by Capt. Durham to New Albany, five miles up the river on the Indiana side, where they were kindly treated by the hospitable citizens.

Christian Magazine of the South

III(January, 1845), 31-32.

Died at Due West Corner of inflammation of the brain on the 5th June last, **Francis George**, son of Rev. J. N. and E. A. **Young**, in his second year.

Departed this life at Due West Corner on the 23d of September last of pulmonic consumption, **Elizabeth Jane**, wife of Rev. J. N. **Young**, leaving one child, an infant son, to feel her loss. The deceased was a native of the State of Ohio, in which she continued to reside until the Fall of 1841.

Died at her late residence in Burke County, Ga., on the 13th June last, Mrs. **Margaret Sarah Robinson**, consort of Mr. Wm. A. Robinson, junr. ..., in the thirty fifth year of her age. She was a member of the Associate Reformed Church. She was the daughter of Mr. Robert Patterson of Jefferson Co. ...an elder in our church.

Departed this life on Wednesday morning the 27th November at his residence on Little River, Fairfield District, **Charles Bell,** Esq., in the 61st year of his age. ...Mr. Bell had been from early life a member of the church. ...and for many years an elder.

Departed this life in Mecklenburg, N. C., on the morning of Sabbath the 8th December, **Deborah Boyce**, in the 64th year of her age.

Departed this life in Fairfield District on the 3d November, Mrs. **Jane Ghisolm**, in the 30th year of her age.

Also, on the 30th of the same month, **Samuel Ghisolm**, husband of the former.

Also, on the 27th December, **Jas. Brice, jr.**, in the 45th year of his age.

III(February, 1845), 63-64.

Died in Abbeville on the 20th February, 1844, Mrs. **Lucretia Kennedy**, wife of Isaac Kennedy, Esq.

On the 21st of May, Mrs. **Sarah Bradley**, the wife of Mr. Archibald Bradley.

On the 25th of June, Mrs. **Margaret Devlin**, the wife of Col. James Devlin, in the 59th year of her age.

On the 19th of August, Mrs. **Jane Little**, the wife of Mr. Archibald Little and daughter of Col. J. Devlin, in the 39th year of her age.

On the 20th of August, Mrs. **Jane Sanders**, the wife of Dr. John Sanders and grand-daughter of Col. J. Devlin.

On the 22d of August, Mrs. **Margaret Brown**, the wife of William Brown.

About the 24th of August, Mrs. **Margaret McFarland** (widow).

On the 16th of September, Mrs. **Jane Patton** (widow), of bilious fever, in the 48th year of her age.

On the 25th of October, Mrs. **Jane M. Kennedy**, the wife of Mr. Archibald Kennedy, of bilious colic, in the 42d year of her age.

On the 9th of November, **James Foster**, Esq., ruling elder, in the 65th year of his age.

On the 6th of December, Mrs. **Jane McDonald**, the wife of Wm. McDonald, Jr., and daughter of Matthew Brown, in the 27th year of her age.

On the 11th of February, Miss **Sarah W. Criswell**, daughter of Thomas Criswell, in the 24th year of her age.

Also, on the 5th of August, **Eliza Criswell**, a second daughter of Mr. T. Criswell's, in the 10th year of her age.

On the 21st of August, **John Lafayette Lindsay**, son of Joseph C. and Sarah Lindsay in the 2d year of his age.

The above named individuals were all in fellowship with the congregation of Cedar Spring and Long Cane, with the exception of the second daughter of Mr. Criswell and the son of Mr. Lindsay, who were baptized members. ... Other individuals connected with the church at Cedar Spring have likewise departed this life during the present year, but the date of their departure has not been ascertained, *viz.*, Mr. **Thomas Kown**, Mr. **Wm. Drennen, Senr.**, **Peter Cook**, son of Wm. Cook, and a little **daughter** of Dr. G. W. **Pressly's** (W. R. H[emphill]).

III(March, 1845), 95-96.

Died in Newberry District, S. C. on the 29th November last, Mr. **John Caldwell**, in the 72d year of his age. Mr. Caldwell had been a member of the Associate Reformed Church from early life; and a ruling elder in the congregation of Cannon Creek near forty years.

Died after a protracted illness at Newberry C. H. in the 24th year of her age, Mrs. Harriet **Summers**, consort of Major John W. Summers and daughter of Major Wm. and Mary Graham.

Died at his residence in Union County, N. C. on the 25th November, 1844, **Andrew McCain**, in the 80th year of his age. The deceased was a native of the county in which he died.

Died in York District, S. C. on the 15th ultimo., in the 29th year of her age, Mrs. **Eliza Killian**, wife of Henry Killian, and daughter of Robt. and Nancy Fee. ...[She is survived by] her husband.... three little children.

Departed this life in Mecklenburg County, N. C. on the 20th December, 1844, Mr. **John Witherspoon**, aged 69 years. ... He had for the last twenty years of his life acted as ruling elder in the congregation of Sardis.

Died in Tipton, Tenn., on the 18th of October, 1844, of congestive chill, **Mary Ann**, daughter of Joseph and Jane **Baird**, in the 10th year of her age.

III(April, 1845), 128.

Departed this life in Jessamine County, Kentucky on Tuesday, the 15th of October last, **Robert Gwynn, Senr.** He was an elder in Ebenezer Church. ... He was the father of a large family, every member of which he lived to see in connection with the church to which he himself belonged.

III(June, 1845), 190-192.

Died at his residence in Newton County, Ga., August 27th, 1844, **Samuel Thompson**, Esq., aged 36 years, 5 months, and 7 days. Having been brought to his bed, 25 days and 9 hours before his dissolution by a sudden and calamitous dispensation of Providence, his team having run off with him, breaking one leg and otherwise mangling his body very much.... He left a wife and five small children. ... was long a member and for some time a deacon in the Associate Reformed Church at Hopewell.

Death by Lightning-- Mrs. **Mary Foster**, the wife of the late James Foster, Esq. was struck by lightning on Wednesday, the 23d of April, and expired immediately. Mrs. Foster was in the 66th year of her age. She had long been a devoted and exemplary member of the Church at Cedar Spring, Abbeville District. At the time of her death, she was sitting alone, in the front room of her house, near to the fire place. The lightning descended the chimney, struck her head, destroying her cap--singeing her temple--injuring her right arm and breast, and descending her person, escaped by her right foot, tearing open the shoe vamp, even to the toe. Her son-in-law, A. P. Lessley, and family from Ohio, were in the adjoining room.

Died on Wednesday the 23d of April, **Ann**, eldest daughter of Thomas C. **McBryde**, aged about eleven years.

Died on Saturday, the 26th of April, Mr. **Matthew Brown**, formerly a member of the Cedar Spring congregation.

Died in February last, **James Harvey** and **Isaac Newton**, sons of M. Brown **Wallace**, Mecklenburg, N. C., one being 7 years, the other 9 years of age. They died within a few hours of each other--the disease being scarlet fever.

Died the 13th March, **Thomas A. W.**, infant son of Col. Wm. **Grier** and Feriba E. Grier of Steel Creek, N. C., aged about 10 months.

Also, on the 19th of the same month of the same disease, **Rufus A. W.**, son of Col. Grier and Feriba **Grier** in the 4th year of his age.

Departed this life December 28th, 1844, at Laurens C. H., S. C., **S. T. H. Todd**, in the 37th year of his age, leaving an aged mother and several brothers and a sister. He was a son of the late Dr. John Todd of this District. His attention was ... devoted to mercantile pursuits.

Died on the 19th of April last, Mr. **James Irwin**, in the 77th year of his age. The deceased was a ruling elder in the Associate Reformed Church.

III(July, 1845), 224.

Departed this life in Oktibbeha County, Miss., on Monday night, the 9th of June, **William C. Bell** (formerly of Fairfield, S. C.) aged about thirty five... [survived by] wife and three children....member of Associate Reformed Church at Starkville.

Died in Chester District, 11th June, **infant** son of Thos. G. and Jane **Bigham**.

III(August, 1845), 256.

Died May 8th, 1845, aged about eight years, **Mary Jane**, daughter of John **Fleming**, Laurens District.

Died, 19th May, 1845, in the 6th year of his age, **Robert McClintock**, son of John **Fleming**.

Departed this life at his residence near Monticello, Fairfield District, on the 2d of July, **William Bell, senr.**, in the 70th year of his age. ... He has left a wife and nine children.

Died some time in April last, Mr. **Reuben Hood,** in the 85th year of his age. ... member of A. R. Church at Sardis, N. C.

III(September, 1845), 288.

Died at his father's residence, Lancaster District, S. C., on the evening of the 5th June, **Robert Freeling**, in the 24th year of his age; and at the same place, on the morning of the 10th of June, **Alexander Boston**, in the 22d year of his age; sons of Robert and Nancy **Nelson**. ...Thus in a few days, were these aged parents bereft of two amiable sons, and Tirzah of two promising members.

Died on the 9th of June at his residence near Shelbyville, Ky., Col. **John Cunningham**, in the 58th year of his age. ...He had long been an elder in the Shelbyville congregation.... While temperately opposed to the ultra notions of the day as to slavery, he was a hearty co-worker in efforts for, the improvement of the conditions of servants, and especially for their religious instruction. ...All his children, four in number, were taken away from him.

Died 27th September, 1844, in Holmes Co., Miss., **Elizabeth Jane**, daughter of Thos. S. **Mealy**, aged 7 years.

Also, two days afterwards, **Sarah Ann**, daughter of the same, aged 6 years. The disease in both cases was congestive chill.

Died 26th July in York District, **Ross Velspasio**, infant son of Dr. J. **McKnight**, aged 10 months.

Died in Pike County, Missouri, **John Carroll**, September 30th, 1844, of violent fever. He had never made a public profession of his faith; but privately had declared his intention to do so by the first opportunity. Also, his sister, Mrs. **Cynthia Ann Findley**, April 22nd, 1845, of inflammation of the brain. ... She has left a bereaved husband and several children. ... Their only surviving parent is Joseph Carroll, formerly of York District, S. C.

III(October, 1845), 319-320.

Died on the 28th of July of chronic diarrhea, Mr. **John Porter**, in the 56th year of his age. ...[member of] A. R. Church at Steel Creek.

Died of congestive chill, 6th September,1844, **Margaret Grizelle Allen,** daughter of John and Margaret Allen [Tennessee] in the 15th year of her age.

Died in Burke County, Ga., on the 6th August, 1845, Mrs. **Eleanor L. Patterson**, aged 66 years and 3 days. ...About ten days before her dissolution, conscious of her approaching end, and the probability that, from the nature of her disease [cancer of the tongue], the faculty of speech might fail her, she requested that all the members of the family, white and black, should assemble around her bed. This done, she called each by name, at the same time extending her feeble hand, and bidding them an affectionate farewell.

Died near Louisville, Jefferson County, Ga., on the 6th of August, 1845, Mrs. **Margaret Manson**, in (perhaps) the fifty third year of her age. ...member of Associate Reformed Church .... She took a formal and affectionate leave of her children, (being a widow) earnestly exhorting them.

III(November, 1845), 351-352.

Died in Chester District on the 7th January, 1844, Mrs. **Katherine Guthrie**, wife of James Guthrie, Esq., and daughter of Ralph and Mary McFadden, in the 46th year of her age. ... member of A. R. Church at Union.

Died at his residence in Chester District, S. C., on the 9th day of April, 1845, **Christopher Strong**, Esq., in the 44th year of his age. The deceased had been a member of the Associate Reformed Church at Hopewell from early life. ...He put in nearly all the days of his church membership in the character of the church's financier, in which capacity he was of great service to the religious society of which he was a member.

Died at her residence in Chester District, S. C., on the 24th of August, 1845, Mrs. **Elizabeth McDaniel**, in the 83rd year of her age. The deceased was the relict of a brave Revolutionary soldier, Edward McDaniel, who was dangerously wounded in the "war for independence." She was born in "County Antrim, Ireland," but emigrated to this country in the 7th year of her age. She was married in the heat of that fearful war. ... She became the mother of her first child whilst the devouring cannon was still roaring... and had to struggle through a long life only partially assisted by her husband, whose wounds ... rendered him unfit to persue [sic] any severe manual employment.

Died the 16th of September, on Catawba River, York District, S. C., **Zillah B. Corethers**, wife of S. D. Corethers and daughter of Joseph and Nancy Miller, in the 30th year of her age, leaving three motherless children.

Died on the 25th of October, 1844, in the 22nd year of his age at Davidson College, **J. Mushatt G. Belk**, eldest son of Thomas Belk, Esq. and Lucinda Belk....At the time of his death, he was a member of the sophomore class, and was prosecuting his studies with a view to the ministry of the A. R. Church, in which communion he was brought up, his parents being members of Shiloh, Lancaster District, S. C.

Departed this life on the 28th August, near Mount Zion, Missouri, Mrs. **Mary Ann Ralston**, consort of Rev. S. S. Ralston, aged 26 years ...[leaves] four motherless children.

III(December, 1845), 381-382.

Departed this life, November 8th, 1845, Mrs. **Martha J. Gordon**, wife of Rev. N. M. Gordon, in the twenty fourth year of her age. ...She was the youngest child of the late James Harris, Esq. of Steel Creek, York Dist., S. C.

Died on the 8th of October of puerperal fever, **Eliza A.**, consort of William **McQuiston**, senr., in the 25th year of her age. ... member of Associate Reformed Church at Salem, Tipton County, Tenn.

Departed this life, October 24th in the 69th year of his age in Providence, N. C., Mr. **John Boyce** .... long been in communion with the Associate Reformed Church at Sardis and for many years a ruling elder. ... seven times did death come up into his dwelling and snatch away a beloved child. The wife of his bosom was long since called. ...

Died on the first inst. in the 31st year of his age, Mr. **James Bigham**, a ruling elder in the Associate Reformed Church, Steel Creek.... The deceased is the third ruling elder that has died in Sardis and Steel Creek, which constitute one pastoral charge during the present year.

Died on the 2nd of October at the residence of her son in Monroe Co., Ga., Mrs. **Margaret McDonald**, relict of John McDonald, in the 71st year of her age. ... during some fifty years was a consistent member at Generostee in Anderson District, S. C. Being left a widow with a large family and most of them young, she had to encounter many difficulties.

IV(January, 1846), 32.

Died at her residence in Abbeville District, S. C. on the 8th of July, Mrs. **Agness McQuirrens**. Mrs. McQuirrens was a native of Abbeville, and for a number of years previous to her departure, had been a worthy and consistent member of Cedar Spring congregation. She was about 48 years old and ... had lived a widow thirteen years.

Departed this life on Little River, Fairfield District, S. C., **James Bell**, son of Thomas Bell, in the 29th year of his age.

Died on Sabbath morning, October 19th, **Edmund**, son of Isaac **Kennedy**, Esq., aged about nine years.

IV(February, 1846), 63-64.

Departed this life at his residence in Starkville, Miss. on the 19th December last, **James Bell**, formerly of Fairfield, S. C., aged 37 years.

Died on the 14th December last, near Cedar Spring, Abbeville, S. C., **William H. Robinson**, in his 33rd year. ... member of A. R. Church.

Died May 25th, 1845 in the 22d year of her age, Mrs. **Emily Craig**, wife of Wm. P. Craig of Union County, N. C. ...It was but five months and four days before her death that she was seen the gay and rejoicing bride.

Departed this life on the 26th November last, after a short and painful illness, Mrs. **Mary Grier**, in the 55th year of her age. ...[early joined] the Associate church at Steel Creek.

IV(April, 1846), 128.

Departed this life on the 6th of January, 1846 at his residence in Iredell Co., N. C., the Rev. **John G. Witherspoon**, aged about thirty four or thirty five years. ... Mr. Witherspoon received his collegiate education at Jefferson College, Pa. and graduated in the Fall of 1831. ...[Ordained and installed pastor of the associated congregations of Gilead, Coddle Creek, and New Perth, N. C., in 1834, but retained Gilead only a few years].

Died on the 26th October, 1844, **Jemina Joanna**, daughter of Mr. A. and Sarah **Nelson**, aged 1 year, 9 months and 25 days.

Also, on 3rd November, 1845, **Robert Davis**, son of William A. and Sarah **Nelson**, aged 5 years and 9 days.

Also, on the 1st October, 1845, of pulmonary consumption, **Isabella**, consort of Robert M. **Nelson**, deceased, in the -- year of her age. ... member of Associate Reformed congregation at Salem [Tenn.] from its first organization.

IV(May, 1846), 159-160.

Died in Mecklenburg Co., N. C. on the 27th May, 1845, Mr. **John Wallace**, leaving an affectionate wife and five small children.

Departed this life in Mecklenburg Co., N. C., Mrs. **Catherine Wallace**, on the 11th June, 1845. [She lost her husband] about twenty years ago, at which time a large and helpless family came under her individual protection.

Mrs. **Margaret Smith**, who had come to lend a soothing hand to alleviate the sufferings of her mother, was seized with disease, and on the 17th of the same month was numbered with the dead.

On the 14th November of the same year, **Isaac Grier Wallace**, son of Catherine Wallace, departed this life.

On the 6th January, 1846, **Wm. Stanhope Wallace**, another son, departed this life, leaving one child and a disconsolate wife.

On the 20th January, 1846, **James McKnight Wallace**, the youngest son, departed this life, lamented by all. Thus within less than a year, a mother and daughter, three sons and a son in law were carried to the grave.

Departed this life in Mecklenburg Co., N. C. on the 19th March, Mrs. **Martha E. Neel**, wife of William Neel and daughter of Thomas and Margaret H. Hunter, in the 29th year of her age.

Departed this life March 25th, 1846, Mrs. **Matilda Elliotte**, wife of Cornelius T. Tribble, aged twenty four years and thirteen days. ... Member of Associate Reformed Church at Providence, Laurens District, S. C. ... She left a disconsolate husband and four small children.

IV(June, 1846), 192.

Died on 4th September last, **Rosanna Emiline**, daughter of Samuel and Ellen **Moffat** of Benton Co., Ala., aged 17 months.

IV(July, 1846), 224.

Died in Chester District, S. C. on the 3d of February, 1846, Miss **Anny Martha**, daughter of David and Sarah **Wilson**, in the 20th year of her age.

Died on the morning of the 30th of March, Mrs. **Hannah Oates**.

IV(August, 1846), 256.

Departed this life on the 27th of May at the residence of Hugh Simpson, Esq., Chester District, S. C., **William Lyle**, in the 28th year of his age. ... member of Associate Reformed Church at Union.

Christian Magazine of the South

IV(September, 1846), 287-288.

Died on the 13th December last, Mr. **Baily Ragan**, son of Mr. Young Ragan, deceased, aged about twenty years.

Died of pneumonia on the 13th of July, 1846, **Wm. Bonner**, in the 77th year of his age. ... elder in Associate Reformed Church. He spent the greater part of his life in Hopewell under the ministry of Dr. John Hemphill. About the year '33 or '34, he removed to Indiana, and became a member of the Session in Rev. W. Turner's charge. He remained there until the Spring of '43, when he removed to the bounds of the writer's charge [Rev. John Wilson in Salem, Tenn.] with a view of spending the remainder of his days with his only surviving daughter, Mrs. Thompson.

Died on the 3d December, 1845, at her residence in Hopewell, Maury Co., Tenn., **Sarah Scott**, in the 83d year of her age. The deceased, early in life became a member of the church, probably in Sharon, York District, S. C.; from which place she emigrated to the region in which she died. She was the wife of Samuel Scott, one of the first and most distinguished members of Hopewell.

Departed this life, January 6th, 1846, Mrs. **Mary Ann J. Marten**, wife of C. C. Marten and only daughter of Thomas and Margaret Galloway, in the 31st year of her age.

IV(November, 1846), 351-352.

Died at Due West Corner on Sabbath, the 27th September, 1846, after a short illness, **Henry L. Lindsay**, son of James and Polly Ann Lindsay in the seventeenth year of his age. ... for some time a student at Erskine College.

Died at the same place on Monday, the 28th of September, **Cornelius E. Lindsay**, brother of the former, in the fifteenth year of his age. ...like the former, had been for some time a student at Erskine College. ...Both were buried in the same grave.

Died at Cotton Plant, Miss. on the 4th August, Mrs. **Margaret Robinson**, consort of Rev. Pressly Robinson of Abbeville, S. C. and daughter of Capt. William Bonner of Wilcox Co., Ala. She had only three months previously [married].

Died in Wilcox Co., Ala. on 12th September, Mr. Enos **Crawford**, formerly of Cedar Spring, S. C. The deceased was about 70 years of age; for the last thirteen a resident of Alabama.

IV(December, 1846), 381-382.

Departed this life after a short illness at his residence in Abbeville District, **John Kennedy**, Esq., aged about 47 years. ... for some time an active and efficient ruling elder in the congregation of Cedar Spring and Long Cane.

Died, October 12th in the 24th year of her age, Mrs. **Deborah C. Ross**, wife of Robert Ross and step-daughter of Capt. Samuel Cox of Steel Creek, N. C.

Died, Mrs. **Margaret McFarland**, on the 5th of April, 1846, after an illness of two weeks, at the house of Mr. A. J. Weed, Abbeville District, S. C. Mrs. McFarland was about 75 years old. ... long in communion with the Associate Reformed Church at Cedar Spring and Long Cane.

Died on the 5th October, 1846 of congestive chill in the eighth year of her age, **Martha Weed**, daughter of Mr. Andrew J. Weed, Abbeville District, S. C.

Died in Tipton Co., Tenn. on Thursday the 15th October of consumption, Mrs. **Elizabeth Strong**, consort of William J. Strong, Esq., formerly of Chester District, S. C., in the 41st year of her age. ...For several years she had been a worthy member of the Associate Reformed Church of Salem.

Also, in the same vicinity, of flux on the 10th October, **Jane**, daughter of Joseph and Jane **Baird**, aged six years.

Died, April 12, 1843, **James Oliver**, aged 2 years, 1 month, and 13 days; March 6th, 1846, **Lucy Ann**, aged 1 month.

Also, September 24th, 1846, **Elijah Alexander**, aged 3 years, 3 months and 12 days; all the children of James and Elizabeth **Robertson,** of Anderson District, S. C.

Died, October 14th, 1846, at his father's residence, Elbert Co., Ga., **Angus M. Gordon**, aged about 21 years. ... He had returned only a short time from Kentucky (where he had spent two years in studies under the direction of his brothers, Revs. G. and N. M. Gordon) and made arrangements to repair to Erskine College at the commencement of the session in November following, with the expectation of entering the sophomore class. . . .while enjoying for a time, the society of his relatives and friends, he was taken with bilious fever.

V(January, 1847), 32.

Died of congestive fever, Lincoln Co., Tenn., the 16th September, 1846, **Mary Ann English**, daughter of Jas. E. and Sarah English, in her 16th year.

Died of bilious congestive fever, **James H. English**, brother of aforesaid Mary Ann English, on the 23d September, 1846, in his 7th year.

Died on the 4th October, 1846 of congestive fever, **Sarah English**, mother of the two above named in her 43d year. This lady had been an exemplary member of the Associate Reformed Church from early life. She was the youngest daughter of Henry Taylor, Senr. and united herself to the church when first organized in this place by the Rev. John T. Pressly, D. D., in 1819. She has left a husband and two children. Of this family, one half is taken, the other left.

Departed this life in Maury Co., Tenn., 23d August, Mrs. **Mary Davis**, wife of James Davis, in the 41st year of her age, leaving a husband and eight children. She is the fourth valuable member which the congregation of Hopewell has lost by death within the last year.

Died at the house of Mr. Samuel Cork, Fairfield District, on the 20th of November, 1846 of consumption, Miss **Martha Glover**. She was born of Christian parents in the County of Antrim, Ireland, and came into this country in the year 1837. She was admitted into the communion of the church in the Associate Reformed congregation of Ebenezer, Fairfield District- perhaps in the year 1838. Lived some time in Winnsboro' as an exemplary Christian in her station. The last two years of her life, she spent in Columbia, where it is supposed by confinement to mantua making, she lost her health, and with Samuel Cork where she ended her worldy career.

V(February, 1847), 63-64.

Died of puerperal fever on the 13th day of August, 1846, **Mary J. W. Dodds**, consort of Isaac Dodds and daughter of John and Margaret Allen, in the 20th year of her age. The deceased had been for several years a member of the Associate Reformed Church at Sardis, Fayette Co., Tenn.

Also, on the 14th of October, **M. J. W. Dodds**, infant daughter of Isaac and M. J. W. Dodds, aged two months and six days.

Departed this life, October 16th, 1846, Dr. **Charles C. Frazer**, elder in Ebenezer, Jessamine Co., Ky., aged fifty eight years. ... We may record with the father, the names of his daughter, **Sarah Ann**, who died August 31st, 1844; and **Rachael Susanna**, who died July 7, 1845.

Died suddenly on the 15th November, **Henry Calvin Simpson**, son of John and Sarah Simpson of Chester District, S. C., in the 6th year of his age.

Departed this life on the 30th July, in the Waxhaw's settlement, Lancaster

District, S. C., Mrs. **Agnes Barton**, in the 86th year of her age. Her father emigrated to America, when she was in her twelfth year, and settled in the vicinity of the Waxhaws, a few years after which she was married to Mr. Barton.

During the former period of the Revolution, she, with her husband, a carpenter by trade, went to Charleston, and settled in the suburbs of the city. It was during her settlement in that city that Mrs. Jackson, the mother of the Hero of New Orleans, went on her errand of mercy to relieve the suffering of the prisoners then incarcerated in that city. In consequence of the fatigue and hardships, endured from making the journey from Lancaster to that place, as it is supposed, she was taken sick shortly after her arrival in the city. And, although a stranger, in a strange land, yet, in Mrs. Barton's heart, she found a welcome, and in her house a home. Night after night did she set by the bed of the stranger, ministering to her wants, and soothing her sorrows, with all the solicitude of an Irish heart. And when she died, she closed her eyes; and although in humble circumstances in the world, yet, she furnished from her own wardrobe the clothes in which the mother of the immortal Jackson was committed to the dust. Her husband, being a carpenter, furnished her coffin, and they two, with the assistance perhaps of a few others, performed the mournful right [sic] of sepulture to the mother of a then future President. ...After the close of the war, Mrs. Barton returned to the Waxhaws. Here, her husband died--and here she spent some forty years of widowhood.... Her family all married and left her, and for the last fifteen years, she lived with her son in law, Thos. Faulkner, second cousin to Gen. Jackson... member of Associate Reformed Church.

V(April, 1847), 128.

Departed this life, March 3, 1847, in Mecklenburg, N. C., Mrs. **Harriet Angelina Fuller**, about 10 years of age...requested her sister to raise her child.

Died in Mecklenburg Co.,N. C.,January 3, 1847, Mrs. **Sarah L. Bigham**, wife of Capt. Wm. M. Bigham of Steel Creek in the 24th year of her age. ... Died on 1st January, aged about one week, an infant daughter of the deceased.

V(May, 1847), 160.

Died in Tipton Co. [Tenn.] on Saturday the 6th of March, 1847 of chronic inflammation of the lungs and bowels, **Martha H. Harper**, consort of Dr. R. B. Harper and daughter of Thomas and Margaret Johnston, in her 27th year.

V(June, 1847), 192.

Died in Tipton Co., Tenn., on the 11th of April, **Archibald Wilson**, son of William and Margaret Wilson, formerly of Chester District, S. C., in the 17th year of his age.

Christian Magazine of the South

V(July, 1847), 224.

Died at her residence in Abbeville District on Tuesday morning, the 18th May, of cholera morbus, Mrs. **Mary Caroline Bradley**, wife of William K. Bradley, in the 26th year of her age. She left an affectionate husband and two small children.

Died on the 3rd of March, **Elizabeth C.**, consort of J. Meek **Watson**, Esq., Pike County, Mo. ... regular member of the A. R. Church since the time of its first organization here. Her father, John Jordan, and the father of Esq. Watson emigrated to this place at an early period, from York District, S. C. The father, the husband and three children ... survive.

Died in Union District, S. C. on Friday, May 28th, 1847, **Margaret Jane McGowan**, daughter of Dr. William and Catherine McGowan, in her 8th year.

Died on the 30th May, 1847, **Mary Adams**, aged about 92 years--the widow of Thomas Adams, who died in S. C. 24 years before. She lived a profession of the faith of the Gospel about three score and ten years, and for about 11 years a member of the Associate Reformed Church of Hopewell in Newton County, Ga.

V(September, 1847), 287-288.

Died of typhoid pneumonia on the 8th of April, **James Knox** of Chester District, S. C. in the 39th year of his age. ... member of the church at Union from his youth. ... left a wife and five children.

Died on the 31st May at his residence in Chester District, S. C., **James Guthrie**, Esq., in the 58th year of his age. ... The community has lost ... an efficient magistrate and Union Church a valuable member. ... Four children, one son, now a volunteer in the army, and three daughters.

Died on the 7th June in Maury Co., Tenn., **Joseph Matthews**, in the 68th year of his age; he connected himself with the A. R.Church at Providence, N. C.

Died in Yorkville on the morning of the 25th May, Mr. **Robison McElwee**, in the 53d year of his age.... elder in A. R. congregation of Bethany.

Died in Jefferson Co., Ga., on the 9th May last, after a short illness, Dr. **Alexander Lowry**, in the 55th year of his age. Dr. Lowry was born and brought up in Fairfield District, S. C., and graduated in the South Carolina College. ... Having made the choice of a medical profession, he removed some 18 or 20 years since to Georgia.

V(October, 1847), 320.

Died of puerperal fever after an illness of eight days in Burke County, Ga. on the 31st August, 1847, Mrs. **Nancy Caroline Patterson**, youngest daughter of the late Rev. Charles Strong, in the 24th year of her age. She was born in Newberry District, S. C. After her father's death, her mother having removed to Mecklenburg Co., N. C., she was educated at the latter place.

Died, August 9, 1847 at Lowndesville, Abbeville District, S. C., Mrs. **Mary Ann Underwood,** consort of James Underwood in the 33d year of her age. ...consistent member of the A. R. Church at Generostee.

Departed this life on the 8th May last, Mrs. **Flora G. Goss**, aged 27 years. From her youth. ... a member of the A. R. Church at Generostee.

V(November, 1847), 352.

Departed this life on the morning of the 1st of October, at his residence in Winnsboro', **Robt. Cathcart.** He has left a widow and two children, an aged father, with several brothers and sisters. ... for some years a member of the Associate Reformed congregation in the village where he lived.

V(December, 1847), 382.

Departed this life in Fairfield District, 1st September, 1847, **Samuel Cork**, aged eighty one years. He was a native of Ireland, County Antrim, having been in this country fifty six years. He was thrice married, leaving a widow, a son, and a daughter ...[member of] Associate Reformed congregation of Ebenezer.

VI(January, 1848), 31-32.

Departed this life in Burke County, Ga., on Wednesday, August 25th, 1847, **Charles Strong**, infant son of Augustin and Nancy Caroline **Patterson**.

Died in Tipton County, Tenn. on the evening of October 7th, at the home of Lusk Davis, Mrs. **Martha Crossett**, aged about eighty years. ... She was a native of Lancaster District, S. C., and had, for a number of years, been a worthy member of the Associate Reformed Church.

Also, in the same vicinity, on the 14th of October, **John Wilson**, son of William and Margaret Wilson, aged about fourteen years. Thus in the wise but mysterious providence of God, have these parents been bereaved of a second son during the present year.

Departed this life on Little River, Fairfield District on the morning of Sabbath, the 5th of December last, Mrs. **Mary Ann Boyce**, the wife of the Rev. James Boyce, in her thirty third year. ... leaving many relatives, a husband, and four children, the youngest of whom commenced its earthly pilgrimage but three hours previous [to its mother's death].

V(<u>March, 1848</u>), 95-96.

Departed this life in Houston, Texas, November 10, 1847, after a short illness from Yellow fever, Dr. **S. O. Young**, aged about thirty years. Dr. Young was born in Abbeville District, S. C. At an early age he removed with his father to Wilcox County, Ala. After a suitable preparatory education, he repaired to Miami University, Ohio, where he graduated in 1839, in conjunction with his brothers, Revs. James M. Young and John C. Young, Esq. He obtained his professional diploma from the Medical College in Charleston. After practicing the duties of his profession for a time in Alabama, in the winter of 1846, he located in Houston, Texas.

Died in Iredell, N. C., Mrs. **Margaret White**, in the 92d year of her age. She was a native of County Tyrone, Ireland. She was confined to her bed for the last 7 years of her life, outliving her husband 19 years. She came to America in 1790, and with her husband settled in Iredell, N. C., where they raised eight children, all of whom were present at her funeral. When she and her husband first came to the country, they, by certificate, joined the Associate Church, and after the Associate Synod passed the act on slavery, they, with all their children except one daughter, united with the Associate Reformed Church.

VI(<u>April, 1848</u>), 128.

Departed this life on the evening of Wednesday, March 1st, at the residence of her mother, Mrs. Jane Bell, on Little River, Fairfield District, Mrs. **Caroline M. Brice**, in the 23rd year of her age.. She left a husband, an infant.

Died at her own residence in Newberry District, S. C. in December last, **Mrs. Jane Renwick**, consort of the late Rev. John Renwick. She was an uncommonly intelligent Christian. She was married to Rev. Bothwell, and left Ireland when about 16 years of age. After the death of Mr. Bothwell, she was married to Mr. Renwick and came to the District where she died. She spent a life of some 70 or more years.

Died in December last in Newberry District, S. C., **William Spence**, son of Capt. James and Elizabeth Spence. He was one of "only" two sons.

VI(May, 1848), 159-160.

Died of pneumonia in Burke County, Ga. on the 20th of February, 1848, after an illness of two days, in the 45th year of her age, Mrs. **Mary Ann Rollins**, consort of John Rollins, junr....leaving a husband and three children.

Died sometime in February, 1848 in Burke County, Ga., Mr. **Daniel Moxly**, in the 80th year of his age. ... a member of the A. R. Church.

Died in Jefferson County, Ga., on the 5th February, 1848, Miss **Eliza Ann Gordon**, in the 17th year of her age.

Died in Jefferson County, Ga., on the 7th February, 1848, **David Oats**, in the 22nd year of his age. ...[member of]Associate Reformed Church.

Died in Jefferson County, Ga., on the 19th February, 1848, **William C. McBride**, in the 22nd year of his age... [member of] Associate Reformed Church at Bethel, Burke County.

Died at his residence near Starkville, Miss., on the 13th of March, Mr. **William H. Montgomery**, after a severe attack of pneumonia. He was in the 36th year of his age. He has left a wife and three children.

Died of small pox on the 18th February last at the residence of her husband in Marshall County, Miss., Mrs. **Mary Ann Therrel**, in her sixty third year.

Died, February 25th in Fayette County, Tenn., Mrs. **Margaret H. Allen**, in the fifty third year of her age. The deceased was a native of Providence, N. C. and daughter of William Matthews. ... she became a member of the Covenanter Church, Rocky Creek, S. C., but returned to the A. R. Church in which she had been baptized and brought up... [left] a husband, one son and daughter.

VI(June, 1848), 192.

Departed this life in Fairfield District on the 22nd January, 1848, **Thomas Kilpatrick**, in his 70th year, leaving an aged widow and four children. ... born in Chester District, and when a young man connected himself with the Associate Reformed Church at Hopewell, and after removing to Fairfield, he united with New Hope.

VI(July, 1848), 223-224.

Died of complicated disease, but chiefly diabetes, at his residence in Butts County, Ga. on the 4th of May, 1848, **Robert Grier**, aged 68 years, 1 month and 25 days. He was a native of Columbia County, Ga. His father, Aron Grier, though not a communing member, with his pious mother, early consecrated him, and all their children, to the Lord, by baptism. Though a friend and contributor to the benevolent operations of the Church of Christ, in several of her departments, the subject of this memoir never made a public profession of faith in Christ. His wife, who is a sister of the late Isaac Grier, D. D., and a member of the Associate Reformed Church of Hopewell, expressed her conviction to the writer [Thomas Turner], that his habit of intemperance, which had grown upon him from the influence of his associations in public life, had been the leading cause of this dereliction from duty. ...The deceased has, for many years, been known to the people of Georgia and South Carolina, as the author of Astronomical calculations for the meridians of those states. He was a man of singular genius, and of eccentricities giving him a strong individuality of character. With a mind of high native powers, he never yielded to the suggestions of ambition, but remained in seclusion, occupying himself in the acquisition of curious lore, and turning science into a recreation to himself, and its results to the benefit of those who came within the sphere of his influence. ... He was a philosopher and a philanthrophist. ... of six children, only one son, Algernon Sydney, survives him..

Departed this life in York District on the 29th of April, Mrs. **Elizabeth Henry**, in the 51st year of her age. .. member of Associate and Associate Reformed Churches about 30 years.

Died in Hopewell congregation, Chester District, March 10th, 1848, **Joseph Whamm**, in the 24th year of his age. ... He was the only son and hope of a widow, and had been married to an interesting young lady only two months before his death.

Died at Erskine College, Abbeville District, S. C., on May 13th, **N. F. Odell**, after an illness of three days. The subject of this notice was a native of Laurens District and the only son of his parents.

Departed this life on Sabbath morning, May 7, 1848, at her residence near Bloomington, Indiana, in the 60th year of her age, Mrs. **Rachel Woodburn**, who had been more than 40 years the amiable consort of D. B. Woodburn. ...[who along with] four sons and five daughters survive.

Died in Memphis, Tenn., on the 8th of October last, **John Hemphill Boyd**, son of William and Mary Boyd of Marshall County, Miss. ... He came to his grave in early life, in consequence of a fall from the bluff at Memphis.

VI(September, 1848), 288.

Died of chronic diarrhea at Cumming, Forsyth County, Ga., at precisely 8 o'clock on Tuesday evening, 25th July, 1848, **Sarah Elizabeth**, the daughter and only child of William A. and Eleanor J. G. **Lewis**, aged one year, nine months and six days.

VI(November, 1848), 350-352.

Died in Gaston County, N. C. of bilious fever, Mr. **William Love, Senr.**, in the 70th year of his age. ...[member of] Associate Reformed Presbyterian Church. ... Ruling elder for about twenty one years.

Departed this life on 2nd of June at the residence of his brother in Jefferson County, Ga., Mr. **G. D. Alexander.** On the week preceding his death, Mr. Alexander left Erskine College, where he was a member of the Senior Class, on account of the very delicate state of his health and returned to visit the scenes of his childhood [died four days later].

Departed this life in the 29th year of her age on 13th August at the house of Neel McAulay, Iredell County, N. C., **Adaline McAulay**, wife of Hugh McAulay and daughter of Robert and Mary Grier of Alabama. The deceased being left an orphan at an early period of life, was brought to this country by Dr. Grier, and was brought up under his care. ... member of Associate Reformed Church at Coddle Creek. ... mother of two children called away before herself. She has left a husband, two brothers and two sisters.

Died on the 14th of June in Lincoln County, Tenn., Miss **Mary Ann Coleman**, in the 19th year of her age.

Died in Rockbridge County, Va., July 17th, 1848 at the residence of her father, Mr. John McKenny, Mrs. **Elizabeth Mary Miller**, consort of W. M. Miller, in the 28th year of her age.

On the morning of the 5th of July, 1848, departed this life, Mrs. **Barbara Matheson**, wife of Donald Matheson. She was born February, 1775. ... about fifty years [ago, she joined] the Associate Church, New Stirling, Iredell County, N. C.

Departed this life August 22nd, **Mary Caroline**, infant daughter of James B. and Nancy M. **Watt**, aged three months and three days.

Died in Tipton County, Tenn., on the 28th of August, 1848 of inflammatory bilious fever, **John Hemphill**, infant son of Rev. John and Arfatia **Wilson**, aged seven months and twenty three days.

Christian Magazine of the South

VI(December, 1848), 382-384.

Died at his residence in Yorkville, S. C., October 3d, 1848, Capt. **John Blair**, aged seventy eight. He was born in Tyrone County, Ireland, November 12th, 1770; emigrated to America in 1796; landed at Georgetown, then directed his way to Yorkville, where he resided until the close of life. ... connected himself with the A. R. Church at Sharon. ... As instances illustrating his benevolence, his love of kindred and country, it may observed that two Parish schools in his native country were established and permanently endowed by him; not less than a score of families were by him induced to emigrate from Ireland to this country, and were comfortably settled here....*Yorkville Miscellany*.

Departed this life at his residence in Chester District, S. C. on the 3d of November, 1848, Mr. **John McDill**, in the 88th year of his age. He was nearly the last of the Revolutionary patriots in his section of the country. ... at the age of 17 he was a soldier in the army of the Revolution. ... Ruling elder in Associate Reformed Church.

Died in Augusta County, Va., on the 29th of June, 1848, Mr. **William McCutcheon,** in the 90th year of his age. A native of Virginia. ... born November 27, 1758. ... at the call of his country, he took up his line of march to the defences of New York. ... In 1806, he united with the A. R. Church at Old Providence in Augusta County and was elected to the office of ruling elder.

Died at the residence of her parents in Abbeville District, S. C. on the morning of the 19th September, 1848, **Jane Elizabeth Chiles**, infant daughter of Gen. P. H. and Jane H. **Bradley**, aged thirteen months.

VII(January, 1849), 32.

Died in DeKalb Co., Ga., September 29, 1848, Mrs. **Mary Stewart**, wife of Joseph Stewart, in the 44th year of her age, leaving eleven children and a husband. ... the deceased was a native of Mecklenburg Co., N. C. ... she removed to Georgia in 1826, and in connection with a few others formed the nucleus of Prosperity, an Associate Reformed congregation. ... was taken with bilious fever the 8th September on her way from North Carolina where she had been visiting her people, but succeeded in arriving at home. She gave birth to a daughter, which survived the mother some two weeks.

Died in Tipton Co., Tenn. of inflammation of the lungs on the 12th of November, 1848, **Jennet Strain**, consort of William D. Strain and daughter of Andrew and Sarah McQuiston, in the 24th year of her age. Two days previous to her death, she had given birth to a still born child which was interred at her side. ... member of Associate Reformed Church at Salem.

VII(February, 1849), 62-64.

Died at his residence in Wilcox Co., Ala. on the 2nd of June, 1848, **W. Lewis Young**, aged about 30 years. ... member of Associate Reformed Church.

Departed this life on the 16th of April, 1848 in Oktibbeha Co., Miss., **John F.**, son of Hugh and Martha **Wiseman**, in the 21st year of his age. ... He volunteered to go to Mexico. Soon after his departure from home, he was attacked by the mumps, then the measles, and these were followed by diarrhea. When the company arrived in New Orleans, his health was so much impaired that it became necessary for him to return home.

Died in Oktibbeha Co., Miss. on the 29th of June, 1848, Mrs. **Nancy M. Gable,** wife of James V. Gable, aged 34 years. ...[left] her husband and five children--the youngest of these, a newly born infant, in a few days followed her.

Departed this life in the 19th of July, 1848 at his residence near Starkville, Miss., Mr. **Robert Bell**, in the 54th year of his age. ... He has left six orphan children to lament his departure. ... his first and second wife, and oldest daughter having preceded him to the tomb.

Departed this life in Monroe Co., Va. on the first of December, 1848, **James Nickell**, in the 67th year of his age.

Departed this life in Monroe Co., Va. on the 8th of December, 1848, Mrs. **Ellen Adair**, in the 89th year of her age.

Also, three days later, Rev. **William Adair**, her husband, in the 90th year of his age. ... had been a member of the Associate Reformed, next the Associate, and then returned to the Associate Reformed Church.

Rev. Adair was born in Antrim County, Ireland in 1758. After obtaining his education in the schools of Scotland, he was licenced. He entered upon the ministry with encouraging prospects, and continued to preach with acceptance, for a number of years in Scotland and Ireland, until he became unexpectedly involved in the Irish Rebellion. Being unjustly suspected for sympathising with the United Irishmen, he was compelled, for safety, to betake himself to their raids; and being found among them he was very much exposed in two engagements with the royal army. This conduct made his concealment necessary for nearly one year, when an opportunity offered for him to enter, in disguise, a vessel bound for the United States. Though, upon entering this ship, cards were seen offering a considerable reward for the head of Rev. William Adair, the Presbyterian, he succeeded in landing safely upon our shores. In a short time after coming to this country, he connected himself with the Associate Reformed Church , in preaching, for many years extended to the states of New York,

Pennsylvania, and Virginia. Finally, he was installed the pastor of New Lebanon congregation, Virginia. His pastoral labors at first seemed to be blessed, many being added to the church. But in a few years, difficulties arose between him and his people, which rendered it advisable for him to demit his charge. And not choosing to break the ties which bound him to Monroe County, Virginia, he requested Presbytery to release him from his obligation to fulfill appointments in other parts of the church. His request was granted. After this, he was known to preach but a few times.

Died suddenly in Lancaster, S. C. on 12th January, 1849, **Alexander J. Nisbet**, Esq., in the 57th year of his age. ... for twenty three years a ruling elder. ... For several years he was a trustee of Erskine College.

VII(March, 1849), 95-96.

Died of chronic bronchitis at his residence in Lincoln Co., Tenn. on the 25th of January, 1849, Mr. **Alexander Wiley**, aged about 50. ... The subject of this notice was a Carolinian by birth. .. made a profession of faith in the congregation of Cedar Spring, Abbeville District, during the interval between the minstrations of Rev. Porter and Dr. J. T. Pressly. About the year 1827, he moved to this State[Tenn.], where he was chosen ruling elder in the Prosperity congregation. ... A widowed wife, two sons and a daughter [survive].

Departed this life in Lincoln Co., Tenn. on the 2d of September, 1848, Miss **Martha Parkinson**, in the 19th year of her age. ... she had been in connection with the Associate Reformed Church at Prosperity for about five years.

Died in Pike Co., Missouri, August 22nd, 1848 in the 72nd year of her age, Mrs. **Rhoda McElwee** of congestive chill. The deceased was the widow of James McElwee, formerly of York District, S. C.

Died in Lincoln Co., Missouri, December 12, 1848, Mrs. **Martha Alexander** of lung fever in the 80th year of her age. She had long been a member of the Associate Reformed Church; and was the companion of our senior elder, James Alexander.

Died in Lincoln Co., Missouri, January 19th, 1849 of pleurisy, Mrs. **Anny Alexander**, aged 58. She was the daughter in law of the above, being the widow of John Alexander.

VII(April, 1849), 128.

Died on the 6th of October, 1848 in her 18th year, Miss **Elizabeth Kennedy**, only daughter of Mr. Archibald Kennedy of Abbeville District.. .

During her illness, her father was absent attending a meeting of the Associate Reformed Synod, her mother had been removed by death a few years ago.

Died in December, 1848, Mrs. **Sarah Criswell,** in her 80th year. The deceased had been a resident of Abbeville District, S. C. until the fall of 1840 when she came to Tipton Co., Tenn. Since that time she has been a member of the church at Salem, and has been entirely dependent upon her daughter for temporal support. She was once in opulent circumstances.

Also, on the 27th December, **James M. Nelson**, in his 18th year after an illness of four weeks.

VII(May, 1849), 159-160.

Died at his residence in Fairfield District, S. C. on the 22nd of March, 1849, Mr. **John Lathan** in the 55th year of his age. The deceased had been in full communion with the Associate Reformed Church at Hopewell, Chester District, from early life; and for the last fifteen years, he had been a ruling elder. ...[leaves an] afflicted widow and bereaved family.

Died near Bloomington, Indiana, **James Turner,** perhaps about dawn of day, January 25th, 1849, aged seventy six years and twenty three days . The deceased was long a member of the Associate Reformed Church at Generostee, S. C. Some twelve years a member and elder of a congregation of the same order on Little Blue River, Indiana; and some five years at Bloomington, under the ministry of his oldest son. ... living with his son in law, John M. Amerman.

Departed this life at his residence on Little River, Fairfield District on Sabbath night, the 29th April, **William Brice**, in the 89th year of his age. Mr. Brice was born in County Antrim, Ireland, in 1760 left Ireland when a young man, and settled in Fairfield District, where he lived until his death. The deceased was a member of the church for about seventy two years. He joined the Presbyterian Church of Ireland when seventeen years of age and was connected with Jackson's Creek Church in Fairfield (Presbyterian) from his first settlement in America until his death, with the exception of the last sixteen years when he united with the New Hope Associate Reformed Church. ... He has left four sons and three daughters.

Died at Lowndesville, Abbeville District, S. C. on the 29th of December, 1849, Mrs. **Matilda McAlister,** consort of L. S. McAlister, in the 36th year of her age. ... eldest daughter of widow Elizabeth Pressly of Abbeville District, who, in the mysterious dispensation of Providence has been bereaved of four of her daughters in about five years and three months. ... member of Associate Reformed Church at Generostee for nearly twenty two years. ... left an affectionate husband, six small children, one of them an infant.

Christian Magazine of the South

VII(<u>June, 1849</u>), 192.

Married on 4th April by Rev. E. E. Pressly, D. D., Rev. **John E. Pressly** to Miss **Martha S. Sherard** of Anderson District.

Also, on the 12th April by Rev. W. R. Hemphill, Rev. **D. G. Phillips** to Miss **Mary I. Hearst**.

At the same time and place by the Rev. Mr. Hemphill, the Rev. **John N. McCain** to Miss **Sarah A. Hearst**, both of Abbeville District.

Departed this life on the 16th of February, 1849 in DeKalb Co., Ga., **Jonathan N.**, son of Joseph and Mary **Stewart** in the 21st year of his age.

VII(<u>July, 1849</u>), 223-224.

Married on May the 24th by the Rev. J. Boyce, the Rev. D. P. Robinson of Lancaster to Miss **Margaret Brice**, daughter of Wm. Brice, Esq. of Fairfield District.

Died in Anderson District, S. C. on the 17th November, 1848 in her 86th year, Mrs. **Ann Pressly**, relict of David Pressly, deceased . ...more than sixty years in connection with the Christian Church--about half of that period in connection with the Presbyterian, and the remaining portion with the A. R. Church. There was one circumstance connected with her spiritual exercises during her last illness, which was forcibly impressed on the mind of the writer [Rev. J. S. Pressly] as he visited her frequently, that while the Scripture Psalms constituted a considerable portion of her meditations, she never once, in his presence, made the most remote allusion to a hymn of human composure.

Also, on the 28th of the same month, Miss **Esther Pressly**, about 75 years of age. She was reared in the Associate Reformed Church, owing to peculiar circumstances she sustained,for some years, a connection with the Presbyterian Church, but had, long since, returned to the A. R. Church.

Died of typhus fever on the 14th of May, 1849 after a protracted, and a portion of the time, severe affliction, **Robert Boyd** in the 52d year of his age, leaving a wife a widow, a large circle of children fatherless, and the A. R. Church of Hopewell, Newton Co., Ga. one less in the number of her members.

Died on the 22d of May, 1849, aged 26 days, an **infant** daughter of Alexander and Mary Ann **Chesnut**.

Departed this life on April 30, **Priscilla**, eldest daughter of Francis A. and

Christian Magazine of the South

Eliza Jane **Ware**, near Starkville, Miss. in the 13th year of her age.

VII(August, 1849), 253-256.

Died on Sabbath evening, July 8th, 1849, Mrs. **Mary Ann** , wife of Alex **Hindman** of Fairfield District, S. C. in the 26th year of her age, leaving a husband and two small children. ...In the enjoyment of her usual health. . .. she was suddenly stricken down by a flash of lighning, within a few paces of her husband, who witnessed the awful scene. ... She was a daughter of Mr. James Ferguson of Chester District, a ruling elder of the church at Catholic.

Died in Jefferson Co., Ga. on the 16th of May, 1849, Mr. **Matthew Marshall**, aged thirty six years, nine months and five days. ... member of Ebenezer A. R. Church.

Departed this life at her residence in Laurens District on the 14th February, 1849, Mrs. **Elizabeth Fleming**, consort of the late Robert Fleming, aged about 74 years. ... Mrs. Fleming was the subject of some severe and trying providences--having once had her family residence, with nearly all of its contents, consumed by fire, and having her husband taken from her, leaving a numerous family dependent upon her for support.

VII(September, 1849), 287-288.

Departed this life in St. Louis on Friday, the 6th of July, the Rev. **W. W. Patton.** ... He fell victim to the cholera. Mr. Patton was born and raised in Cedar Spring, Abbeville District, S. C., graduated at Oxford, Ohio, studied theology at Erskine Seminary, Due West, was licensed by Second Presbytery of the Associate Reformed Synod of the South, and preached extensively in S. C., N. C., Georgia, Alabama, Mississippi, Tennessee, Kentucky, and in the winter of 1845 or 1846, in company with Rev. James M. Young of Alabama, by direction of Synod, explored Texas. Wishing to effect a settlement of the North or West, he spent the spring and part of the summer of last year in New York and New England. Thence through Ohio to St. Louis. Thence to Springfield, Ohio where he spent the winter. In the month of June, he returned to St. Louis, and there fell a victim to the plague. His age was about 26 or 27.

Died at his residence in Marshall County, Miss. on the 30th of June, 1849 of chronic diarrhea resulting in typhoid fever, **Wm. J. McClurd** in the 25th year of his age. ... native of Lincoln Co., N. C. Thence he moved to Chester District, S. C., and last fall removed to Marshall Co., Miss. ... member of A. R. Church at Hopewell, Chester District.

Departed this life in Winnsboro on the 28th of June, Mrs. **Priscilla**

Lyons, wife of George Lyons, in the 36th year of her age, leaving three children and a husband. ...member of Associate Reformed Church in Winnsboro.

Died on the 8th of July at her residence in Stuart Co., Ga. of dropsy of the chest in the sixty first year of her age, Mrs. **Katherine**, consort of John **Kennedy**. Early in life ...[a member] of Ebenezer Church, Jefferson Co., Ga. for the last ten years held membership in Smyrna, Stuart County ..[left] aged husband and two daughters.

We are informed that **Thomas Ware**, the colored man, our missionary in Africa, is dead. Of the particulars of his death, we have heard nothing.

VII(October, 1849), 320.

Departed this life in Fairfield District, June 16th, 1849, Mrs. **Jane Stevenson**, wife of William Stevenson, Jr. and daughter of Francis and Elizabeth Land, aged twenty three years, nine months and twenty one days. ...[left] a husband ...and an infant son about three weeks old, which soon followed her to the grave. She had been a member of the Baptist Church.

Departed this life, July 15, 1849, **Francis Walter**, infant son of William **Stevenson**, Jr. and Mrs. Jane Stevenson, aged two months and one day.

VII(November, 1849), 351-352.

Departed this life on the 10th September in York District, Mrs. **Rachel S. Boyce**, wife of William Boyce and daughter of Joseph and Nancy Miller, aged 30 years. ... She has left three young children and a husband.

Died July 29, 1849 of cholera, after less than one day's illness, Mrs. **Georgiana Guyn**, wife of Samuel R. Guyn, elder of Ebenezer congregation, Ky.

Died July 31, 1849 of cholera, after lingering ten days, Mrs. **Mary Ann Guyn**, wife of Robert Guyn, elder of Ebenezer congregation, Kentucky. ... They were sisters. The first, while attending the sufferings of the other.

Died at his father's on the 2d of July, 1849, **Robert Simonton Wilson**, son of David and Sarah Wilson, having nearly finished his sixteenth year.

Departed this life on Little River, Fairfield District on Thursday evening, 6th September, Mrs. **Mary Ann McElroy**, wife of Robert McElroy and daughter of James and Elizabeth Lama, in the 24th year of her age. ... member of Associate Reformed Church at New Hope ... [left husband and] one child.

Departed this life on Sunday, 18th inst. at the residence of her husband in Cabarrus, Mrs. **Martha M.**, wife of R. L. **Cochran**, Esq. ... she was aged 21 years, 7 months and 3 days, and for some time a member of Back Creek Church.

VII(December, 1849), 382-384.

Departed this life in Oktibbeha Co., Miss., **Susan Bryson** in her 29th year

Departed this life in Oktibbeha Co., Miss., September 2nd, 1849, Mr. **Hugh Montgomery** in the 53d year of his age.

Departed this life near Starkville, Oktibbeha Co., Miss., October 15th, 1849, Mrs. **Lethe Ann Pressly**, wife of Rev. David Pressly and daughter of James and Ann Fair of Abbeville District, S. C. in the 24th year of her age. ... she has left a husband and three children (the youngest about eleven hours old).

Died on the 27th of September at Timber Ridge, Rockbridge Co., Va., Miss **Eliza McClung**, daughter of James McClung, deceased.

Died at the residence of his father in Marshall Co., Miss. on the morning of the 18th of October, 1849 of croup, an **infant** son of Rev. James A. and Mrs. Sarah A. **Sloan**, aged 5 days and 8 hours.

VIII(January, 1850), 31-32.

Died at the residence of her son, Dr. C. C. Dickson, near Portersville, Tipton Co., Tenn., on the night of the 18th of October in her 62d year, Mrs. **Martha Dickson**, formerly of Dickson County, and daughter of Major C. Strong.

Died in Gilmer County, Ga., October 8, 1849, Mrs. **Martha H. James**, aged 32 years. ... The deceased was a daughter of Francis and Margaret Henry, and a grand-daughter of Rev. Wm. Dixon. . .for many years pastor of Bethany and connections, York District, S. C. ... a husband and four children are left.

Died at his residence in Lancaster, S. C. of pneumonia, on the 8th ult., **Alexander Nesbit**, in the 56th year of his age.

VIII(February, 1850), 62-64.

Died on the 15th of June, 1849, **Robert Miller**, aged 56 years and eight months; formerly of Chester District, S. C., but a resident of Newton County, Ga. for twenty two years before his death, and a conscientious member of Hopewell congregation from its organization till his death.

Died on the 1st of July, 1849, **John Cowan,** aged forty years and eight months. Formerly a member of Union congregation, Chester, S. C., and for about four years before his death, a member of Hopewell, Georgia. Like the preceding, he left a widow and several orphan children.

Died by sudden calamity, **Lucy B. Orr**, aged twenty nine years and two months, on the 8th of November, 1849, leaving her husband, William Orr, three small children, one at the breast; her parents, James and Elizabeth Stewart. ... and the church at Hopewell, of which she was a member, to lament her loss. Her neck was broken in endeavouring to escape from a carriage with which a mule was running.

On the 25th of December last, Mr. **Alexander Miller**, a very respectable citizen and a worthy member of the church at Due West, S. C., was killed by the discharge of his own gun. He and a neighbor were in quest of game on Christmas day, and he is supposed (as no one was near him at the fatal moment) to have stepped upon a fence to look for approaching game, and to have set the butt of his gun on a round pole on the opposite side of the fence from this position the gun is supposed to have slipped, striking the lock against the pole, bursting the cap and discharging the contents of one barrel just below the ear, causing immediate death.

Departed this life on the 8th December, Mrs. **Jane Grier**, a resident of Steel Creek, Mecklenburg Co., N. C., in the 67th year of her age. At an early period of life, she connected herself with the Associate Church, Steel Creek.

In Munroe County in the month of October, **Hamilton Dickson**, in the 29th year of her age, departed suddenly this life. ... He left a wife and two little children.

At her residence on Clear Creek, Jessamine Co., Ky., on Monday morning, November 19th, Mrs. **Sarah January**, relict of Ephramin January, in the 87th year of her age. She was one of the very few survivors of the first settlers of Kentucky. With her husband and father, Andrew McConnell and his family, she emigrated to Kentucky from Pennsylvania in the year 1780, descending the Ohio River to Louisville and located themselves for a few months in the Fort at Spring Station, about six miles from Louisville, and thence went to the Fort at Harrodsburgh, where they lived about one year, from which place they removed to the Fort at Lexington, where they lived until after the memorable battle of Blue Lick, in which her father was killed. She resided in the Fort at Lexington when the first in that Fort was born, (which child was the late Mrs. Robert Wickliffe, and daughter of Col. Todd, who also fell at the Blue Lick Battle). In the fall of 1783, or spring of 1784, she removed to the farm on Clear Creek, thirteen miles from Lexington, where she resided up to the time of her death, a period of about sixty six years. At an early period she and her husband became members of the Associate Reformed Church, located on their farm, called Ebenezer, (on ground given to and conveyed to the church by her husband) at the time under the care of Rev. Adam Rankin, and afterwards Rev. R. H. Bishop, D. D. ... For nearly twenty seven years she was left a widow, her husband having died in 1823. She was the mother of a large family and reared eleven children, five sons and six daughters, all of whom have married and settled in three or four different states, and all are members of some branch of the Church of Christ.

VIII(March, 1850), 96.

Died at Lannahasse, Georgia, on the 20th of September, at the residence of her son, T. L. Irwin, Esq., Mrs. **Jane Irwin**, aged eighty two years, one month and sixteen days. She had been upwards of sixty years a member of Christ's mystical body, holding connexion near forty five years at Bethel, Georgia, the remainder at Smyrna, Marion County, Ga. She left three ...[living] out of nine children.

Also, on the 24th of July at his residence in Marion County, Ga., **John Pendry**, aged seventy one years. He had witnessed a good profession before many witnesses for about fifty years; the former part at Bethel, the latter at Smyrna, Georgia. He has left behind eight children. . . . the former was a sister in law, and latter a nephew to the Rev. Robert Irwin, a name so dear to many readers of *The Christian Magazine of the South.*

VIII(May, 1850), 158-160.

Died March the first in the twenty fourth year of her age, Mrs. **Lauretta L. Strong**, consort of W. J. Strong and daughter of John and Laura Bernard of Tipton Co., Tenn.

Died at the residence of his father, James Wright, in Tipton County, Tenn. on the 18th of February, **William Wright**, in the 22nd year of his age. ... The deceased had been for about three years a consistent member of the Associate Reformed Church at Salem.

Also, on the 12th of January, **John Allen**, at his residence in Fayette County [Tenn.] in his 66th year; disease, inflammation of the bowels. Mr. Allen was a native of York District, S. C., and lived for some time in Mecklenburg, N. C. Early in life he attached himself to the Reformed Presbyterian Church, and remained in that connection until the dissolution of that body in the Carolinas. After moving to Tennessee and remaining for some years detached from the church, the writer of this notice [John Wilson] was providentially led to visit him and a few other families in connexion with

Brother Turner, and to spend a night with them. In answer to their earnest petition, they were supplied with preaching during the winter and spring of 1836. In the month of May the congregation of Sardis was organized, and Mr. Allen was elected and ordained as one of its elders.

Died March 11th of the effects of cholera, terminating in an affection of the lungs, **Robert Gwyn**, elder of the Ebenezer congregation, Kentucky. He was attacked in August last, just after the death of his wife, of the same disease. ... A family of helpless children are thus bereaved.

Died in Pickens County, Ala. on the 17th of February, **Margaret Conor**, wife of Robert J. Conor and daughter of Mr. James S. and Nancy Smith of Starkville, Miss.; aged fifteen years. ... she has left a husband, a tender infant.

Died on the 4th of January, Mrs. **Jennet Millen**, wife of Robert Millen, in the thirty eighth year of her age. ... She connected herself with the church at Union, Chester District, S. C. in her youth. ... She has left a husband and three children, one daughter and two sons.

Died in Chesterville, on Sabbath the 13th of January, **Charlotte**, only daughter of Maj. W. D. and Julia **Henry**, aged three years and one day.

Died in Newberry, S. C. on the 26th of February of pneumonia, Mrs. **Elizabeth Caroline Aul**, aged about thirty one years; leaving a husband, two children, one of which is only a few days old, and the small congregation of Prosperity, of which she was a consistent member, to mourn their loss.

Also, in the same District, and near the same time, Mrs. **Mary Hunter**, daughter of Robert Carmical, of pneumonia. She left a husband and five children; and was also a consistent member of the same congregation.

VIII(June, 1850), 192.

Died in Mecklenburg County, N. C. on the 26th of April, 1850, Mrs. **Esther Walker**, in the seventy fifth year of her age. The deceased survived her husband about eight years. ... She has left eight children.

Departed this life at his residence in Little River, Fairfield District, S. C. on the 15th March, 1850, **Thomas Bell**, aged sixty four years and some months. ... A widow, a son and three daughters [survive].

III(July, 1850), 224.

Departed this life April 19th in Panola County, Miss., Mrs. **Martha**

Matilda Orr, wife of Mr. Jonathan Orr and daughter of Capt. Hugh Harris of York District, S. C. in the 27th year of her age.

Died at the residence of her father in Chester District, S. C. on the 5th of May, 1850, Mrs. **Martha Morgan**, wife of James Morgan and daughter of Robert and Nancy Fee, in the 26th year of her age. ...[member of] the Church at Union.

Departed this life at the residence of her husband, Mr. Samuel A. Boyce, in Mecklenburg, N. C. on the 15th ult., Mrs. **Sarah E. Boyce**, in the 22nd year of her age. ... Not only a fond husband and a helpless infant son . . . . experience in her death an irreparable loss, but the Church at Sardis.

VIII(August, 1850), 264.

Departed this life in Muray Co., Ga. on the 28th April, 1850, Mrs. **Sarah S. Stevenson**, (wife of Mr. Wm. Stevenson) aged 37 years and 10 months. The deceased was born in North Carolina, and admitted by baptism into the pale of the visible Church by Rev. Wm. Blackstocks. In 1831, she in connexion with her mother's family, removed to DeKalb County, Ga. and was thence admitted into the full communion of the Church by Rev. Mr. Bryson. In 1841, she, in connexion with her husband, removed to Muray County, Ga. ... she has left a husband, two children.

Died at his residence in Chester District, S. C. on the 17th November, 1849, **James Strong**, Esq., for a long time a ruling elder in the Associate Reformed congregation of Hopewell. ... aged 67 years.

VIII(September, 1850), 295-296.

Died on Sabbath, May 26th, 1850 at the residence of her husband, T. C. Moore, in Tipton Co., Tenn., **Sarah A. Moore**, in the 28th year of her age. ... disease, pulmonary consumption. The deceased was a native of South Carolina, Lancaster District, where both her earthly parents died. In the fall of '41, she moved out to Tennessee, in company with her two brothers, Thomas and Richard Cousar. In the spring of '42, she connected herself with the Associate Reformed Church at Salem. ... She has left a husband, four children.

Departed this life on the 22d of April last, Mrs. **Susan Hart**, consort of Wm. Hart, in the fifty fourth year of her age. The deceased had for many years been a consistent and exemplary member of Old Providence Church. ...[leaves] an afflicted husband and son.

Mrs. **Mary L. Wylie**, wife of Samuel Wylie and daughter of Mrs.

Strong, died at the residence of her mother in Chester District, on Sabbath the 2d of June, 1850. ...Mrs. Wylie was only 17 years and 2 months old--had been married nine months and ten days when she died.

Died at the residence of his mother in Chester District, S. C. on the 2d of August, 1850, Mr. **Charles Strong**, son of the late James Strong, Esq. in the twenty sixth year of his age.

VIII(November, 1850), 360.

Died of typhoid fever after a protracted illness of twenty five days, October 1st, 1850, Miss **Margaret Caroline**, daughter of James and Jane **Sloan**, aged 15 years, 10 months and 7 days.

VIII(December, 1850), 395-398.

Died at his residence on North River, Rockbridge County, Va. on the 22nd of September, Mr. **John McKenny, sr.,** in his 70th year . ... a ruling elder over the united congregations of Timber Ridge and Ebenezer more than forty years.

Departed this life, September 28, 1850, at his residence in Rockbridge County, Va., Mr. **Thomas Lackey**, in the 41st year of his age. ... He was also an elder in the Associate Reformed congregation of Ebenezer. He left behind himself a bereaved wife and three orphan children.

Died in Green County, Ohio, in July last, at the residence of her son in law, Mrs. **Mary McClung**, widow of James B. McClung, deceased, aged 71 years, 8 months and 18 days. She was a resident of Timber Ridge, Rockbridge County, Va. and had gone to pay a last and much desired visit to her friends in the West. ... She is mourned by an only son and daughter. ... having buried in the short space of six years a kind husband and four amiable daughters.

Mrs. **Elizabeth McWilliams**, wife of David C. McWilliams and daughter of the late Robert Harbison of Indiana, departed this life on the 14th of October, 1850. She had advanced a few days into the 33d year of her age. ... She was a member of the Associate Reformed Church at Hopewell.

Departed this life July 18th, 1850, **Robert Walter**, infant son of R. F. and J. V. **Taylor**, aged three months and eighteen days.

Departed this life in York District, S. C. on the 14th August, 1850, **James H. Black**, son of Joseph and Martha Black, aged nineteen years and three days.

Died of congestive fever at his residence in Marshall County, Tenn. on the

31st August, 1850, Major **John M'Clain**, after an illness of about ten days, aged about fifty five years. The subject of this brief notice was born in Guilford Co., N. C., and at an early period of his history, removed to Tennessee and settled in Williamson County where he resided up until 1842, when he went to Marshall County in the vicinity of Head Spring where he connected himself with the Associate Reformed Church.

Died at the house of Dr. Brice, Fairfield District, S. C. on the 9th of October last, **John A. Beattie**, son of Francis Beattie, Gaston County, N. C. ... only twenty one years of age.

Departed this life in Mecklenburg County, N. C. on the 9th of October, 1850, **John Calhoun**, infant son of Arthur and Martha **Grier**, aged one year .

IX(January, 1851), 31-32.

Died at his residence in Lincoln Co., Mo., on the 30th of August, 1850, **James Alexander**, in the 84th year of his age. Father Alexander was a native of Rockbridge Co., Va. Thence he emigrated to Shelby Co., Ky. and thence to this place. From early life he had been a member of the A. R. Presbyterian Church and for many years he had acted in the capacity of an elder. ... was an uncle to Rev. Archibald Alexander, D. D. of Princeton. ... Two sons and two daughters survive the patriarch.

Departed this life near Charlotte, Dixon Co., Tenn. on Friday the 22nd of November last, **Christopher Strong.** He was born in Ireland the 20th of January, 1760, and consequently his age was 90 years, 10 months and 2 days. He removed at an early age to Chester District, S. C., and after remaining there for a term settled in Dixon Co., Tenn. where he lived about half a century. He joined the church (the Associate Reformed) in early life, and was a member some 70 years and a considerable part of that time a ruling elder.... In his last will and testament he has bequeathed ($2,000) two thousand dollars for the endowment of Erskine College at Due West, S. C., ($2,200) two thousand two hundred for Foreign Missions, ($2,200) two thousand two hundred for Domestic Missions, and ($1,000) one thousand for the education of indigent young men, who are or may be preparing for the Gospel ministry, and the Associate Reformed Church, all of which he gives to the Southern Synod (the Associate Reformed Synod of the South) the control of for their specific purposes. He has also emancipated all his slaves and provides for them to be sent to Liberia. ... Mr. Strong was a soldier in the Revolutionary War.

IX(February, 1851), 64.

Died of pneumonia in Mecklenburg County, N. C. on the 22nd of November last, Mrs. **Eliza McGinnis**, wife of Major Charles B. McGinnis, in the fiftieth year of her age. She lived for thirty two years a member of the church at Back Creek. ... leaving her husband and seven children.

Departed this life in Chester District, December 16th, 1850, **James Strong,** infant son of James and Mary Strong, aged 10 months.

IX(March, 1851), 95-96.

Died in Mecklenburg County, N. C. on the 22nd of January, 1851 of dropsy in the chest, Mr. **Alexander Wallace**, aged about fifty four years. He was for many years a member of the A. R. Church at Sardis. He has left a large family.

Died of typhoid fever in Union County, N. C. on the 13th of December, 1850, Mrs. **Sarah D. Wilson**, wife of Hugh Wilson and daughter of James D. Craig, deceased, and Elizabeth Craig, in the 28th year of her age. ... at an early age was admitted to full communion in the Associate Reformed Church at Tirzah, Waxhaw. .. a bereaved husband, an infant son ... have been left.

Departed this life December 9, 1850 at the residence of her father in Oxford, Ohio, **Anna G.,** eldest daughter of Mr. **David Christy**, aged twenty three.

IX(April, 1851), 126-128.

Died on the 28th of February at the residence of her husband in Jefferson County, Ga., Mrs. **Mary Isabella Phillips**, wife of Rev. D. G. Phillips and daughter of John Hearst, late of Abbeville District, S. C. ... Only a year had passed away since she saw her first born son and daughter laid together in a coffin, and when called away herself, she left an only child not three days old. ... Member [at Cedar Spring, S. C.] until the 12th of April, 1849. Then, assuming the trying duties of a Christian minister's wife, she moved her membership to Ebenezer, Jefferson Co., Ga., whence in less than two years she has been called to rest from her labours, at the age of 26 years, 9 months and 24 days.

Died on the 20th of September last, **Thomas France**, in the 92nd year of his age. ... member Associate Reformed Church... ruling elder. ... He removed from Fayette County, Pa. about the year 1814, and located in the vicinity of New Washington, Guernsey County, Ohio.

Died at the residence of his son, Thomas Walker, near Savannah, Ashland County, Ohio, on the 18th February, Rev. **James Walker**, supposed to be in his 92nd year, and it is presumed, the oldest minister in the A. R. Church.

Christian Magazine of the South

IX(May, 1851), 158-160.

Died in Jefferson County, Ga. on the 27th February, 1851, Mrs. **Jane Boyd**, aged 35 years. In her youth she professed faith in Christ at Bethel, Burke County.

Died at the residence of William D. Stone, Esq. in Jefferson Co., Ga. on the 15th March, 1851, **John Hearst**, infant son of Rev. D. G. **Phillips**, aged 18 days.

Died at the residence in Jefferson County, Ga. on the 27th March, 1851, Mr. **William Whigham, sr.**, aged about 83 years. He had been for many years a member of the Ebenezer Church.

Died in Lincoln County, Tenn. on the 1st of March, **Mary Ann Spence**, wife of James L. Spence of bronchitis, aged about 35 years. She left a husband and a daughter by a former marriage. ... She was from her youth a consistent member of the A. R. Church at Bethel.

Died on the 2nd of April, 1851 in Tipton County, Tenn. in the 26th year of his age, **Cyrus W. Hutchison**, after a severe illness of three weeks. Disease, typoid fever ... member of Associate Reformed Church at Salem.

Died at his residence in Chester District, S. C. at 4 o'clock on the 14th inst., **William Moffatt**, in the 65th year of his age. ...[early member of] Hopewell, Chester District; but removed some thirty five years since to Union .

IX(June, 1851), 191-192.

Died on the 5th of January, 1851, Hon. **Alexander Reid,** in the -- year of his age. He was a native of Kentucky; but emigrated to Lincoln County, Mo. at the time of organizing the congregation at Mount Zion, Mo., he was elected and ordained to the office of ruling elder. ... At the time of the last canvass, he was elected as a Representative in the State Legislature, and accordingly he took his seat in the Legislative Hall at Jefferson City on the last Monday of December, but on the Wednesday following he was attacked with pneumonia and died on the 8th day.

Departed this life near Starkville, Miss, 1st of December, 1851, **Nancy Elizabeth Bell**, in the 11th year of her age.

Departed this life on the 25th February, 1851, **Mrs. N. H. Irwin**, consort of R. H. Irwin of Viney Grove, Tenn. in the 22nd year of her age.

Christian Magazine of the South

IX(July, 1851), 222-224.

Died in Rockbridge County, Va. on the 25th of November, 1850, **Christiana Harper**, daughter of John and Jane Harper in the 11th year of her age.

Died at his residence in Chester District, S. C. on the 10th inst., **John Lynn, sr.**, in the 71st year of his age. He had been a member of the church at Union for many years. ... He has left a large family to mourn their loss.

Died at his residence in Chester District on the 5th inst., **John Wiley, senr.**, in the 86th year of his age. From his youth he was a member and for many years a ruling elder in the Associate Reformed Church.

Died March 28th, Mrs. **Louisa Miller**, wife of Joseph Miller of the New Sterling congregation, in the 46th year of her age. ... left a tender husband and three affectionate children.

IX(August, 1851), 253-256.

Erskine College, June 24, 1851. It has pleased God in his wise Providence to remove from our midst a beloved fellow student, **S. B. M'Clerkin** (a member of the Sophomore Class), a young man of ardent piety, and unblemished reputation. Our deceased brother (a native of Fairfield, but at the time of his death a citizen of Tennessee) entered Erskine College in 1847, but owing to an act of dyspepia, he was constrained to abandon his literary pursuits for a time. Having recruited his health, he returned to college in the fall of 1850, but pursuing his studies with greater ardor and closer application than his physical strength would permit, his disease returned, and it terminated his life on the 21st instant.

March 17th, died at his residence (Bath Co., Ky.) Dr. **Joseph Berry** in the 62nd year of his age. ... He attended Lexington Academy.... read medicine with Dr. Warfield of Lexington. ... attended Medical Lectures at Philadelphia... volunteered in the War of 1812 under Gen. Harrison, and was promoted to a place on the Medical Staff. After the war he devoted himself successfully to the practice of his profession.

Mr. **Robert G. Hays** departed this life with chronic pneumonia on the 9th of June, 1831, at his father's house in Lincoln Co., Tenn. in his 28th year.

Died of pulmonary consumption in Jefferson County, Ga. on the 20th June, 1851, Mrs. **Mary Burke**, relict of the late Michael Burke, aged about 74 years. ... for many years a consistent member of the Ebenezer Church.

Died in Rockbridge Co., Va. on the 4th of April, Miss **Hannah E. Lackey** in the 17th year of her age.

Died on Thursday morning the 12th of June of an inflammation of the brain, **Fanny**, infant daughter of J. B. and Nancy M. **Watt**, aged one year and six months.

Died in Chester District on the 29th June after an illness of whooping cough of four weeks and two days, **John Edward**, son of J. Y. and Sarah J. **Miller**, aged two months and nineteen days.

IX(October, 1851), 316-320.

Departed this life on Wednesday the 13th of September on Little River, Fairfield District, Mrs. **Elizabeth Stevenson**, wife of Robert Stevenson, in the 51st year of her age. ... For the last fifteen or twenty years she was in communion with the Associate Reformed Church at New Hope.

Died on the morning of 31st July at his residence in Chester District, S. C., Rev. **Warren Flenniken**, after protracted and painful illness, in the 47th year of his age. ... He was born Jan. 9th, 1805 in Mecklenburg County, N. C. His education until near the period of manhood, was such only as is usually obtained at our primary schools. At this period he entered the Academy at Ebenezer, York District, S. C., at that time under the supervision of Rev. E. Harris. After having completed his academic course, he went to Jefferson College, Pa., and was there graduated in 1829. . . . .His theological studies were pursued under the direction of Rev. Dr. Grier, and partly, under Rev. James Lowry. Hopewell and Union being at that time vacant by the death of Rev. Dr. Hemphill, presented a call to him to become their pastor, which he accepted, and was ordained and installed pastor of the congregation at Hopewell in Nov., 1832. From this period till 1839, he labored with fidelity in these congregations, at which time he demitted Union.

IX(November, 1851), 352.

Died October 10th, 1851 at the house of John Simonton in Fairfield, S. C. in the 23rd year of her age, his daughter, Mrs. **Margaret Jane Boyce**, wife of Rev. E. E. Boyce of Gaston, N. C. ... Two hours before her departure, she was delivered of a still born son, which reposes on her arm in their lowly place.

IX(December, 1851), 381-382.

Died in Obion County, Tenn. on the 21st of August, 1851, Mrs. **Elizabeth Galloway**, consort of Robert Galloway, in the 29th year of her age. Early in life she connected herself with the Associate Reformed Church at Prosperity, Mecklenburg County, N. C. Immediately after her marriage in '45, she removed with her husband to Maury County, Tenn. ... left a bereaved husband and two motherless children.

Departed this life in Chester District, S. C. on the 20th of October, Sarah **Isabella**, daughter of the late Rev. Warren and Jane **Flenniken** in the 15th year of her age--disease, the typhoid fever.

Mrs. **Sarah Warnock** died at her residence in Burke County, Ga. on the 29th August, 1851, after a painful and lingering illness of many months. She was 55 years old and had been a worthy and consistent member of Bethel Church.

Died of bilious colic at her residence in Burke County, Ga. on the 9th of September, 1851, Miss **Mary Patterson**, aged 67 1/2 years. ... member of Bethel Church.

Died in Wilcox County, Ala. on the 21st of October of whooping cough, **Samuel Pressly**, infant son of Rev. John and Sarah **Miller**, aged seven weeks and a day.

The Erskine Miscellany

Died in the village of Anderson on the 16th inst. from constipation of the bowels, Miss **Permelia Adeline Jordan**, youngest daughter of Capt. Bartholomew and Margaret Jordan of this District.

Died on the 6th March inst., **Mary McBryde**, a daughter of Thomas C. McBryde of this District. This lovely child was nearly five years and a half old.

February 7, 1851

Died on the 21st of December last at her residence near the junction of Little and Broad Rivers, Fairfield District, S. C., Mrs. **Jane Watt**, in her 82nd year. ... consistent member of Associate Reformed Church for the space of 60 years.

March 7, 1851

Died at the residence of his mother near Laurensville, on the 12th ult., **James P. Kennedy**, in the 34th year of his age.

Died at his residence in the lower part of Greenville District on Tuesday morning, the 11th ult., Mr. **John Simpson Peden**, son of Capt. Robert Peden, in the 35th year of his age.

Married on the 4th inst. by Rev. James Dannelly, Mr. **Henry H. Harper** to Miss **Elvira**, daughter of John **Brownlee**, Esq., all of this District.

Married on the 6th ult. by Rev. D. Pressly, **Robert Holmes**, to Miss **Jane T. Weed**, daughter of N. and Mary Weed of Oktibbeha Co., Miss.

Married on the 23d ult. by Rev. Barnette Smith, Maj. **G. W. Connor** of Laurens to Miss **Mary Jane**, daughter of Dr. W. L. M. **Austin** of Greenville District.

Married on the 25th ult. by Rev. P. J. Shrud, Mr. **John A. Wharton** of Texas to **Miss E. P. Johnson**, daughter of ex-Governor David Johnson of this State.

May 2, 1851

Married in Tipton County, Tenn. on the 5th inst. by Rev. J.Wilson, Mr. **John R. M'Daniel** and Miss **Martha McQuiston**.

Married on the 1st ult. by Rev. Horatio Thompson, Rev. **W. M. M'Elwee** and Miss **Anna R. Harvey** of Lexington, Va.

May 23, 1851

Died at Louisville, Ga. on the 15th April, 1851, Mrs. **Harriet J.**, wife of Wm. S. **Lowry**, and daughter of Jennings O'Bannon, late of Barnwell, S. C. ... She left an infant son, a husband, and an aged mother. ... She had been. ... received into membership in the Baptist Church, where she continued to adorn her profession by a godly walk and conversation until her death in her 27th year.

June 27, 1851

Married on the 19th inst. by Rev. J. C. Williams, Dr. **James Donald** and Miss **Mary Lyon**, all of this District.

The Due West Telescope

April 23, 1852

Departed this life on the 6th of April in Wilcox Co., Ala., Mrs. **Elizabeth Young**, wife of Samuel Young, Esq., aged 62 years and 8 days.

Married on the 25th March by Rev. W. H. Harris, Mr. **W. P. Young** and Miss **Mary E. Newman**, all of Carroll County, Miss.

Married on the 20th inst. by Rev. W. R. Hemphill, Dr. **E. Gaines** of Pickens and Miss **Vashti Sharp** of Abbeville District.

June 25, 1852

Married on the 22d June, inst. by Rev. J. C. Williams, Col. **Samuel Donnald** to Miss **Emily Seawright**, all of Donnaldsville, S. C.

July 2, 1852

Died on the 31st of May at the residence of his mother in law in Jefferson Co., Ga., Mr. **James C. Trimble**, aged about 25 years. He has been for several years a consistent member of the Methodist Church. ... His death has left a widow and three small children.

Died at his residence in Jefferson Co., Ga. the 19th of June, Mr. **A. B.**

Smyth, aged about 37 years. He also left a widow and four small children.

Married on the 26th of May at Bordeaux by the Rev. Mr. Chiles, Mr. **J. H. Britt** to Miss **Susan J.**, second daughter of J. L. **Bouchillon**.

July 16, 1852

Departed this life on Friday morning the 25th June at the residence of her mother, Mrs. Jane Bell, Little River, Fairfield District, **Isabella J. Bell**, in her fourteenth year. ... She was preceded on her passage out of this life by her sister, Mrs. **Celia Brice**, on the preceding Saturday. The death of the one was on Saturday, that of the other was on Friday following--the disease in both being the same--typhoid fever.

Died June 10th of typhoid fever at his father's residence on Fishing Creek, York District, S. C., **John Thomas**, formerly of Chester District, S. C., aged 25 years and 3 months. The subject of the above notice had connected himself with the A. R. Church at Union, Chester District.

August 6, 1852

Married on the 31st, inst. by Rev. J. C. Williams, Mr. **Ebenezer Sharp** and Miss **Letitia Razor**, all of this District.

August 20, 1852

Died at Ebenezer, Tippah Co., Miss., Miss **Mahala Bryson**, wife of Matthew H. Bryson and daughter of Benjamin Pulliam of Abbeville District, S. C. ... She was the mother of six children, two of which had gone before her.

Died in Perry County, Ala. on the 17th of July last, Mr. **John Cunningham**. He was a native of Laurens District, S. C.--was born on September 17th, consequently had nearly completed his 56th year. ... member of Presbyterian church (from the *Southern Presbyterian* by request).

November 26, 1852

Departed this life at St. Clair, Illinois, on the 9th of August, 1852, Mrs. **Jane Lyons**, aged about sixty eight years. Mrs. Lyons was born in County Antrim, Ireland and was brought up in Kilwrath Church. She emigrated to South Carolina in 1805, where she resided until 1833, at which time she moved to the State of Illinois. For a greater part of her life, she was a member of the Covenanter Church. ... Her husband still lives. . . . as also several children.

Due West Telescope

Died on the 18th of Sept., 1852 of fever at the residence of her husband in Tipton Co., Tenn., **Sarah McQuiston**, consort of Andrew McQuiston and only daughter of William and Jane Hemphill, in the 60th year of her age.

Married on 21st September by Rev. Thomas Ketchen, Mr. **George Lyons** to Miss **Mary Elder**, both of Winnsboro.

------ on the 10th inst. by Rev. D. D. Hamilton, Mr. **Wm. Johnston** of Dallas County, Ala. to Miss **Amanda Jane Staten** of Mobile County, Ala.

------ on the 16th inst. by Rev. Hugh Dickson, Mr. **J. M. Benson** of Greenville to Miss **Sarah M. Davis** of Due West.

------ on Thursday 18th inst. by Rev. H. Dickson, Col. **W. A. Williams** to Miss **Catherine**, daughter of Dr. Samuel **Marshall**, all of this District.

December 24, 1852

Died on the 21st of September, 1852, **Albert G. McCain**, in the 27th year of his age, disease, typhoid fever.

[Died] on the 7th of October, 1852, in the 30th year of her age, Mrs. **Margaret H.**, consort of David H. **McQuiston**, and daughter of James and Margaret Wright. The deceased has been an exemplary member of the Associate Reformed congregation at Salem Church, Tipton Co., Tenn. from her youth. She left a husband and four children.

[Died] in York District, S. C., 30th November, Mrs. **Nancy Emeline**, consort of Rev. R. A. **Ross**. The deceased wanted but a few days of completing her 24th year; she left three children, the youngest being but a few weeks old.

Married on the 11th inst. by Rev. J. C. Williams, Mr. **George Morrow** and Miss **Luvenia Pruit**, all of this District.

----- on the 2d inst. by the Rev. Mr. Gamewell, Dr. **M. Tucker** to Miss **Adeline Nesbitt**, all of Spartanburg District.

January 7, 1853

Departed this life on December 21st, **Fanny**, infant daughter of Rev. J. B. and A. M. **Watt**, aged 1 year.

Died on the morning of the 6th ult. (of consumption) Miss **Sarah Gibson**, aged 34 years, 1 month and 16 days. ... member of Long Cane, Abbeville Dist.

[Died] on December 15th, 1852 after a protracted illness of measles and whooping cough, **Sarah Margaret**, daughter of Rev. N. M. and Catherine **Gordon**, aged 15 months and 9 days.

Died at his father's, Matthew Strickland, in Anderson District, Mr. **James B. Strickland**, in the 32nd year of his age.

Married on Thursday evening, December 2d by Rev. John Wilson, Mr. **William Huey** and Miss **Jane Baird**, all of Tipton Co., Tenn.

----- on the 23rd ult. by Rev. J. C. Williams, Mr. **J. N. Seawright** and Miss **Jane Cowan**, all of this District.

----- on Thursday the 23rd December by Rev. W. Banks, Mr. **John R. Westbrook** and Miss **Sarah M. Ross**, all of Chester District.

----- on the evening of the 21st ult. by Rev. H. L. Murphy, Mr. **W. Reynolds** and Mrs. **Nancy Jane Holder**, all of this District.

----- on the 115th December, 1852 by Rev. Jas. Douglass, Mr. **Robert McDowel** and Miss **Margaret Johnston**, all of Chester District.

-----also, at the same time and place, Mr. **Wm. Dunbar** of Fairfield and Miss **Nancy Johnston**.

August 26, 1853

Died in Laurens District on the 10th of July, Mrs. **Judith Blakely**, wife of David Blakely, in her 34th year .... [leaves] a bereaved husband and six children.

Married on the 28th July in Cahaba, Ala. by Rev. J. M. Young, Mr. **W. H. Quarles** and Miss **Lucy H. Bell**.

-----on the 11th August by the same in Orrville [Ala.] , Mr. **H. C. Hatcher** and Miss **M. W. Alexander**.

October 14, 1853

Died on the 3rd inst. at her residence at Fairfield District, S. C., Mrs. **Jane Elliot**, in the 89th year of her age. ... was a native of County Antrim, Ireland. ...When twenty one years old, she and her husband, **Francis Elliot**, bid adieu to their native land, embarking for the wilds of America. The strangers in a strange land then settled on Rocky Creek, and shortly afterwards connected themselves with the A. R. Church at Hopewell.... in the Fall of 1826, Mr.

Elliot was summoned to that land from which no weary traveler returns.

November 4, 1853

Married on the 27th October by Rev. Jas Moore, **B. W. Williams** and **Rosa Ann E.**, daughter of John T. **Haddon**, all of Abbeville District.

----- on the 24th October by Dr. E. E. Pressly, **Mr ----Bowen** and **Patsy Ann**, daughter of Andrew **Pruit**, all of Abbeville District.

----- on the 25th October by Rev. J. E. Pressly, Mr. **W. L. Benson** of Cabarrus Co. and Mrs. **Sarah Sloan** of Iredell, N. C.

November 25, 1853

Married on Thursday evening the 17th inst. by Rev. George W. Moore, Mr. **William C. Moore** and Mrs. **Elizabeth Shillito**, all of Abbeville.

----- on the 17th inst. by Rev. J. Boyce, Mr. **Andrew Strong** of Chester and Miss **Elizabeth Chisolm** of Fairfield District.

March 3, 1854

Died at the residence of her sister in Maury Co., Tenn., November 4th, 1853, Miss **Sarah**, daughter of Samuel and Sarah **Scott**, in the 60th year of her age. The subject of this notice was born February 10, 1794 in York District, S. C. Her parents left that county in 1804, resided a few years in Blount County, East Tennessee, and from thence they moved to Maury County in 1810.

Married on the 2d of January by the Rev. J. Wilson, Mr. **Joseph Strain** and Miss **Jane Forsythe**, both of Tipton, Tenn.

-----on the 30th December by Rev. T. S. Lee, **W. McClintock, Jr.** to **Miss M.--- Thompson** of Nicholas Co. --[next two notices are illegible].

-----on Tuesday, 7th ult., by the same [Rev. L. McDonald], Dr. **Walter Brice, Jr.** and Miss **Mary**, daughter of D. G. **Anderson**, Esq., all of Chester.

March 10, 1854

Died on the 9th of February at the residence of Capt. James McDill in Chester District, Mr. **Samuel Moffatt** in the 85th year of his age. He was for many years the oldest man in connection with the A. R. Church at Hopewell.

Due West Telescope

Died of pneumonia on the 3d inst. at the house of Mrs. Young, Miss **Jane Spence**, in the 23d year of her age. . . . [member] the church of Long Cane.

Married on Thursday the 9th inst. by Rev. J. N. Moore, Mr. **R. A. Belle** and **Miss M. E. Letcher**, all of Perry County, Ala.

-----on the 23d inst. by Henry Harris, Esq., Mr. **Andrew L. Scott** and **Miss E. W. McCain**, all of Maury County, Tenn.

September 1, 1854

Died in Mecklenburg County, N. C. on the 5th day of August, 1854, Mr. **John Q. Cochran** in the sixtieth year of his age. He was a ruling elder in the A. R. congregation at Back Creek for 15 years. ... A wife and ten children, many of whom are heads of respectable families in our community, mourn their loss.

Married on the 10th of August by the Rev. J. Wilson, Mr. **James Wiley** and Miss **Jane Davis**, both of Tipton Co., Tenn.

October 27, 1854

Died after a lingering illness in DeKalb Co., Ga. on the 17th of August, 1854, Mrs. **Mary G. Jeffers**, consort of Robert D. Jeffers and daughter of Samuel and Mary McElroy, in the 41st year of her age. ...[member of Prosperity, DeKalb Co.]. She has left two aged parents and 2 orphan children.

Died at the residence of E. M. Alexander in Lafayette, Miss. on the 15th of August, 1854, Mrs. **Margaret Wilson** in the 81st year of her age. ... native of Sugar Creek, Mecklenburg County, N. C.

Died on the 17th of October near Due West at her son in law's, E. Ellis, Esq., Mrs. **Molly Wright**, at an advanced age.

[Died, also near Due West] on the 23d of October, **Lewis**, son of John **Cowan**, about six years of age.

[Died] on the 24th of October, **Vashti Cowan**, sister of the above, aged near 16. Both died of dysentery, after several weeks of illness.

Died October 1st near Portersville, Tipton Co., Tenn., Mrs. **Margaret S. McCain**, wife of W. R. McCain and daughter of William Simonton in the 39th year of her age. ... was born in Chester District, removed with her father to this country in 1831 and was married to W. R. McCain, March 11, 1836. ... she leaves a husband, four daughters and three sons.

Due West Telescope

Died in Jefferson County, Ga. on the 6th of October, 1854, Mrs. **Margaret Cotter**, wife of Isaac Cotter. Mrs. Cotter died in the prime of life, leaving a husband and family of little children. ... member of Church at Ebenezer.

Died at her residence near Palestine, Anderson Co., Texas on the 15th of September after a short and painful illness of sixteen days, Mrs. **Sarah Ranson**, consort of John Ranson, in her fifty second year. Early in life she connected herself with the A. R. Church in Laurens District, S. C. In the Fall of 1824, she, with her husband, emigrated to Lawrence Co., Ala., where they united with the O. S. Presbyterians, under the pastoral care of Rev. Barr. After a sojourn of only six years in Ala., they moved to Lincoln Co., Tenn. and there united with the A. R. Church under the care of Rev. H. Bryson in which she remained a pious and devoted member until the Fall of 1849, at which time she went to Texas and there lived until the time of her death. ... she was the mother of three sons, the youngest of whom . . . [died in] 1850.

Married on the 8th of November, 1854 by Rev. Thos. Ketchen, Mr. **Henry L. Elliott** of Winnsboro, S. C. and Miss **Tirzah C. Ketchen**, daughter of the above named Thos. Ketchin, Cleveland County, N. C.

Married in Harris County, Ga. on the 5th October, 1854 by Esq. Passmare, Mr. **D. P. Lowry**, Esq. of Jefferson County and Miss **Ruth Darley** of Harris County, Ga.

Married on the 23d of October by the Rev. J. Wilson, Mr. **John McCaughan** and Miss **Margaret Allen**, both of Lafayette County, Tenn.

----- also, on the 11th of October by the Rev. Edward Green, Mr. **J. McClaughlin** and Mrs. **Nancy White**, both of Tipton County, Tenn.

Died of consumption at the residence of her father near Mt. Hill in Abbeville District, S. C. on the 11th of January, 1855, Miss **Mary Margaret Rasor**, aged 14 years and 6 days. She was the youngest child of Ezekiel and Permely Rasor. Nine months before her death, she entered the Johnson University at Anderson C. H., apparently in the best of health.

Departed this life near Starkville, Miss. on the 8th of December, 1854, Mr. **John M. Bell**, the only son of the late Robert Bell. He was killed from the fall from his horse. He had gone alone on a visit to a married sister. ... [He had] nearly attained his twentieth year.

Married on the 6th of December, 1854 by Rev. David Pressly, Mr. **William Perry** and Miss **Helen O. Miller**, all of Oktibbeha County, Miss.

May 25, 1855

Died of pneumonia in Newberry District on the 26th of April, 1855 in the 6th year of her age, **Sara Euphemia**, daughter of Rev. J. and M. **Galloway**.

Died of pneumonia in Newberry District on the 18th of April, 1855 in the 9th year of his age, **Joseph Erskine**, son of Samuel and Susanah **Reid**.

Also, of the same disease, on the 19th of April, **Susanah Galman [Reid]**, daughter of the same parents in the 12th year of her age.

Died in Tippah Co., Miss. on the 4th day of April, 1855--Miss **Amanda Arabella Rodgers** in the 16th year of her age.

Died of laryngitis on the 22nd March at the residence of her husband in Steel Creek, N. C., Mrs. **Mary Grier**, consort of J. E. Grier, aged 42 years.

Married on the 16th inst. by Rev. J. C. Chalmers, Mr. **James H. Walkup** of Abbeville to Miss **Margaret Y. Ranson** of Anderson District, S. C.

June 1, 1855

Departed this life at the residence of his father in York District on the 5th of September, 1854, **Irving Blair Moore**, second son of C. W. Moore in the 13th year of his age of typhoid fever.

September 14, 1855

Died in Wilcox County, Ala. the 10th of August, Miss **Margaret Smith**, daughter of Solomon and Jane Smith, aged 21 years.

Died the 12th of August in Wilcox Co., Ala., **Florence Courtland Bonner**, eldest daughter of Dr. Joseph H. and Sarah Bonner, aged 9 years. Two months since, these parents were called to give up an infant son.

October 5, 1855

Died in Tippah Co., Miss. on the 16th of August, **James G. Stewart**, Esq. in the 48th year of his age. The deceased was a native of Anderson District, S. C., and was, if we are not mistaken, the youngest son of the "patriarch-elder," to whom allusion was made in a former number of the *Telescope* by J. S. P.

He had gone to explore Drew Co., Ark. where he was attacked by a bilious fever which terminated his earthly existence in three days after he reached home.

Died in Lafayette Co., Miss. on the 6th of September, **Thomas Andrew**, youngest son of John N. and Martha J. **Spence**, aged 1 year, four months.

Died in Pope Co., Ark. on the 6th day of August, Monday, 12 o'clock, Mr. **John Falls**, aged seventy years. Mr. Falls had been in the communion of the Church forty seven years and held the office of ruling elder twenty six years; first in the Associate and afterwards in the A. R. Church. He resided in the Pisgah congregation, Gaston Co., N. C. until the Fall of 1852, when he emigrated with his family to Pope Co., Ark., and when the congregation of Pisgah, Arkansas was organized in January, 1853, he was chosen one of the ruling elders.

Married on the 30th July by Mr. A. W. Smith, Esq., Mr. **Nathan McCormic** and Miss **Julia Hindman**, all of Tipton County, Tenn.

----- on the 15th of September by the Rev. J. K. Boyce, Mr. **Joseph A. Dickson**, one of the Alumni of Erskine College, and Miss **Mary C. McCain**, all of Tipton County, Tenn.

---- on the 6th of September by Rev. J. Wilson, Mr. **R. R. Simonton** and Miss **Margaret McQuiston**, all of Tipton County, Tenn.

November 16, 1855

Deaths--**John Brown**, for a number of years a ruling elder of Mt. Carmel Church died at the residence of his father in Marshall County, Miss. on the morning of the 23d of October. ... he leaves a young widow.

March 7, 1856

Deaths ... of whooping cough in Abbeville District, S. C. on the 26th of February, 1856, **infant** son of Marshall and Nancy **Sharp**, aged 24 days.

Married on the 13th of February by Rev. J. Wilson, Mr. **William R. M'Cain** and Mrs. **Letitia Simonton**, daughter of John and Martha Strong, all of Tipton Co., Tenn.

April 11, 1856

Died March 30th after five days illness of pneumonia, Mrs. **Ann Stewart**, wife of John Stewart, Senr. of Anderson District, S. C., aged about sixty years.

... consistent member of the A. R. Church at Little Generostee.... She has left an affectionate husband, three sons and five daughters.

Departed this life on the 29th of March, 1856 at her residence in Anderson District, S. C., Mrs. **Martha Smith**, about eighty years of age or upwards. Mrs. Smith has been a member of the Associate Reformed Church at Concord during a period of some 45 or 50 years--having united, it is believed, under the ministry of the Rev. Robert Irwin.

May 2, 1856

Died in Yorkville of pulmonary disease, Mrs. **Catherine I. Enloe**, wife of Maj. John G. Enloe and daughter of Mr. Hugh and Mrs. Violet Allison, in the 33d year of her age.

September 5, 1856

Died at Abbeville village on the 15th ult., **Harriet Bethany**, youngest daughter of Basil M. and Elizabeth V. **Blease**, aged almost one year.

Died in Tippah Co., Miss., August 8, 1856, **Mary Jane**, daughter of Maj. James and Mary N. **Wiley**, aged one year, five months and sixteen days.

Departed this life at his residence in Tishomingo Co., Miss., on Sabbath morning, August 10th, 1856, Mr. **James Wilson Agnew** in the forty second year of his age. ... born in Abbeville District, S. C. on the 13th day of August, 1814. ... the Spring of the year 1838, he united with the A. R. Church of Due West.... [After ten years] he changed his business and removed with his family to Lincoln Co., Tenn., into the bounds of Prosperity congregation. ... elected and ordained into the office of ruling elder [and served until] the Fall of 1855 when he removed to his late residence in Miss. Here he located in the bounds of Bethany congregation (a part of J. L. Young's pastoral charge). ... He left a wife and eight children.

Thomas Chisolm of New Hope, Fairfield District departed this life on the 11th of August of typhoid dysentery after an illness of 16 days. Mr. Chisolm was born in County Antrim, Ireland, near Larne, on the 25th of October, 1791, which made him not quite 62 years of age at his death. He left Ireland for the United States in 1819, and spent the two first years of his residence in America in Chester District, where he, on a certificate from the Presbyterian Church in Ireland, united with Hopewell under the ministry of Dr. John Hemphill. Thence he came to Fairfield and settled within one mile of the spot he died. From that time until his death, he was a member of New Hope. ...About the year 1831, he was ordained a ruling elder at New Hope .... gave two sons a collegiate education, left his surviving children and widow a competency.

October 10, 1856

Died in Marshall County, Tenn. on the 12th of July, 1856, Mrs. **Margaret Blair**, consort of John Blair, Esq., in the 44th year of her age.

Her infant son **Hamilton [Blair]**, the object of her solicitude in the hour of her death, followed her on the 2d day of September, aged 9 months.

Died in Lincoln Co., Tenn. on the 5th September, 1856, Mrs. **Louisa Ann Tate**, wife of Dr. A. A. Tate in the 31st year of her age. ... in her death, her husband has lost the partner of all of his joys; five children, one an infant of a few days, have lost a kind and tender mother, their best friend.

Died of consumption on the 15th of September, Mrs. **Sarah E. Nisbet**, wife of John C. Nisbet and daughter of Hannah Nisbet, in the 28th year of her age. ... [survived by] two small children, ... mother, husband... .[member] the Associate Reformed Church at Tirzah, Union County, N. C.

Died at the residence of her son Robert on the 25th September, Mrs. **Jenny Elder** in the 83d year of her age--the oldest member of the A. R. Church of Hopewell, Chester District.

January 9, 1857

Died in Alexander County, N. C., Dec. 27th, 1856, **J. Curtis Moore**, aged 33 years, disease, typhoid fever. ... communicant at Sterling Church. ... Survived by an aged mother, an invalid wife, and two infant children.

Died at the residence of her son, A. B. Boyd, in Abbeville District, S. C. on the 22nd of December, ult., Mrs. **Ann Boyd**, aged 65 years, 8 months and 9 days. She had been a widow for 27 years.

Died in the 59th year of his age on the 11th of December, 1856, Dr. **John Berry** of Butt Co., Ky. with neuralgia plura pneumonia affection. ... He was an active member of Christ's Church for 20 years at Mount Olivet.

Married on the 1st inst. by Rev. H. T. Sloan, Mr. **Joseph Lindsay** to Miss **Jane Robinson**, all of Abbeville District.

Married on the 23rd ult. by the Rev. B. F. Corley, Dr. **W. K. Griffin** to Miss **Octavia R.**, daughter of Dr. Peter **Moon**, all of Newberry District.

Married on the 10th of December by Rev. J.H.Bryson, Mr. **N. P. Wilburn** of Alabama to Miss **Emma J.**, daughter of Henry **Harris**, Esq. of Maury Co., Tenn.

February 13, 1857

Married on the 6th of January by the Rev. J. Wilson, Mr. **Abner Hanna** and Miss **Mary E. Wiley**, both of Tipton County, Tenn.

----- on the 22nd of January by the Rev. F. H. Green, Mr. **Charles Strong** and Miss **Martha A. Dickson**, both of Tipton Co., Tenn.

February 20, 1857

Died in Iredell County, N. C., Jan. 15, 1857 with apoplexy, Mr. **Jas. W. Emmons** in the 32nd year of his age. Mr. Emmons came to this country from Culpepper, Va. in the year 1849. He married a daughter of Mr. Jas Davidson and settled in the congregation of Sterling with which church his wife and [two] children by baptism are connected.

In Alexander [Co, N. C.] on January 28th, 1857, **infant** daughter of James and Martha **Grey**, aged 1 year and three months.

It becomes our melancholy duty to record the death of the much lamented Dr. **William J. Watt**, who departed this life on the evening of the 4th inst. at his newly purchased residence in Mecklenburg, N. C. The subject of this notice was born in Fairfield District, S. C. in 1823. .... [He] sought his fortune in the West. ... found a home in Starkville, Miss.; here he resided for some years; here he married; here he connected himself with the A. R. Church in 1849 of which he was a consistent member until his death. But filial affection called him away to watch over the declining years of his widowed mother. ... In 1854, he returned to the home of his childhood, at which time he became a member by certificate of the Ebenezer Church. ... leaves a wife and three children.

February 27, 1857

Died at his residence in Fairfield District, S. C. on the night of the 13th inst., Mr. **Jas Harper**. ... [He] was born in Ireland, County Antrim, in 1776. He emigrated to this country in1810 with his family, consisting of a wife and two children, and settled on the Wateree, thence he removed to the place of his death where he resided near seventeen years. This brought him within the bounds of the Ebenezer congregation. ... the aged companion with whom he had spent so many happy days and four of his children were with him [at his death].

Married on the 25th of December, 1856 by Rev. D. McDill, Mr. **Wm. B.**

Cooper to Miss **Jane Baird**, all of Randolph County, Illinois.

Married by Rev. L. McDonald on the evening of the 18th inst. at the house of the bridegroom's mother, Mr. **T. Henry Moffatt** of Chester District, S. C. to Miss **Mary S. Lowrie** of New York.

Married on February the 19th inst. by the Rev. S. C. Millen, Mr. **Samuel N. Miller** to Miss **Eliza J.**, eldest daughter of James **McElwee**, Sr., all of this District.

March 6, 1857

Died, January 23, of fever, **Shannon Reid** of Shelbyville, Ky., aged 49 years. The deceased was a member of the A. R. Church.

March 13, 1857

Died in Mecklenburg, N. C. on the 9th of February, 1857, Mrs. **Ann Hunter** in the 43rd year of her age. Her disease was rapid consumption. The deceased was a most exemplary member, and had been for many years, of the Associate Reformed Church at Sardis, and was one of a large family of people who have been somewhat noted for their humble piety and Christian zeal ... sister of Dr. James Boyce and Rev. E. E. Boyce.

Died in Mecklenburg, N. C. on the -- of January, 1857, **J. Newton Irwin**, aged about 29 years. The deceased was a member of the A. R. congregation of Sardis.

Died in Chester District, S. C. at the residence of his father in law, R. Boyd, Sr., on 25th February, Mr. **William Strong** in his twenty sixth year.

Married March 5th by Rev. L. McDonald, Mr. **J. Alexander Roseborough** to Miss **Isabella H. Moffat**, all of Chester District, S. C.

March 20, 1857

Died in Anderson District, S. C., March 14, 1857, **William Ranson** in the seventy first year of his age. The deceased connected himself in early life, in Ireland. ... with the Irish Presbyterian Church and on his arrival in this country, forty odd years ago, he attached himself at once to the Associate Reformed Church in the South. ... He was the father of Rev. A. Ranson.

Died at this residence in Lincoln County, Tenn., November 30th, 1856, Mr. **James Hays**, in the eightieth year of his age. He was a native of

Antrim, Ireland. ... In his youth he connected himself with the Presbyterian Church of Ireland. Emigrating to South Carolina in 1818, he attached himself to the Associate Church--and then removed to Tennessee in 1833; was received in the communion of the A. R. Church at Prosperity. A native impetuosity frequently drove him into excesses which for a long time rendered uncertain his Christian character. This, however, was one of those rare cases in which church discipline was really seen to be a blessing by its effects upon his life. For years he has been an ornament to the church, and lived long enough to put an end to all peradventures about his piety.

March 27, 1857

Died of pneumonia in Dallas County, Ala. on the 25th of February, **John Chesnut** in the 49th year of his age. The deceased was an elder in Prosperity.

Also, of the same disease, a short time previous, **W. C. Moore** in the 40th year of his age.

Died November 2nd, 1855 in Obion Co., Tenn., Mrs. **Rosannah Harper** in the eighty first year of her age. She was born December 25th, 1774. She was a widow above forty years. She first connected herself with the Presbyterian Church in the Waxhaw settlement, S. C., and when she moved to the West, she identified herself with . . . . the A. R. Church at Troy, Tenn.

Died in Mecklenburg County, N. C. of old age on the 23d of January, ult, Mrs. **Majora Cochran**, aged 85 years. ...[member of] Back Creek.

April 3, 1857

Married in Wilcox Co., Ala., the 17th of March by Rev. John Miller, Mr. **Green Dunham** to Miss **Lizzie Dale**.

April 10, 1857

Died March 22nd, 1857 at the residence of her father, John Young, Esq., in Iredell, N. C., Mrs. **Margaret Ann Bell** in the 28th year of her age. ... was for eleven years member of the Associate Reformed Church of New Perth.

Died in Maury County, Tenn. on the 24th of March, Mrs. **Esther Coffey,** aged about 84 years. She was originally from Lancaster District, S. C., settled in this country at an early day.

Married on the 31st ult. by Rev. S. C. Millen, **S. M. Johnson** and **Margaret Frances**, daughter of R. M. **Pressly**, Esq. of York District, S. C.

Due West Telescope

Died in Wilcox Co., Ala., March 23rd, Mr. **Solomon Smith** in the 56th year of his age. ... three of [his] children were taken in quick succession last Fall. ...[he] experienced the trials and privations connected with the first settlements of Ala. His youth was passed in frontier life, and as a consequence, under influences adverse to piety. It was not until after his alliance in marriage to one of the families of Lebanon, that his religious convictions were matured.

(from the *United Presbyterian of the West*) Died in Chicago in the evening of the 18th of March, **Thomas McCalla**, Esq. of the banking firm of Messrs. Davidson, McCalla & Co. ... Born in Chester District, S. C. in 1813, Mr. McCalla moved to Bloomington, Indiana in 1837, where he engaged in mercantile pursuits, he resided until 1852 when he came to Chicago. ... He was one of the individuals engaged in promoting the organization of the Associate Reformed Church in Chicago. ... an elder and also superintendent of the Sabbath School. ... nephew of Rev. W. R. Hemphill, Due West, S. C.

Died at her residence in Anderson District, S. C. on the morning of the 13th instant, in the twenty sixth year of her age, **Nancy Wilbanks**, consort of Henry M. Wilbanks and daughter of Nathaniel and Margaret Moore. The deceased was born in Abbeville District. ... member of Little Generostee...leaves husband and three small children.

Died of scarlet fever in Anderson District, S. C. on the 11th of April, 1857, **Jasper N. Partain**, son of J. H. and Elizabeth Partain; aged four years, two months and twenty three days.

Married on the 7th inst. by Rev. J. E. Pressly, Mr. **James M. Rodgers** and Miss **Sarah Isehower** of Cabarrus Co., N. C.

Married on the 7th inst. by Rev. D. G. Phillips, Mr. **Robt. Boyd** to Mrs. **Jane P. Darley**; the former of Muscogee County, Ga., the latter of Jefferson County, Ga.

Married on the 2d April by Rev. Jno. Miller, Dr. **J. H. Pressly** of Wilcox County, Ala. to **Miss McMillen**.

Died of scarlet fever on the 23d of March, **Katherine**, little daughter of John C. and Elizabeth **Sloan**, in the 2d year of her age.

Died, March 26th of scarlet fever, **Mary Olivia**, daughter of Samuel H. and Martha J. **Sloan**, about two years old.

Died of scarlet fever, April 4, **Ann**, youngest daughter of Rev. H. and H. **Bryson**, about two years of age.

Married at Pine Grove, Augusta County, Va. on Thursday the 16th of April by Rev. J. C. Hensell, Mr. **Jacob Lotts** from near Old Providence church to Miss **Eliza J. Armstrong**, all of Augusta County, Va.

May 8, 1857

Died in Mecklenburg, N. C. on the 2d of March, Mrs. **Nancy P. Stewart** in the 33rd year of her age. ... She leaves a bereaved husband and several small children. She was a member of Sardis Church.

Also, in Mecklenburg, N. C. on the 14th of April, 1857, (a member of the congregation with the above) Mrs. **Elizabeth Edwards**, aged about 21 years.

Died at the residence of J. W. Craig in Orrville, Ala., **Margaret Johnson** in the 78th year of her age. ...[member of] Prosperity Church.

Married in Rutherfordton, N. C. by Rev. Thomas E. Davis, Mr. **M. L. Ford** (the foreman of the *Telescope* office) to Miss **Nancy L. Oliphant** of Rutherfordton.

Married by the Rev. H. Quigg on the evening of the 21st instant, Mr. **Charles H. Paul**, Mississippi to Miss **Mary A. E. Wheeler**, Newton County, Ga.

Married by Rev. J. E. Pressly, April 14th, Mr. **James H. Smith** of Cabarrus and Miss **Abigail Johnson** of Mecklenburg County, N. C.

Married on the 1st of April, 1857 by Rev. W. B. Pressly, Mr. **H. Clodfelter** and Miss **Isabella J. Miller**, both of Alexander County, N. C.

-----by the same on the 23d of April, 1857, Mr. **G. A. McCoy** and Miss **Nancy C. White**, both of Iredell Co., N. C.

May 15, 1857

Died in Newton County, Ga. on the morning of the 19th ult., Mr. **Neal McDonald** in the 82d year of his age   ... A native of the Scottish Highlands.

Departed this life on the 1st of May at the residence of her father, Dr. **M. Thomson**, in Tuscaloosa County, Mrs. **Rachael Mariah Singletary**, wife of Rev. W. H. Singletary. ... member of Presbyterian church.

Married in Yorkville on Tuesday morning 5th instant by Rev. W. W. Carothers, Mr. **Samuel W. Melton** of the Enquirer and Miss **Mary Helen Goore**, both of that place.

Married on the 5th instant by Rev. H. T. Sloan, Mr. **E. Cowan** to Miss **Sallie**, daughter of Samuel **Jordan**, Esq., all of Abbeville.

Married by Rev. Mr. Potter, April 21st, Dr. **Samuel Boyd** to Miss **Sallie A. Riley**; the former of Harris County, the latter of Talbot County, Ga.

May 22, 1857

Died of consumption in Lancaster District on the 29th ult., Mr. **James Harvey Nesbit** in the 21st year of his age, leaving a disconsolate wife. ... member of the Associate Reformed Church at Tirzah, Union County, N. C.

Married on the 28th of April in Orrville, Ala. by Rev. J. M. Young, Mr. **John A. Patton** to **Miss M. E.**, daughter of Dr. **Thomason**.

June 5, 1857

Died in Iredell County, N. C., Mr. **John F. McAulay**, son of John McAulay, in the 17th year of his age. ... member of Coddle Creek Church.

Died at her residence in Anderson District, S. C. on the 29th April last, Mrs. **Mary Watt**, consort of James D. Watt, aged forty five years. ... member of Little Generostee. ... leaves a husband and a numerous family of children.

Departed this life on the 21st of May, Miss **Mariah Marshall**.. . .[lived] with Mr. William Brice. ... member of the A. R. Church at Winnsboro, S. C.

Married on the 21st ult. by Rev. E. E. Pressly, D. D., Mr. **John C. Chalmers** to Miss **Emma E.**, daughter of Capt. James Maffett of Newberry.

Married on the 14th ult. by the Rev. Albert A. Morse, Mr. **J. I. Jolly** to Miss **Martha**, daughter of Mr. Reuben Richey, all of Anderson District.

June 12, 1857

Died after a short illness in Alexander Co., N. C., May 25th, 1857, Mr.

James McDaniel, aged about 60. ... He leaves a wife and six children.

Departed this life in Tippah Co., Miss., April 30, 1857, Mrs. **Martha Wiseman,** consort of Hugh Wiseman, elder of the Ebenezer congregation. ... Her father, William Fleming of Head Spring, Laurens, S. C., having moved to Alabama while she was but a youth, she was cut off from the church of her fathers and her choice until the removal of her husband and family to Starkville.

Mrs. **Samuel Young** departed this life on the 12th of May in the twenty second year of her age, leaving a disconsolate husband and a tender infant. ... member of Long Cane A. R. Church.

Died on Sabbath evening, the 24th of May, Miss **Martha Thomas Willis**, daughter of Mrs. W. K. **Bradley,** aged 13 years, 2 months.

June 26, 1857

Died in Cabarrus County, N. C. on Thursday, the 28th of May, Mr. **Houston Cochran** in the 22nd year of his age. The deceased met with his death from the accidental discharge of a gun held by his own hand. In the evening of the day on which he was killed, his family being from home on a visit to the house of some friends, taking his gun in hand, he walked to a blacksmith's shop, about one mile from his residence.... Upon arriving there, he met the proprietor in front of the shop, and a conversation, somewhat protracted, being introduced, Mr. Cochran, to secure some support in his standing posture, leaned upon his gun. The conversation being ended, Mr. Cochran started in the direction of the door; but in taking up his gun, which had been placed inadvertently between the spokes of a buggy wheel standing by his side, one of the hammers caught in a spoke, and was raised enough to burst the cap as it sprang to its place, and caused the whole load to be poured into his right eye. ...He leaves a wife, a little child and an only brother.

Married on the 10th of June by Rev. W. B. Pressly, Mr. **A. M. Walker** and **Miss M. L.Miller**, all of Alexander County, N. C.

Married on Tuesday morning the 2d of June by Rev. J. M. Young, Rev. **H. Quigg**, pastor of Hopewell Church, Newton County, Ga., to **Miss S. A.,** daughter of R. G. **Craig**, Esq. of Dallas Co., Ala.

July 3, 1857

Died on the 4th of June of Typhoid dysentery, **Joseph Daniel**, infant son of Capt. Matthew and Mrs. Emily **Lynn**, aged one year, four months and eighteen days.

Due West Telescope

Died at the residence of his father in Fairfield District on 21st of June last, Mr. **Franklin Gibson** in the 25th year of his age. Died about the same time and in the same neighborhood, Dr. **J. Glenn**, a young physician.

Died, June 11, 1857, Mrs. **Jane Gwyn** of Ebenezer congregation, Kentucky, aged eighty three years. The deceased, early in life, was married to Robert Gwyn, who died during the meeting of Synod among us in 1844, and settled on the farm where her life was spent. She was the mother of eleven sons and two daughters who became heads of families.

Died in Yorkville on Friday morning, 25th ult., Mrs. **Margaret C. Lester**, wife of Rev. A. H. Lester, the South Carolina Conference [Methodist], aged 22 years, 11 months and 4 days.

Married on the 14th ult. at 9 o'clock by Rev. W. B. Telford, Dr. **Nathaniel Hart** of Cartersville, Ga. to Mrs. **Margaret E. Goodman** of Laurens, S. C.

Married on the 30th ult. by the Rev. H. T. Sloan at the residence of her uncle, Dr. R. Devlin, Miss **Sallie J. Walker** to Mr. **E. Westfield**, all of Abbeville District.

We have to record the death of Mrs. **Mary Faulkner**, wife of John Faulkner, on the 8th inst. ... in the 31st year of her age.

Died on Tuesday morning the 21st inst., little **Charlie**, first born and only child of Dr. A. G. and Mrs. M. A. **Cook** of Generostee, Anderson District, S. C. Charlie was between two and three.

Died from bowel affection on the 17th of July, 1857, **William James,** son of Rev. J. and M. **Galloway**, aged six months and thirteen days.

Married on July 23d by Rev. E. E. Pressly, **James W. Richey** to Miss **Nancy Martin**, all of Abbeville District.

Died July 29th, 1857, **William Love**, an elder of Pisgah, Gaston County,

N. C... [Rev. E. E. Boyce writes] the bloody flux is sweeping over my congregation with fearful power. Within a few days it has done the following work in addition to the above: a child of Thomas **Ferguson**, the youngest of Samuel **Wilson**, of James **Carson**, of Robert **Love**, of Robt. **Adams**, of George **McAlister**, and of others.

Died in Murfreesboro, Oktibbeha Co., Miss. on the 2nd ult. from the effects of a pistol shot received on the evening of the 29th of June, **David M. Thompson**. ... He was the youngest son of Major John Thompson of Oktibbeha Co., Miss. and formerly of Fairfield District, S. C. ... He was about 25 years of age.

Departed this life on the 16th of July, 1857, Mr. **Andrew Stevenson** who for the last fifty four years was a constant resident of what is now Anderson District. Mr. Stevenson was born in Mecklenburg Co., N. C. on the 30th of August, 1783, and was nurtured by parents belonging to the Associate Reformed Church... ruling elder in the Church at Concord.

Died of brain fever in Cabarrus Co., N. C., July 21st, 1857, **Minnie Linette**, daughter of Rev. J. E. and M. S. **Pressly**, aged 2 years and 8 months.

August 21, 1857

Died at his residence in Abbeville District, S. C. of pneumonia on the 24th of July, **Samuel Reid**, Esq. in the 69th year of his age. ... ruling elder in Presbyterian church.

Died of measles, March 11, 1857, at his residence in Mecklenburg Co., N. C. , **Robert Hunter, Sr.**, aged 68 years, 5 months and 12 days. He connected himself with the A. R. Church at Prosperity in early life, and was for many years an elder in that congregation.

Married in Lincoln Co., N. C. on the 16th ult. by Rev. Drury Lacey, D. D., Major **T. J. Jackson**, Major in the Military Institute at Lexington to Miss **Mary Anna**, daughter of Rev. R. H. **Morrison**, D. D.

----- at the University of Va., July 10th, by Rev. W. H. McGuffey, Rev. **A. D. Hepburn** and Miss **Henrietta McGuffey**, second daughter of the officiating clergyman.

----- at Lexington, Va., August 3d by Rev. Dr. **Junkin**, President of Washington College, Rev. **J. T. L. Preston** of the Virginia Military Institute and **Margaret**, eldest daughter of the officiating clergyman.

Due West Telescope

Died in Chester District on the 22d of August. .. **J. P. Lathan**, Esq., in the 36th year of his age. ...[belonged to] A. R. Church of Hopewell of which he was a ruling elder. ...[He was] civil magistrate, postmaster, and agent of the Chester & South Carolina Railroad at Blackstock's Depot. Departed this life at Oktibbeha Co., Miss. on the 5th inst., Mrs. **Elisabeth Brown**, wife of William Brown, aged 51 years, 9 months and 9 days. Mrs. Brown was a native of Fairfield District, S. C. and a daughter of John Weldon. ... She has left a husband, three daughters and one son.

Married on Monday morning, 26th of August, by Rev. R. W. Brice, Mr. **Wm. M. Martin** to Miss **Margaret**, daughter of William **Stevenson** of Fairfield, S. C.

September 11, 1857

We are again called upon to mourn the loss of an esteemed and valued member of Cedar Spring Church, **Mrs. James I. Morrow**, died of typhoid dysentery, July 17th in the forty ninth year of her age. ... She has left a bereaved husband and five children. Died at Lowrysville in Chester District on the 24th ult. of bowel affection, J. **Paul Miller**, infant son of J. G. and E. **Lowry**, aged three months. Died on the 11th of August, 1857 in the third year of his age at Little Generostee, Anderson District, S. C., **Wilston**, the youngest child of Thomas and Eliza Ann **Stevenson**.

September 18, 1857

Departed this life near Starkville, Miss. on the 27th of August, Mrs. **Jane M. McKell**, wife of Mr. James McKell, in the 47th year of her age. She was the daughter of Dr. Benjamin Harris, late of Columbia and the grand-daughter of Capt. Hugh Miller of Fairfield District, S. C. She has left a disconsolate husband and seven children (six of them under ten years of age).

Married on Thursday evening, 10th September, by Rev. R. W. Brice, **J. L. Gaston**, Esq. of Chester to Miss **Margaret B. Hemphill** of Fairfield, S. C.

October 2, 1857

Died on the 18th of September in Fairfield District, S. C., Mr. **William B. Lathan** in the 24th year of his age. This is the third member of this family who has fallen this summer. William was assiduous in his attentions to his brother (J. P. Lathan, Esq.) during his illness and a few day s after he was buried, we hear of William being prostrated with the same disease, typhoid fever. ...[member of] Hopewell, Chester District.

Died on Little River, Abbeville District, S. C. on Sabbath evening the 20th of September, Mrs. **Mary Robinson**, wife of Hugh Robinson and daughter of John Clinkscales, Sr. Member of Baptist Church at Little River. ... and about 29 years old.

October 9, 1857

Died at her residence in the upper part of Abbeville District, S. C. about the 13th of August last, Mrs. **Margaret Carlisle**. The deceased was about ninety five years of age and had been a zealous and consistent member of the Associate Reformed Church at Little Generostee.

October 16, 1857

Died of flux in Gaston County, N. C. on the 14th of September, 1857, **William Boyce**, son of Thomas M. and Esther R. **Hanna**, aged fourteen months and one day.

Died at his residence in Laurens District, S. C. on the 21st of September, Mr. **Robert Sloan** in the 71st year of his age. The deceased made a public profession of his faith in Christ by connecting himself with the A. R. Church at an early period of his life.

Died in Camargo, Tenn., August 11th, 1857, Miss **Margaret A. McClough** in the 24th year of her age. ...She was an orphan.

Rev. and Dear Brother: I perform a painful service, in forwarding you the following brief notices. These persons have died in my congregation during the prevalence of a distressing disease this summer, yours &c. James L. Young:
Departed this life in Itawamba Co., Miss., July 19th, 1857, **Letitia Jane**, infant daughter of David and Martha J. **Lemon**, aged one year and four months.
On the morning of the 30th July, **Mary Ann**, the daughter of David and Martha J. **Lemon**, aged six years and nearly five months.
Departed this life in Itawamba Co., Miss. on the 30th July, **Samuel Lafayette**, son of Samuel and Jane **Bryson**, aged ten years and five months.
On the 30th of July, Mrs. **Jane Bryson**, wife of Samuel Bryson and daughter of the late John Milan of Laurens District, S.C. ... had for more than twenty years been a consistent member of the A. R. Church. ... She was about forty five years of age.
On the 6th of August, Miss **Sarah Elizabeth**, oldest daughter of Samuel and Jane **Bryson**, aged about eighteen years.

On the 10th of August, **Eliza Green**, infant daughter of Samuel and Jane **Bryson**, aged about six years.

Departed this life, Tishmingo Co., Miss, August 21st, **Ida Young**, infant daughter of Alfred and Margaret **O'Shields**, aged one year and five months.

On the 22nd of August, **Mary E. D.**, daughter of Alfred and Margaret **O'Shields**, aged about two months.

In Tippah Co., Miss on the 7th of August, Mrs. **Martha Bryson**, wife of Thomas Bryson and daughter of the late John Milan of Laurens District, S. C. ..[became member] of Providence, Laurens District, more than twenty years ago. ... was about fifty years of age, and has left a husband and five children.

Departed this life in Pontotoc Co., Miss. on the 14th of August, **Wm. Millen**, second son of A. M. and the late Mrs. Nancy **Galloway** in the seventeen year of his age.

On September 3rd, **Eliza Savannah**, infant daughter of A. M. and Martha E. **Galloway**, aged five months and 24 days.

On the 31st of August, **Thomas Wiley**, oldest son of A. M. and the late Nancy **Galloway**, aged about eighteen years.

On the 17th September, **Robert Spence**, son of A. M. and Martha E. **Galloway**, aged two years, two months and 5 days.

Departed this life on the -- of August, **Wm. Caldwell**, eldest son of F. A. and Elvira **Young**, in the twenty first year of his age. ...[member of] church at Bethany.

Departed this life in Tippah Co., Miss. on the 16th of August, **Euphemia Caroline**, daughter of James and Nancy **Turner**, aged six years and nearly three months.

On the 19th of August, **Harriet Amanda**, youngest daughter of James and Nancy C. **Turner**, aged about four years.

On the first of September, Miss **Nancy Eleanor**, second daughter of James and Nancy C. **Turner** in the 19th year of her age. ...[member of] A. R. Church at Bethany.

On the 10th of September, **Ebenezer Erskine**, youngest son of James and Nancy C. **Turner**, aged one year, two months and two days.

Departed this life in Tishomingo Co., Miss. on the 12th of September, Mrs. **Rachel Crocket**, wife of John F. Crocket, aged sixty five years. She had for many years been a member of the A. R. Church.

The disease which terminated the earthly existence of all of the above was dysentery or flux in a very malignant form; many of them did not survive a week after they were attacked.

Departed this life in Tippah Co., Miss. on the 15th of September, Mr. **Eli Crocket** in the thirty ninth year of his age, leaving a wife and seven children to mourn their loss. The disease which terminated his life was bowel affection..

October 23, 1857

Died at his residence in Yorkville on the 22nd of September, in the 58th year of his age, Col. **Wm. Wright**. His father, Samuel Wright, was among the first settlers of Yorkville. The subject of this notice early in life embarked upon the business of merchandise. By close attention to business, combined with a business talent, and at a period in the history of our country, when there was but little competition compared with the present, before having reached the decline of life, he had come into possession of a considerable amount of worldly substance. . . . .Early in life, he connected himself with the Associate Church, of which his parents were members, of Bethany, York District. ...Although he could not sing a single tune, yet in the family and in the sanctuary, he never, (as but too many in this age of improved refinement are found doing) sat with his lips closed while the praises of God were sung. But in his own way, like Father Blackstock, he joined in the employment of the upper Sanctuary.

It has been more than once stated, through mistake, in the Telescope, that Col. Wright was an elder in the church. Although repeatedly and earnestly solicited to allow his name to be put in nomination for the office of ruling elder, his consent could never be obtained, it is believed by the writer, entirely in consequence of the very low opinion he had of his qualification for so responsible and important a station. ...

In his last will and testament, we have learned that he did not forget the A. R. Synod of the South and her institutions, which had before partaken of his liberality. For the A. R. Church in Yorkville which owes its existence to his zeal and munificence, he also made provision.

Henry Moffatt, third son of Rev. Jas. A. and Mrs. Sarah **Sloan**, died at the residence of his father in Marshall Co., Miss. on Friday, 2d of October, 1857, aged four years, seven months and eleven days.

Died on the 9th October, 1857, **Martha Emeline**, wife of John M. **Grier**, in the 40th year of her age. The deceased left a husband and two children to mourn her--one child by a former and other by her latest marriage. ... member of the Associate Reformed Church at Steel Creek.

Married on the 15th instant by Rev. R. W. Brice, Mr. **Wade W. Lewis** to Miss **Elizabeth McKown**, both of Fairfield District, S. C.

October 30, 1857

Death has again visited our little flock [written by Rev. C. B. Betts of Winnsboro] , and carried off not the aged, not the shock to human appearance ripe for the sickle, but the tender lamb. ... On Tuesday morning, the 14th inst., little **Lawrence**, son of James M. and Ann **Elliott**. ... Had he lived three days longer he would have numbered fifteen months.

Due West Telescope

Died on Friday morning, 23d of October at his father's house in Lexington, Rockbridge Co., Va., of consumption, **William Lindsay**, son of James Lindsay, Esq., in the --year of his age. He was an only son.

Departed this life on Monday, 2d inst., Mrs. **Elizabeth Webb**, consort of John Webb, Sr., in the 72d year of her age. In early life, Mrs. Webb connected herself with the A. R. Church in Due West. She lived to see her descendants in the third generation. Her husband died several years previous--her children were all settled in life and for some time she was left alone.

November 20, 1857

Died in Yorkville, S. C. on the 5th inst., Mrs. **Jane Elder**, wife of Prof. M. Elder in the 38th year of her age. ... she leaves a husband and four children.

November 27, 1857

Died at his father's house in Generostee, Anderson District, S. C. of typhoid dysentery on the 17th October, 1857, **James Chalmers Wilbanks**, son of Elijah and Nancy Wilbanks. ... sixteen years, nine months and 5 days old.

Died of consumption on the 27th August, 1857 at the residence of her brother in Knox Co., Tenn. in the thirty seventh year of her age, Miss **Martha Jane Woods**, ... consistent member of the A. R. Church at New Salem.

Died of flux, Mecklenburg Co., N. C., **Margaret Louisa**, youngest child of Maj. **McGuinis**, and the only child of its mother, one year and five months.

Died of breast complaint on Sabbath evening, November 15th, **William Nelson,** in the -- of his age. ... He early made a profession of religion in the Associate Reformed Church, under the ministry of Rev. I. G. McLaughlin, then of Monroe Co., Va. He afterwards returned to Rockbridge, his native county, and established himself as a merchant of high repute in the bounds of Rev. Wm. McElwee's congregation where he was elected ruling elder. ... Two years since he changed his residence for a location in Old Providence, Augusta Co., Va.

Died, Nov. 7th, after a protracted and painful illness, Mrs. **Mary Bradley,** wife of Archibald Bradley, near the 60th year of her age. ... consistent member of the A. R. Church at Long Cane.

Married on the 18th inst. by Rev. C. B. Betts, Mr. **John H. Cathcart**, to Miss **Nancy Madden**, all of Winnsboro, S. C.

Married on the 12th inst. by Rev. H. T. Sloan, Mr. **H. T. Oliver** of Mississippi to Miss **Sallie C. Frazier**, daughter of James W. Frazier, Esq. of Abbeville, S. C.

Married on the 11th inst. by Rev. R. W. Brice, Mr. **Robert N. McCaw** of Chester and Miss **Narcissa Blain** of Fairfield District.

Married by Rev. J. M. Young on the 4th inst., Mr. **J. C. Hodges** of Wilcox to Miss **Martha A. Craig** of Dallas Co.[Ala].

December 4, 1857

Died at his residence in Decatur Co., Ind., October the 24th, 1857, in the 70th year of his age, Mr. **James McCrackin.** The subject of this notice was born and raised in Kentucky. In early life, he connected himself with the A. R. Church at Lexington, under the care of Rev. Adam Rankin. ... Mr. McCrackin emigrated to the precise spot where he died upward of 30 years ago, when this country, now so densely populated, was a wilderness, he being among the first settlers. The main design for emigrating here, according to his own statement, was the earnest expectation of soon enjoying church privileges, a thing of which, he was about denied in that part of Kentucky in which he lived at the time of his removal. And it was not long ere this expectation bid fare [sic] to be realized, in as much as a considerable number of A. R. people moved out of Kentucky to his neighborhood, about and after the time he came, probably some few before. He and the rest went to work as one man and built a commodious log church, and obtained supplies from the A. R. Church West. But when they proceeded to form an organization, Mr. McCrackin could not obtain church privileges, in consequence of his views upon the subject of slavery, which were opposed to those of the Western A. R. Synod. Time and again he attempted to adjust and compromise the matter, so as to obtain membership, but all in vain, since he was still required to make an acknowledgement relative to the subject, which he could not conscientiously do. Finally he became disheartened at his abortive attempts and despaired of ever obtaining privileges in the A. R. Church West. Hence, he, in connection with some others, applied to individual members of the Southern Synod, to come and supply them. Rev. N. M. Gordon first visited them and after him Rev. G. Gordon, later eventually organized the Clarksburg Church, in which Mr. McCrackin was chosen a ruling elder.

Died in Lincoln Co., Tenn. on the 7th of November, ult., Mr. **William Givens**.... He had passed his four score, being 82 years and fifteen days old. ... He was born in Mecklenburg Co., N. C., but had been in Tennessee many years. He had been a consistent member of the A. R. Church for 35 or 40 years.

Robert Samuel, infant son of Rev. A. S. and Mrs.L. G. **Montgomery**, died in Richmond, Ind. on Tuesday the 8th of September, 1857, aged two months and 23 days.

Married on the 24th inst. by Rev. H. T. Sloan, Mr. **Thomas Fell** to **Miss --- Wilson**, all of Abbeville District.

Married on the 26th inst. by the same, Mr. **J. L. White** to **Miss M. F. Lipford**, at the residence of her mother in Abbeville District.

December 11, 1857

Died of croup in York District, S. C., **Laura Jane**, daughter of William and Emeline **Boyce**, in her 4th year.

Married by Rev. H. Quigg on the 3rd ult., Mr. **Henry McDaniel** to Miss **Nancy M. Stewart**, daughter of James Stewart, Esq., all of Newton Co., Ga.

December 18, 1857

Died at the residence of his father in Drew Co., Ark. on the 4th of October, **William**, the son of Samuel and Elizabeth **McDaniel**, aged about 25 years.

Died also on the 22nd November, **Margaret Ann**, only daughter of Samuel and Elizabeth **McDaniel** of the same disease (typhoid fever) after the illness of twelve days, aged about 20 years.

Married on the 28th of October by Rev. Reuben Burrow, Mr. **John R. M'Cright**, merchant of Mt. Zion, Tipton Co., Tenn. and **Miss Kandas W. Hilliard** of Fayette Co., Tenn.

Married on the 29th of October by Rev. F. H. Green in the vicinity of Portersville, Mr. **George Wilkins** and Miss **Nancy**, daughter of the late Andrew **Shaw**, both of Tipton Co., Tenn.

Married on the 14th of October by Rev. F. H. Green, Mr. **David Fight** and Miss **Ellen Banks**, both of Tipton Co., Tenn..

Married on the 11th of November by the same, and in the vicinity of Portersville, Mr. **Jas. Huffman** and Miss **Nancy**, daughter of the late Hugh **Thompson**, both of Tipton Co., Tenn.

Married by the Rev. A. D. Montgomery on Thursday evening the 10th inst., Mr. **W. H. Hood** and Miss **Mattie McCaughrin**, all of Newberry, S. C.

Due West Telescope

Died on the 16th of October last, after a few days illness, Mr. **Thomas Bell**, in the 57th year of his age. The subject of the above notice was a native of Ireland. He emigrated to South Carolina where he resided several years--thence to Newton Co., Ga., where he settled in the neighborhood of Hopewell Church. In this church for several years he held the office of deacon.

Died on the morning of the 7th ult. in Newton Co., Ga. of typhoid pneumonia, Mrs. **Sarah L. Bell**, wife of A. S. Bell, in the 35th year of her age. ... member of Hopewell church....[left] a husband and four tender children.

Died on the 5th ult. in Butts Co., Ga. of typhoid pneumonia, **Mrs. E. A. Stewart**, wife of James T. Stewart, having lately entered her 27th year. The deceased was the younger sister of Mrs. Bell mentioned above. ...They were the children of John and Lucy McClelland.

Died in Tippah Co., Miss., the 14th of September, 1857, **W. A. A.**, infant son and only child of John A. and Margaret L. **Whitington**, aged 14 months.

Also, on the 18th of October, **William Nathan**, infant son and only child of Robt. and Martha **Jones**, aged about 8 weeks.

Miss **Ann Amanda Boyd** died of typhoid fever in Jefferson Co., Ga. on the 7th of November, 1857, aged 19 years. . . . a member of Bethel Church.

Married on the 24th of November by the Rev. J. R. Castles, Mr. **J. M. Whiteside** of York and Miss **Margaret M. Castles** of Fairfield, S. C.

Departed this life on the 6th of December, 1857 at his residence in Hart Co., Ga., **John McCurry** in the 82nd year of his age. The deceased united with the A. R. Church at Generostee about the time that Rev. R. Irwin took charge of the same. He was for many years a regular attendant although the church was 15 miles distant. ... While in the service during the War of 1812, his health was so impaired that he was removed home under difficult circumstances. During this trip he contracted an aversion to riding in any kind of vehicle which never left him, so that he rarely left home unless to attend church, an election, or where he thought his duty demanded his presence on which occasion he generally walked. ... He leaves a widow, a large number of children and grandchildren.

Married on the 14th ult. by the Rev. J. E. Pressly, Mr. **Hiram Deaton** and Miss **Clarissa Overcash** of Rowan Co., N. C.

----- by the same in Cabarrus Co., N. C., December 31st, Mr. **John Pope** to Miss **Christena Seaford**, of the same county.

January 22, 1858

Died in Lounds Co., Ala., December 2d, 1857 of disease of the heart, Mr. **Matthew Shanks, Sen.**, in the 80th year of his age. He was the head of a little band of Christians near Mt. Willing, by whom he was looked up to for counsel. In early life, he joined the A. R. Church in Abbeville District, S. C., was afterwards (about 1824) chosen an elder in Long Cane Church; in 1840 or ' 41 moved to Alabama, where he continued to act as ruling elder.

At the same place on the 5th December, 1857 of the same disease, Mrs. **Nancy Shanks**, wife of Matthew Shanks, deceased, aged about 76. She early joined the A. R. Church in Abbeville District, S. C.

Died in Wilcox Co., Ala., November 26th, 1857, of apoplexy, **J. Lewis Stewart**, in the 31st year of his age. He joined the A. R. Church at Wilcox in 1848. ... His wife, **Mary A. Stewart**, joined the church at the same time, died June 23d, 1857, aged 28. They left small children to the care of his widowed mother.

Married on the evening of the 12th inst. by Rev. C. B. Betts, Mr. **James Boyd, Sr.** of Chester District to Miss **Mariah R. McDowel** of Fairfield.

Married on Tuesday evening, the 19th January, 1858, by Rev. J. l. Bonner, Mr. **R. Beatty Parker** of Anderson village and Miss **Mary A.**, daughter of Major W. **Dickson** of Abbeville, S. C.

Married on the 22nd of December by Rev. J. F. Stewart, Mr. **Samuel Brown** to Miss **M. B. Marshall**.

----- also, on the 23rd last by the same, Mr. **Samuel T. Weir** to **Miss M. P. Cooper**, all of Randolph Co., Illinois.

January 29, 1858

Died on the 11th of January at the residence of his mother, four miles north of Ripley, Miss., **Willis J. Elliot** in the 28th year of his age.

Died on the morning of the 9th of December, after a short illness, Mrs. **Emily H. Lynn**, wife of Elder Capt. Matthew Lynn, in the 29th year of her age.... member of Church at Neely's Creek. ..leaves a husband and four children.

Married by Rev. L. McDonald on the 14th inst., Mr. **W. B. Simpson** and **Miss M. F. Millen**, all of Chester District, S. C.

Married by Rev. J. E. Pressly in Iredell Co., N. C. on the 14th inst., Mr. **John M. Gray**, Esq. and Miss **Nancy McNeely**, both of said county.

Married by the same on the same day in Cabarrus Co., Mr. **Wm. Isehower** and Mrs. **Susannah Cashin**, both of Cabarrus Co., N. C.

Married on the 13th inst. by Rev. T. A. Hoyt, Mr. **J. Fraser Livingston** and Miss **Fannie McCaw**, all of Abbeville District.

Married on the 5th inst. by Rev. T. L. McBryde, D. D., Rev. **D. Chalmers Boggs** of Pickens and Miss **Henrietta R.**, daughter of Rev. J. L. **Kennedy** of Anderson.

February 5, 1858

Departed this life in Oktibbeha Co., Miss. on the 7th of December, Mrs. **Elizabeth Cooper**, wife of James H. Cooper, aged 49 years. ... she leaves a husband, six children, and eight step-children.

Married on the 27th inst. at Albemarle, the residence of Mrs. John C. Singleton, by the Rev. P. J. Shand, **Wade Hampton, Jr.** to **Mary Singleton**, daughter of the late Gen. George McDuffie.

February 12, 1858

Died, December 4th, 1857, Mr. **John Robinson** in the 60th year of his age. During the early and greater part of his life, he was a consistent member of the the church, practically religious and diligent in his attendance upon ordinances; but for some years he seemed to walk with us no more. When talked with and entreated by the writer [Rev. H. T. Sloan] to consider his ways and to turn unto the Lord God, whom he had so long professed to love and serve, he wept as men seldom weep, confessing his sin and thanking me for the admonition; but a few months only glided by, until his sun went down and to us, behind a cloud.

Died, December 10th, 1857 of pneumonia, Mrs. **Rachel Harvely**, daughter of John Robinson, aged about twenty three years and three months. ... She left a husband and child.

Died in Chester District, S. C., the 21st January, Miss **M. M. Thomas**, daughter of Mrs. Jane Thomas, widow, in the 18th year of her age.

<u>February 19, 1858</u>

Died at her residence in Warren Co., Iowa, **Margaret Ann,** wife of Joseph **Henderson**, in her 51st year. She was born in Chester District, S. C. on the 11th of April, 1827; emigrated with her father, Mr. Wm. Fee, to Bloomington, Ind. in 1830. She became a member of the Associate Reformed Church at the age of sixteen, and was married to Joseph Henderson in 1848. She was a consistent member of the church at Bloomington until 1854, when she removed with husband and young family to Iowa.

<u>February 26, 1858</u>

Death of a Student. Our community was startled on last Sabbath afternoon by the announcement of the death of **D[avid] M. West**, member of Senior Class in Erskine College. ... It is supposed death came from a latent disease of the lungs or brain, or perhaps both. The funeral procession on Monday was one of the largest that we recollect to have seen in Due West.

Died, November 13th, 1857, Mrs. **Mary Renwick**, wife of James Renwick, Esq. and daughter of the late John Cunningham, elder of the Mt. Olivet congregation, Ky. ... She leaves a husband and one infant child.

Died in Decatur Co., Indiana on the 19th of December, 1857, Mrs. **Mary Anderson**, wife of Samuel Anderson, in the 57th year of her age. Mrs. Anderson emigrated from Kentucky with her father, (a distinguished elder in the A. R. Church in its early history) and married shortly after she arrived. Although she and her husband had both been reared by pious parents, yet they did not connect themselves with the church for many years after their marriage; not because they did not have an attachment for the church of their fathers, and a desire to connect themselves with it long before they did, but because neither of them could conscientiously subscribe to the stringent law of the A. R. Church West, upon the vexed subject of slavery. But so soon as they met with a chance of connecting themselves with the A. R. Church under the care of the Southern Synod, they joyfully availed themselves of the opportunity, and had all their children baptized at once, except the eldest who was grown and married. Mrs. Anderson joined the A. R. Church at Clarksburg when it was organized by Rev. G. Gordon, some ten or twelve years ago. [Rev. A. S. Montgomery].

Married in Pope Co., Arkansas on the 4th ult. by Hugh Taylor Esq., Mr. **Robert B. Whitesides** and Miss **Elmina Jane Blackwood.**

Due West Telescope

Died in Maury Co., Tenn. on the 22d of January, Miss **M. Adaline Lusk**, aged 21 years, one month and 7 days.

Died in Maury Co., Tenn. in the seventh year of her age, **Nancy L.**, youngest child of A. B. **Walker**.

Departed this life in Union Co., N. C. on the 18th of February, 1858, Mrs. **Mary Stewart**, wife of John Stewart, Esq., in the 61st year of her age. ... She was, for something more than forty years, a consistent member of the Associate Reformed Church, at Shiloh, in the Waxhaws.... [survived by] an aged husband, two sons and five daughters.

Married on the 3d by D. W. Hawthorn, Esq. at the residence of James Weir, **Lorenzo Dow Wright** and Miss **Lucinda Burnett**, all of Abbeville Dist.

Married on the 1st December by Rev. J. Wilson, Mr **John Moore** and Miss **Mary J. McClerkin**, all of Tipton Co., Tenn.

Married on the 8th December by the Rev. Mr. Wilson of the Methodist church, Mr. **James Tucker** of Fayette Co., Tenn. and Miss **Laura**, daughter of T. N. **Carothers**, Esq. of Tipton Co., Tenn.

Married on the 15th December by Rev. John Wilson, Mr. **Alexander J. Wilson** and Miss **Eliza Hemphill**, second daughter of W. R. **McCain**, all of Tipton Co., Tenn.

Married on the 29th December by the same, Mr. **Wm. Wilson** and **Mrs. McCullough**, both of Tipton Co., Tenn.

Married on the 2nd February by the same, Mr. **James Hindman** and Miss **Sarah**, eldest daughter of John **Linn**, all of Tipton Co., Tenn.

Married on the 25th February by Rev. C. B. Betts, Mr. **John T. Huey** of Abbeville District to Miss **Mary C. Bell** of Fairfield District, S. C.

Died of scarlet fever on the 2nd of February, 1858, little **"Sallie,"** youngest daughter of Mr. and Mrs. John **Chiles** in the 4th year of her age.

Died in the residence of her mother in this District on the 4th ult. in her 34th year, Mrs. **Ann E. Pressly**, wife of David A. Pressly and daughter of Andrew and Grizza Gillespie, after an illness of some four months.

Married on the 25th of February by Rev. H. L. Murphy, Mr. **Adams Rutherford** and Miss **Harriet Caldwell**, all of Newberry District, S. C.

Married by Rev. J. E. Pressly on the 25th ult. in Iredell Co., N. C., Mr. **Ninian Robinson** and Miss **Catherine E.M. White**, both of said county.

March 26, 1858

Departed this life on Sabbath evening the 14th inst. at the residence of her son in Mecklenburg, N. C., Mrs. **Rebecca McDowell**, in the 78th year of her age.

Died at his residence in Mecklenburg Co., N. C., March 11th, **John M. Porter**, a deacon of the A. R. Church of Steel Creek in the 45th year of his age. ... [member of] A. R. Church at Bethel about twenty years.

April 2, 1858

Married on the 11th inst. by the Rev. D. G. Phillips, Mr. **D. P. Lowry** of Jefferson County to Miss **Jane A. Netherland** of Burke Co., Ga.

Married in Rowan Co., N. C., March 10th, by Rev. J. E. Pressly, Mr. **Robert F. Cavin** of Iredell and Miss **Theresa Overcash** of Rowan.

Died on Wednesday night the 31st ult., **Jessie Hearst**, a little daughter of Dr. E. E. and Mrs. Mary **Pressly**, not quite two years. She died of measles.

Died in Rockbridge Co., Va. on the 12th of March, Mrs. **Patsy Harper**, wife of Jas. F. Harper, Esq. in the 52nd year of her age.

Married by Rev. H. Quigg on the evening of the 23d inst. at the residence of the bride's father, Dr. **John McKown** to Miss **Madora A. Sims**, daughter of Dr. Sims of Henry County, Ga.

Married on the 11th inst. by Rev. H. T. Sloan, Mr. **William Butler** to Miss **Mary Ann Martin**, all of Abbeville District, S. C.

Married at the residence of Mr. W. J. Dunbar on the 18th inst. by Rev. M. Peden, Mr. **James Jammison** to Miss **Sallie Johnston**, all of Winston Co., Miss., formerly of Chester, S. C.

April 9, 1858

Married on the 17th of March by Rev. J. E. Pressly, Mr. **Thomas D. Graham** and Miss **Mary A. McKnight**, of Iredell Co., N. C.

April 16, 1858

Mrs. **Margaret G. McCaughan** died, at the residence of her husband in Fayette Co., Tenn. on the 18th day of March last. She was in the twenty fifth year of her age. She connected herself with the A. R. Church of Sardis, Tenn. at the age of fifteen and remained a consistent member. ... She leaves a husband and two small children.

Died in Cabarrus Co., N. C., March 6th, Miss **Sarah S. Cochran**. She had nearly completed her forty eighth year.

Died in Rockbridge Co., Va. on the 31st ult., Miss **Mary Ann Anderson**, in the 45th year of her age.... member of A. R. Church of Ebenezer.

April 30, 1858

Died on the morning of the 2nd of January, 1858, **David McWilliams**, in the 74th year of his age. The day before his death, he appeared as well as usual--more cheerful--went to the village of Lynville in the neighborhood where three of his sons reside. ... Mr. McWilliams was born in Chester District, S. C. in the year 1784. He was the youngest son of Jno. and Jane McWilliams, natives of Ireland, ... [members of] A. R. Church, Hopewell. ... He removed with his family to the State of Indiana, Gibson County, in the year 1837, and with his wife, were the first members of the A. R. Church in the eastern part of said county, where there is now a flourishing congregation of over seventy members, with Rev. R. Gray, pastor.

Married on the 17th of March by Rev. David Pressly, Mr. **Henry P. Fowler** to Miss **Sallie Pearson**, all of Oktibbeha Co., Miss.

----- on the 15th inst. by Rev. R. W. Brice, Mr. **William Boyd** to Miss **Sarah White**--all of Chester District.

----- on the 30th of March by Rev. J. H. Bryson, Dr. **A. A. Tate** to Mrs. **Jane Galloway**, all of Lincoln Co., Tenn.

May 7, 1858

Died at his residence in Tipton Co., Tenn.., October 28th, 1857, **Thomas D. Kilpatrick**, aged 40 years and 17 days. In 1837, he and his wife together connected themselves with the Church at New Hope, Fairfield District, S. C. . . . of which church they continued members until the fall of 1848, when they moved to Tipton Co.,Tenn. where they immediately became members of Salem.

May 21, 1858

Died in Due West on the 12th of May with measles and erysipelas, **Martha Fillen**, youngest child of Rev. J. N. and E. F. **Young**, aged about 15 months.

Departed this life on the 14th of May, at the residence of her brother, Esquire Ellis, near Due West, Mrs. **Margaret Burton**. ... member of Methodist Church ... widow and childless.

Departed this life in Orrville, Dallas Co., Ala. on the 23d of April, 1858, **Thomas Craig**, in the eighty second year of his age. When quite a youth, on his passage to this country, he was deprived of his father. ... He was an early settler of Alabama and among the first to erect the standard of the A. R. Church in this state. ...[member of] Prosperity Church.

Married on the 2nd of March, 1858, by Rev. N. M. Goodman, **Samuel McCaulay** and **Martha H. Gwyn**, of Jessamine Co., Ky.

----- by the same, May 6th, **Robert Garrett** of Woodford and **Margaret Wilmore** of Jessamine Co., Ky.

May 28, 1858

Killed-- A well grown **son** of Thos. **Stevenson** of Abbeville District was killed instantly on last Sabbath by a fall from a mulberry tree. He fell only ten or twelve feet, but the head striking the ground first, the neck was dislocated. Boys, remember the Sabbath!

Aged old **Mrs. Gantt**, long a worthy member of the Little River Baptist Church in Abbeville District died at her residence on Little River on the 22nd inst. at an extreme old age being in her one hundred and third year.

Died at his residence in Rockbridge Co., Va. on the 10th inst., Mr. **Richard Gibs**, a worthy member of the A. R. Church.

Departed this life in Jefferson Co., Ga. in December last, Miss **Nancy I. Cotter**, the only daughter of Mrs. W. Cotter . ... she was followed by her brother **Stephen Cotter**.

Married on the 6th of May by Rev. J. H. Bryson, Mr. **J. L. Alexander** to Miss **Louisa**, daughter of P. G. **M'Mullen**, Esq., all of Lincoln Co., Tenn.

The village of Due West has been called this week to mourn the death of two of its promising youth. ...[**William H.**] **Drennen** died on the 30th of May, the day of his birth just as he had completed his twentieth year. ... He was a student of Erskine College--a member of the Freshman Class, making the fourth student of the college which has yielded to the stroke of death during the present session. ...[buried at family burying ground at Cedar Spring]

Little [**John**] **Cleaveland** [**Sharp**], the only son of Mr. R. C. Sharp ... died on the 31st of May. He had entered on his tenth year.

Died on the 23rd of May, **David M'Cray**, of Rockbridge Co., Va. For about twelve of the last 36 hours of his life he labored under an abberation of the mind--talking incessantly--and what is so remarkable in his case, was that nearly all his talk was in rhyme, (or original poetry, principally of long metre verse), delivered too in the most eloquent manner, the most of which contained sensible ideas. ... the deceased was born in Rockbridge Co., Va. on the 25th of April, 1803.

Miss **Margaret E. Bonner**, a sister of the Editor, departed this life on yesterday, the 10th. ... she was a member of the A. R. Church.

Died of a complication of diseases on the 22d of April, **John Calvin Lynn**, son of the late Joshua Lynn of Chester District, S. C. in the 12th year of his age.

Married in Greensboro', Ga. on the 27th May by Rev. Mr. Houston, Mr. **Robt. A. Irwin** and Miss **M. R. Miller**.

Died of consumption at the residence of her brother in Due West on the 10th inst. Miss **Margaret Bonner** in the twenty third year of her age. Margaret was a native of Wilcox Co., Ala. ... the youngest child of James and Mary P. Bonner. ...[She was] in childhood left an orphan.

Died at the residence of her father, Jas. McElwee, York District, S. C., May 31st,1858, Mrs. **Eliza Jane**,wife of S. N. **Miller**, in the 28th year of her age.

William Henry, infant son of Thomas and Mary A. **Castles**, died at the residence of his father in Fayette Co., Tenn. on the 27th of May last, aged two months and three days.

Died at the residence of H. Quigg, **Mary E.**, commonly called "Willie," only child of Mrs. Mary L. **Barron**, relict of the late William A. Barron, of Percy Co., Ala, aged 2 years, 4 months and 15 days.

Died in Rockbridge Co., Va. on the 11th inst., **William Moore**, aged about 75 years. The deceased was one of our most respectable citizens and had as few enemies as is common with men. He was kind even to a fault. As a husband and parent, he was self-sacrificing and indulgent. The church was never permitted to call him a member by profession; and yet all of its pecuniary claims he responded to with more than ordinary freedom. He lived and died within little more than a mile of Old Providence Church and his remains sleep with a numerous connection in the churchyard of his fathers.

<u>July 2, 1858</u>

Died on the 9th inst. at the residence of her brother in Albany, Miss **Mary D. Robertson**, on her return from her residence in Due West, Abbeville District, to that of her father, Alexander Robertson, at Fort Miller, Washington Co., N. Y. in the 36th year of her age. By a residence of some years at the South, she had contracted the disease peculiar to that climate, usually so fatal to those whose constitutional habits have been formed under the influence of higher climate, the flux, or affection of the bowels.

Married . . . 26th May by Rev. J. B. Watt, Rev. **W. B. Pressly** and Miss **Lorenna E.**, daughter of the late Dr. Jno. Moore **Harris** of Mecklenburg, N. C.

Married by the Rev. Milton Carr on the evening of the 4th of May at the residence of the bride's father, **Alexander I. Owens** to Miss **Martha J. Goens**, only daughter of Jesse Goens, Drew Co., Arkansas.

<u>July 9, 1858</u>

Died in Abbeville village of the consequences of scarlet fever on the 13th June after an illness of, and just five weeks after the death of her little brother Willie, **Eliza Thomson**, daughter of R. A. and M. A. **Fair**, 5 years, 7 months and 9 days old.

Died in Cabarrus Co., N. C., Mrs. **Catherine M. McGinnis** in the thirtieth year of her age, on the first day of June, 1858. Mrs. McGinnis was a member of the A. R. Church at Back Creek.

Died on the 19th of June, 1858 at the residence of her father, **Sarah E. B. Milliken**, aged about two years, disease--typhoid fever.

July 16, 1858

Died of consumption on the 21st of June at the residence of his sisters in Laurens District, S. C., Mr. **James Fleming**, in the 42d year of his age. ...[member of] A. R. Church at Bethel about twenty years.

Died at the residence of her father, James Martin, in Panola Co., Miss., June 16th, Mrs. **Sarah Jane Painter**, wife of Thomas L. Painter, in the 32d year of her age. She joined the Methodist Church at Anderson C. H. in 1842. She was the mother of five children, two having gone before her; the third one, an infant daughter, **Sarah Ugenia [Painter]**, ten days after her.

Died on the 29th of June of typhoid dysentery, Mrs. **Jane Turnbull**, in the fifty second year of her age. ...she was the daughter of Francis and Nancy Young, and spent most of her earlier days in Abbeville District, S. C., the place of her nativity, but emigrated with her husband and family in 1837 and settled in Oxford, Miss., where the remainder of her life was spent. Four of her children preceded her to the grave; and one, her first born, who emigrated to Texas some years ago, her eldest daughter who sustains the relations of wife and mother, and her husband and two daughters, of the homestead, remain to mourn their loss.

Died near Williamsport, Maury Co., Tenn. on the morning of June 10th, Mrs. **Jane D. M'Caw**, wife of David M'Caw and daughter of John and Mary Torbit of Chester District, S. C. She was in the 40th year of her age, had been married over 19 years, and left three children, the youngest, eight years old.

August 6, 1858

Died on the 21st of July in the 25th year of her age Miss **Isabella Young**, only surviving daughter of Mr. John Young, Esq. of Iredell Co., N. C.

Died at the residence of her husband in Harris County, Ga., June 26th, 1858, Mrs. **Mary Brown**, wife of Mr. -- Brown, in the 63rd year of her age. Our departed sister was born in Jefferson Co., Ga. in the year 1795, and lived in that county till the year 1836, when she removed to western Georgia. ... By her first marriage (with Mr. Samuel Fleming of Jefferson County) she had a number of children who survived her. ... After the death of her first husband (Mr. Fleming) she married Mr. -- Brown of Harris Co., Ga. who survives her.

Married on the 20th of July by Rev. J. E. Pressly, Mr. **H. Goodnight** and Miss **M. E. Morrison** of Cabarrus Co., N. C.

Due West Telescope

Died on the 30th June, 1858, at his residence in Tipton Co., Tenn., **Wm. A. Kirk**, aged 31 years, disease--typhoid fever. ... member of the Associate Reformed Church at Salem. ...has left a widow and four small children.

Mrs. **Martha McGill**, wife of Thomas McGill, elder of Mount Nebo, N. C., departed this life July 19th, 1858 in the 64th year of her age. She had been a member of the A. R. Church at Old Pisgah for 36 years.

Also, on the 23rd July, at her father's house, Gaston, N. C., **Mrs. Holland**, wife of Jasper Holland and daughter of Jane Quinn.

Died at his residence in Union Co., N. C. on the 27th ult., **John Walker**, Esq. in the 78th year of his age. ... in early life connected himself with the congregation worshipping at Tirzah. He was three times married and raised a tolerably numerous family. ... A few days before his death he walked out to the graveyard which was near, in company with Mrs. Walker, and was observed to contemplate with more than usual solemnity, the last resting place of loved ones, till at length struggling emotion vented itself in a flood of tears. He then remarked to Mrs. Walker, " I have been three times married have lived about 11 years with each of my wives; I now think our separation is near."

Mrs. **Mary Hadden**, widow and pensioner of the late William Hadden, decd., a Revolutionary soldier, departed this life in Louisville, Jefferson Co., Ga. on the 7th of August, 1858 . . . . in the 88th year of her age. ... a member of the A. R. Church at Old Bethel, Burke Co. for nearly "three score and ten."

Died on the 17th January, 1858, **James Stewart**, infant son of James and Margaret **Cooper**, aged six weeks and one day.

Died in Maury Co., Tenn. on the 11th of August, **Samuella Jeannie**, infant daughter of J. B. and M. **Galloway**, aged 1 year, 7 months and 18 days.

Died in Henry Co., Ga. on the 2d instant, **John Adolphus**, son of James T. **Stewart**, aged 1 year, 5 months and 7 days. ...He was taken home, after the demise of his mother last fall, and kept by his grandmother, Mrs. Lucy McClelland.

Departed this life, July 27th, 1858, **Mary Ann Sylvania**, infant daughter of J. W. and M. A. **Allen**. She was born March 19th, 1858. ..Macon, Tenn.

Died at Troy, Tenn. on the morning of the 22d of July, **Nancy Jane**, wife of A. P. **Moffatt** and daughter of James McClerkin of Tipton Co., Tenn. ... in the 29th year of her age. ... She leaves a husband, an infant daughter.

Died of pneumonia on the 28th of April, **Elvirah**, wife of R. M. **McEwen**, and daughter of John V. and Leanna Moore. ... she had been married eight years and a few months, and was the mother of four children, one of whom died in '54, and another a month old at his mother's death, has since died, aged three months. ... She was a member of the A. R. Church, Salem, Tipton Co., Tenn.

Died in Knox Co, East Tennessee, on the 26th of July, 1858, **Mary Amelia**, only daughter of James and Martha J. **Kennedy** in her 10th year.

Married on the morning of the 1st instant by Rev. H. Quigg, Dr. **J. S. Middlebrook** to Miss **Laurie Garlington**, all of Newton Co., Ga.

September 3, 1858

Died on the 14th of August, 1858, at his residence in Shelby Co., Tenn., **Matthew Wilson**, aged 70 years. ... Long a member of the A. R. Church; for many years at Bethel, Lincoln Co., and for the last 5 or 6 years at Salem, Tipton Co. He leaves an aged and afflicted companion to mourn his loss. His children are dispersed and are not known to the writer.

Died in Wilcox Co., Ala. on the 17th of August, Dr. **William C. Smith**, in the 32d year of his age. ... He was a graduate of East Tennessee University at Knoxville and known to many of the readers of the *Telescope* as a pupil at Erskine College. ... leaves a widow and three little orphans.

Died on Sabbath morning the 8th of August, 1858 at the residence of her husband in Tipton Co., Tenn., **Margaret Wright**, consort of James Wright, in the 65th year of her age. The deceased from early life had been a member of the Associate and the Associate Reformed Church. For the last twenty two years, she had been a consistent member of the A. R. Church at Salem, being received with her husband at its first organization..

Departed this life in this district on the 23d day of May last, **William Stevenson**, son of Thomas and Mary Ann Stevenson, at the age of twenty years, eleven months and two days.

Died on the 2d of July, Mr. **Samuel Patterson**, formerly of Washington Co., Pa. He died at his residence, Shepherd's Dale, Bedford Co., Va. ... it is believed that he was upwards of 60 years. Mr. Patterson was born and educated at West Middletown, Washington Co., Pa. where a great part of his family still reside. About the year 1848 he came to Va. with a view of seeking a milder climate. ... He was an excellent farmer and a successful wool grower. [member and ruling elder of the A. R. Church] he procured at his new home among the wild and majestic mountains of Bedford a minister of his own denomination to labor statedly for the benefit of his family and neighbors.

Married on the 31st of August by Rev. W. R. Hemphill, Mr. **J. Marion Pruit** to Miss **M. Myrtle Pratt**, daughter of John Pratt, Esq.--all of Abbeville District, S. C.

Married on the 21st of July by Rev. A. P. Sillaman, Mr. **James M'Kell** of Oktibbeha Co., Miss. to Miss **Isabella J. Mayes** of Green Co., Ala.

Married by Rev. David Pressly, 4th of August, Mr. **Pleasant J. Wray** to Miss **Sarah J. Cooper**, all of Oktibbeha Co., Miss.

Married on the 5th of August by the same, Mr. **William McCann** to Miss **L. W. Nichols**, all of Oktibbeha Co., Miss.

Married on the 12th of August by the same, Mr. **John C. Cooper** to Miss **Margaret L. Cooper**, all of Oktibbeha Co., Miss.

September 10, 1858

Died on the 11th of August after a very protracted illness, old **Mrs. Miller** in the 84th year of her age. ... consistent member of the church of Christ at Cedar Spring since the days of Dr. John T. Pressly's pastorate.

Died of cholera at the residence of her parents in Pickens District, June 22nd, **Mary Estelle**, infant daughter of Col. and Mrs. P. H. **Prather** and grandchild of Mr. and Mrs. Drennon, aged 10 months and five days.

[Died] after illness of five days, July 22nd in Pine Bluff, Arkansas, **R. Henry Drennon**, Esq., son of Capt. Wm. T. and Mrs. M. D. Drennon, aged 22 years and 3 months. ... A graduate of Erskine College at the early age of nineteen, Mr. Drennon commenced the study of law, [but] only for a few months under Genl. McGowan and Perrin at Abbeville Court House...[and] in December, 1857, he was admitted to the practice of law, and the February following left his native state to pursue his profession at Pine Bluff, Arkansas.

On the third of August, **James W. Shaw** rose early in the morning in good health, and unusually cheerful, repaired to a pen in which he had some sheep enclosed, and was assisting to catch one, when the sheep attempting to make its escape inflicted a blow in the chest which terminated his life in some three hours. ... leaves a widow and two interesting little children, both daughters.

Died in Newton Co., Ga. on the 28th of June, 1858, Mrs. **Eleanor Sarvice** in the 79th year of her age. She was for 50 years a member of the church of Christ and for 48 a widowed mother. ... Originally she belonged to the Associate Church and held her membership at Smyrna, Chester, S. C. ... A few years ago she removed herself to this place ...[and joined] Hopewell Church.

Married on the 19th August by Rev. L. McDonald, **Jno. W. Baird** of Marengo, Ala. and Miss **Sarah**, daughter of Jno. **Simpson**, Esq. of Chesterville, S. C.

Married on the 31st of August by Rev. J. Boyce, D. D., **I. P. Moffatt** of Troy, Tenn. and Miss **Mary F. Brice** of Fairfield District, S. C.

Married on the 1st instant by Rev. J. C. Williams, Mr. **Hugh D. Brownlee** and Miss **Eugenia --- Barmore**, all of Abbeville.

September 17, 1858

Esther P., wife of Hugh **Hemphill**, died July 28th, 1858, near Bloomington, Ind. The subject of this notice was born in Chester District, S. C., August 16, 1813. ... She left a kind husband and a lonely daughter.

October 15, 1858

Rufus Cain died on the 15th of July last, lacking four days of being 30 years old. About 10 years ago he made a profession of religion at Sharon Church, York District, S. C.

Departed this life at the house of Mr. Ferbrick Nane in Pontotoc Co., Miss., July 10th, 1858, Mr. **Alfred Agnew**, in the 31st year of his age. Mr. Agnew was the youngest son of the late Mr. Samuel and Melinda Agnew of Abbeville District, S. C. He never made a public profession of religion, yet there were some things in his conduct during the last three or four months of his life, which afford some grounds to believe that his spiritual interests were not overlooked. ... much of his time was spent in reading the Bible.

Married on the 7th instant by Rev. H. T. Sloan, Mr. **J. A. Myers** of N. C. and Miss **Sallie Morris** of Cedar Spring, Abbeville District, S. C.

Married on the 7th instant by Rev. R. W. Brice, Dr. **Stirling W. Blain** to Miss **Sarah**, daughter of Wm. **Knox**, all of Chester District, S. C.

Married on the 21st September by Rev. S. S. Ralston, Mr. **W. Bruce Brown** (formerly of North Carolina) and Miss **Mary M. Reid**, both of Lincoln Co., Mo.

Married on the 15th of September by Rev. R. H. Morrison, **George Little**, Esq. to Miss **Martha King**, all of Lincoln Co., N. C.

Married on the 7th of October by the Rev. W. T. Pharr, **William B. Osborn** to Miss **Nancy Ann L. Beard**, all of Mecklenburg Co., N. C.

December 3, 1858

Died in the city of Lynchburg of asthmatic pulmonary on the 20th of July, 1858, **Andrew Kinnear**, Esq. in the 57th year of his age. He was a native of Ireland, County Monaghan. ... He had made a profession of religion in Ireland, a certificate of which he retained; but for reasons known to himself did not unite with any branch of the church from his emigration to the United States in 1827, until October, 1857 when he united with the A. R. Church of Old Providence, Augusta Co., Va., a distance of 50 miles. ...[left] two orphan daughters.

Died at her residence in Monroe County, Va. on the 1st of November, Mrs. **Emily Patton**, wife of Robert A. Patton, in the 27th year of her age. ...member of the A. R. Church, New Lebanon congregation, Monroe Co. Va. She leaves a husband and two lovely children, Eliza Ellen and Thompson McElwee.

Died of croup in Tippah Co., Miss. on the 17th of October, **Thomas Wilson**, infant son of W. J. and J. C. **Patterson**, aged 6 months and 17 days.

Died of pnuemonia on the 1st of November, Mrs. **Eliza Louisa**, consort of James **McBryde** in the 47th year of her age. ...[God] had spared her to see both her sons united with the church of Christ and expressing a strong hope that an only little daughter would at an early age follow their example.

Died in Newberry District, S. C. of congestive fever, **J. W. Renwick**, son of Col. J. S. and Mary Renwick, in the 20th year of his age. The deceased was spending the vacation with his parents and friends when the summons came that Washington must leave this world. ... he had connected himself with the church during the revival in Erskine College last summer; and several of his fellows in college were present to pay their last kindness in ministering to his comfort while alive, and in following to its clay house in King's Creek graveyard, his body after death.

Married on the 9th of November by Rev. H. L. Murphy, Capt. **J. F. Cromer** to **Miss M. C. E. Crosson**, all of Newberry, S. C.

Married on the evening of the 11th of November by Rev. H. Bryson, D. D., Mr. **John S. McCown** to Miss **Kezia Taylor**, all of Lincoln Co., Tenn.

Married on the 10th November by Rev. C. B. Betts, Mr. **Franklin Elder** and Miss **Henrietta Shaw**, all of Winnsboro, S. C.

December 10, 1858

Died at his residence in Pope Co., Arkansas on the 28th of October, 1858, Mr. **John Oats** in the seventy third year of his age. The subject of this obituary was born in Lincoln Co., N. C., July 17, 1786. He was nurtured in the Associate Church, and when about 21 years of age was received in the communion of that church. About the age of 31, he was chosen to the office of ruling elder in the congregation at Pisgah, then under the care of Rev. William Dickson. After this, the congregation came under the care of Rev. Joseph Banks, but he soon left them because of their opposition to the Act of Synod concerning slaveholding. In the Autumn of 1851, he with some others, principally from Pisgah, emigrated to Arkansas. ... in about twelve months after their arrival at their new home, a minister was sent to them, they were organized and he was chosen one of the ruling elders.

Died in Abbeville District, S. C., November 30, 1858, Mrs. **Isabella Pressly**, wife of Dr. George W. Pressly, aged 52 years, 8 months and 2 days. ... Several children preceded Mrs. Pressly to the tomb, but three survive her whom she had the satisfaction of seeing following her footsteps as members of the church of Christ at Cedar Spring.

Died on the 31st of October at his residence in Tipton Co., Tenn., **Joseph H. Strain** in the 30th year of his age. ... But a short time his brother in law, **W. A. Kirk**, had died, leaving a widow and four small children. And now another of the same family is cut down leaving a widow and one child.

Married on the 23d of November by the Rev. Mr. Griffin, Mr. **R. G. M'Elwain**, late of Lancasterville, S. C. and Miss **Laura L. Pullin**, all of Tipton Co., Tenn.

Married on the 23d of November by the same, Mr. **J. S. Slaughter Caruthers** and **Miss J. F. Hill**, both of Shelby Co., Tenn..

Married on the 10th November by the Rev. D. H. Cummins near Covington, Tipton Co., Tenn., Mr. **Robt. Hall** and **Miss Still**, all of that county.

Married on the 19th October by the Rev. M. M. Brown, Mr. **John S. Burrow** of Jackson County and **Miss D. J. Cooper** of Randolph County, Illinois.

December 24, 1858

Died October 16, 1858 in Iredell Co., N. C., Miss **Sarah Allison** in the 20th year of her age.

In the same county, September 20th of typhoid fever, Mr. **Albert T. White** in the 22nd year of his age; and November 22nd, Mr. **John A. White**, a brother, of the same disease, in his 24th year. Died, November 28th, Mrs. **Sarah White**, the mother of the above, in the 54th year of her age.

Died, August 5th, 1858 of congestive fever, **Samuel Shannon** of Shelby Co., Ky. ... member of the A. R. congregation of Shelbyville.
Died, October 28th, 1858, **Samuel James**, son of Moses C. **Gwyn**, of Ebenezer congregation, Ky. ... aged seventeen years.

On the 4th of December, 1858, near Bloomington, Tenn., **John W. Allen** in the 23rd year of his age.

Married by Rev. J. C. Boyd on the 16th of December, Mr. **Abram Carmical** of Georgia and Miss **Jane G. Carmical** of Newberry, S. C.

----- on the 16th inst. by Rev. R. W. Brice, Mr. **Leonard L. Rataree** and Miss **Sarah E. Dorrough**, all of Chester District, S. C.

----- by Rev. H. L. Murphy on the 16th inst., **J. S. Reid**, Esq. and Miss **Dallas C. Boyd**, all of Newberry, S. C.

----- by Rev. J. E. Pressly, December 3rd, Mr. **H. C. Malcolm** of Salisbury and Miss **Judith F. Black** of Cabarrus Co., N. C.

Married in Sumter, S. C. on the 2d December by the Rev. D. McQueen, Rev. **James Douglas** of Winnsboro and Miss **Margaret**, daughter of the late Davidson **McDowell** of Georgetown District.

Married by Rev. J. G. Richards on Thursday evening, 25th November, **Andrew B. Wardlaw** of Abbeville and Miss **Sallie E.**, daughter of J. S. **Thompson** of Liberty Hill, Kershaw District.

----- on Tuesday evening the 8th by Rev. Wm. Banks, Mr. **John P. Bell** of Fairfield to **Miss I.H.**, daughter of Wm.**Caldwell** of Chester District.

January 7, 1859

Died in Chester District, S C. on the 28th of November, Mrs. **Martha**

Hamilton, aged 88 years. She came to this country from Ireland in the year 1792. ... [member of] A. R. Church at Hopewell.

Died in Chester District, S. C. on the 30th October last, Miss **Nancy Dickey**, aged about fifty years. ... member of A. R. Church at Hopewell.

Married by Rev. J. I. Bonner on the 23rd December, Mr. **W. L. Pressly** of Due West and Miss **Fannie**, daughter of A. **Wideman** of Long Cane, S. C.

Married on the 22nd ult. by Rev. James M. Chiles, Mr. **R. F. McCaslan** to Miss **Mollie E. Carter**, all of Abbeville, S. C.

Married on the 23rd December, 1858 by Rev. W. R. Hemphill, Mr. **Matthew R. Cochran** and Miss **Nancy J. Greer**, all of Abbeville District.

Married, December 16th by Rev. J. E. Pressly, Mr. **Levi Bell** and Miss **Mary J. von Pelt** of Cabarrus Co., N. C.

----- by the same at the same place and time, Mr. **Caleb M. B. Goodnight** and Miss **Asenah J. Bell.**

Married on the 24th of November, by ----- Mr. **Malcus Hooks** of Tipton Co., Tenn. to **Miss Bonds** of Shelby Co., Tenn.

----- on the 30th of November by Rev. Jno. Wilson, Mr. **James English** to Miss **Martha Prince**, all of Tipton Co., Tenn.

----- on the 16th of December by the same and near Bloomington, Tipton Co., Tenn., Mr. **William McKinstry, Junr.** of Fayette County to Miss **Eliza Davis.**

----- on the 23rd of December by the same, Mr. **Wm. Allen** of Fayette County to Miss **Jane** -----, daughter of N. H. **Nelson** of Tipton Co., Tenn.

Married on the 14th of December by Rev. J. M. Young, Mr. **E. S. White** to Miss **Margaret J. Chisolm**, all of Dallas Co., Ala.

Married on the 21st ult. by Rev. D. F. Haddon, Mr. **Albert Anderson** of Spartanburg and Miss **Sarah A. Bryson** of Laurens.

January 14, 1859

Died at his residence in Abbeville, Lafayette Co., Miss. on the 7th December, Mr. **John Irwin**, in the 65th year of his age. The deceased was ordained a ruling elder in Mecklenburg Co., N. C. by Rev. Isaac Grier, D. D. about the year 1829, and up to the time of his peaceful departure was actively and faithfully employed in the duties of that sacred office. By his death the little congregation of Shiloh has lost an invaluable member. ... once possessed of an ample fortune, he saw the most of it swept away from him by the winds of adversity.

Died in Iredell Co., N. C., November 19th, 1858, **Mary R. Gibson**, oldest daughter of Levi Gibson, aged twenty years and 10 months. ...[member of] New Sterling.

Departed this life, October 23rd, 1858, Mrs. **Margaret**, wife of Alfred **O'Shields**, and daughter of Mrs. E. A. Bryan, aged thirty nine years, seven months and nineteen days. ... Last year she was called, by the providence of God, to consign to the silent grave two of her children, one of them twelve years old. ... She has left a very kind husband, five children, an aged mother, twelve brothers and sisters.

Died in this county on the 18th December, 1858, Mr. **James Taylor**, in the eightieth year of his age. This worthy citizen of Rockbridge, Va. was among the oldest and most respected of our inhabitants. ... In the War of 1812, he was a soldier in defence of his country. ... For many years he was a ruling elder in the church at Timber Ridge.

Married on the 23rd December, 1858 by Rev. H. T. Sloan, Mr. **Samuel P. Young** to Miss **Rebecca,** daughter of F. B. **Robinson**, all of Abbeville.

Married in York District, S. C. on the 4th inst. by Rev. W. B. Pressly, Miss **Fannie L.**, daughter of John **Barron**, Esq. and Mr. **F. C. Harris**, both of the same district.

Married by Rev. J. M. Young on the 4th January in Dallas Co., Ala., Dr. **J. McBoyd** of Wilcox Co., Ala. to **Mrs. M. L. Barron**, daughter of R. G. and Mary Craig.

January 28, 1859

Died In Dallas Co., Ark. on the 30th November last, Mr. **Robert Elder** In the 42d year of his age....He left Chester District on the 15th of November, with his family, consisting of a wife and five small children to go to Arkansas with a view of locating in that new country, traveling by public conveyance, they arrived at Pine Bluff, Ark. at the beginning of the next week. Here Mr. Elder was taken sick with typhoid pneumonia, but being met there by a brother in law he was able to get to his house, a distance of sixteen miles, but it was only to lie down on his death bed....He was a member of the A. R. Church at Hopewell.

Due West Telescope

Died in Princeton, Indiana, January 3rd, 1859, Mrs. **Elizabeth H. McCalla**, wife of David McCalla, in the seventy eighth year of her age. Her father died before she was born. ... In the year 1804, she was married to David McCalla; thirty two years they lived together in South Carolina, and then moved to Princeton, Goshen Co., Ind., where they lived together twenty two years.

February 11, 1859

Departed this life on the 31st of January, Mrs. **Martha Robinson**, aged 26 years, one month and 18 days. ... left an infant ... but two weeks [old].

Married on the 3rd inst. by Rev. H. T. Sloan, Mr. **Wm Harvely** to Miss **Lizzie Robinson**, step daughter of Mr. Geo. Davis.

Married on the 3rd February by Rev. H. L. Murphy, **Joseph Caldwell** and Miss **Angelina Turnipseed**, all of Newberry, S. C.

February 18, 1859

Died on the 18th of January, 1859, **Sarah**, only daughter of Joseph H. **Strain**, deceased, and Jane Strain, in the fifth year of her age.

Married at Rock Hill on the 20th ult. by H. Simpson, Esq., Mr. **Wm.D. Marks** and Miss **Laura Keistler**, formerly of North Carolina.

Married by Rev. R. W. Brice on the 3d inst., Mr. **Wm. Estes** to Miss **Sarah**, daughter of James **Boyd**, Sr., all of Chester District, S. C.

Married by Rev. R. W. Brice on the 10th inst., Mr. **Wm. Casky** to Miss **Mary Jane**, daughter of D. C. **McWilliams**, all of Chester District, S. C.

Married at Memphis, Tenn. the 14th of December by the Rev. R. C. Grandy, Mr. **J. Churchell Wright** to **Mrs. M. Seler**, both of Tipton Co., Tenn.

----- on the 20th of January by Esq. Dickison, Mr. **Alexander Irwin** of Tipton Co. to **Miss Griffith** of Shelby Co., Tenn.

----- on the 20th of January by the Rev. Mr. Griffin, Mr. **Freelin Appleberry** to **Miss Shaw**, all of Tipton Co., Tenn.

February 25, 1859

Died, February 5th, **Mary Ellen**, infant daughter of Rev. N. M. and C. M. **Gordon**.

Died, February 6th, **John W.**, son of Joseph M. and Ann **Patterson** of Jessamine Co., Ky., aged two years.

Died in Anderson District, S. C. on the 24th December, 1858, aged one month and two days, **David Luther**; also, on the 7th January, 1859, ------------ ----------, aged one month and fifteen days; infant sons of William and Mary Ann **Stewart**, members of Little Generostee Church.

Departed this life at his residence in Tippah Co., Miss., January 5, 1859, Mr. **John Watt**, in the fifty seventh year of his age. Mr. Watt was a native of Anderson District, S. C., and the most of his years were spent not far from the place of his birth. He made a public profession of religion and united with the Associate Reformed Church at Generostee under the ministry of Dr. E. E. Pressly. And about eleven or twelve years ago, he removed with his family to Tippah Co., Miss. and at the organization of the Associate Reformed Church at Bethany, he was received by letter. ... He leaves a wife and five children.

Died at his residence at Obion Co., Tenn. on the 26th of January, 1859, **John Moffatt**. The deceased was born January 17, 1783. He lived the greater position of his life in Chester District, S. C., and was long a member of Hopewell Church under the pastorate of Father Hemphill. For a number of years preceding his death, he was a member of the A. R. Presbyterian Church at Troy, Tenn. His death breaks one more of the links which connect the present generation with the past. He was a man of good powers of mind and of great decision. At times he might have seemed almost stern and inflexible, yet he had a kind and genial heart, and much charity for others, which rendered him a valuable friend. Born and reared in an age when the intoxicating bowl was a token of hospitality and friendship in too many families, he acquired intemperate habits, which for a number of years seriously marred his Christian character and impaired his usefulness. But for several years preceding his death, he appeared to have overcome these evil habits, seldom permitting them to gain the ascendancy.

Departed this life at the residence of his father at Holmes Co., Miss., **Robert M. Mealy**, aged 23 years, 3 months and 10 days--disease, pneumonia.

Married on the evening of the 5th inst. by Rev. M. I. McWilliams, Mr. **J. D. McNeill** to **Miss M. J. Griffith**, all of Wilcox, Ala.

----- on the evening of the 8th inst. by Rev. A. C. Ramsay, Mr. **L. R. Smith** of Choctaw Co., Ala. to Miss **Susan Williams** of Wilcox, Ala.

Married at the residence of Mr. James Carson of Rockbridge Co., Va. by the Rev. Horatio Thompson, D. D., Mr. **John Callison** to **Miss Archie C. Carson**.

----- on the 17th January last at the residence of E. S. Coppock, Esq. in Newberry village, **James H. Johnson**, Esq. of Ocala, Fla. to **Mrs. R. N. Schumpert** of the former place.

March 4, 1859

Died at his residence in Lancaster District, S. C. on Sabbath the 13th ult., **Alexander Montgomery**, in the 105th year of his age. .... Mr. Montgomery entered the Continental army in 1780; but was soon discharged on account of sickness. After he returned home, his health was restored, and he then joined himself to the troops under Sumpter. ... He was in the battles of Fishing Creek, Eutaw Springs, and Blackstock; and his conduct in the hour of danger reflected credit on his family and merited the gratitude of his country. Mr. M. was a man of considerable wealth, but never asked office of his country. He was a very moral and upright man, and although not a member, his sympathies were with the A. R. church. Although he lived to an extreme age, he was never married.

Died at Walkersville, Union Co., N. C. on the 27th ult., after a protracted illness of 4 months, Mrs. **M. Adaline**, consort of **Hugh Wilson**, Esq.... Her maiden name was Nisbet.

Departed this life on the 24th of January near Relf's Bluff, Ark., Mrs. **Isabella Jane Spencer**, in the 24th year of her age. The daughter of John and Margaret Wilson, the wife of Jonathan Spencer.... several years ago ... [she joined the church at] Hopewell, Chester District, S. C. ... Emigrating west she came with her husband to Drew Co., Ark. in December, 1856. ... She has left an affectionate husband ... and little "Willie," who is too young to know...

Died on the morning of the 14th of February at the residence of his brother, near Monticello, Ark., **Thomas Allen**, a young man, the son of Samuel and Mary Allen of Shelby Co., Tenn. Only a few weeks have passed since he separated himself from his parents and came to this country. ... member of the church at Sardis.

Married on the 17th inst. by Rev. H. T. Sloan, Mr. **William P. Kennedy** to Miss **Margaret J. McClain**, daughter of David McClain, Esq., all of Long Cane.

Married on the 24th ult. by Rev. I. D. Durham, Mr. **Franklin G. Stansell** of Abbeville to Miss **Ellen K. Hiett** of Greenville.

----- on the same evening by Rev. B. F. Mauldin, Mr. **B. F. Griffin** of Williamston, Anderson District to Miss **Hattie C. McLane** of Spartanburg.

Due West Telescope

March 11, 1859

Married on the 17th February by Rev. R. W. Brice, Mr. **Augustus P. Moffatt** of Troy, Tenn. and Miss **Jane**, daughter of Samuel **Lathan** of Fairfield, S. C.

Married, February 24th at the residence of the bride's father, Camden, Ala., by Rev. W. W. Spence, Mr. **John A. Henry** of Bell's Landing and Miss **Lizzie F.**, eldest daughter of John D. **Caldwell** of the former place.

March 18, 1859

Died, February 13th ult. in Mecklenburg Co., N. C., Mrs. **Jane Quay**, widow of our deceased brother A. Quay, in the thirtieth year of her age. ... she left an only son, Lester Howie, a bright and promising boy of three or four.
Died in Laurens District, S. C. on the 12th of February (pneumonia), Miss **Elizabeth M. Reed**, daughter of Jonathan and Jane Reed in the 20th year of her age. ...[member of] the A. R. Church at Head Spring.

Married on Thursday the 24th ult. by Rev. J. C. Williams, Mr. **J. W. Tolleson** of Spartanburg District to Miss **Sallie Pratt** of Abbeville District

March 25, 1859

Married, March 15, 1859 at Dr. T. A. Wideman by Rev. H. T. Sloan, Mr. **John Henry Wideman** to Miss **Kate Patton**, all of Abbeville District.

Married on Wednesday evening, 9th March, 1859 by Rev. James F. Hendrick, Mr. **Stephen Campbell** to Miss **Margaret Ann Butler**, daughter of James Butler, deceased, all of Fleming Co., Ky.

Married on 8th of March by Rev. David Pressly, Rev. **Henry S. Holliday**, Choctaw Co. to Miss **E. Jane Boyls** of Oktibbeha Co., Miss.

----- also, by the same on 10th of March, Mr. **John H. Cooper** to Miss **Martha Ann Martin**, all of Oktibbeha Co., Miss.

Married in Tishomingo Co., Miss. by Rev. J. L. Young, **B. M. Latimer** of Due West, S. C. and Miss **Hester A. Agnew** of the former place.

April 1, 1859

Died of scarlet fever on the 10th of Feb. in Tippah Co., Miss., **Mary Martha Alice**, daughter of N. M. and Jane **Leslie**, aged 3 years, 6 months.

Also, on the 29th of February of the same disease, **Nancy**, youngest child of Hugh **Wiseman**, in the 11th year of her age.

Also, on the 12th of March of the same disease, **John William**, and on the 15th, **Hugh Silas**, only children of J. A. and Mrs. Jane **Barkly**.

Married by Rev. J. H. Bryson on the 17th March, Mr. **J. W. Kerr** to Miss **Sallie E.**, daughter of Andrew **Scott**, Esq., all of Maury Co., Tenn.

----- by J. E. Pressly, March 16th, Mr. **James A. White** and Miss **Margaret A. H. Barringer** of Iredell Co., N. C.

----- on the 16th inst. at Inorna, the residence of Albert Miot, Esq., Columbia Co., Fla. by the Rev. Basel Lanneau, Mr. **Joseph Davis Miot** of Columbia to Miss **Pamela E. Moore** of Newberry, S. C.

April 8, 1859

Mrs. **Elizabeth Wiseman**, wife of James Wiseman and daughter of Wm. Fleming, died at the residence of her husband in Marshall Co., Miss. on Wednesday evening 8th of March last. Mrs. Wiseman was in the forty ninth year of her age. She had been a regular member of the A. R. Presbyterian Church, the last 8 or 10 years of her life she was connected with the Mt. Carmel congregation, Miss.

Departed this life of typhoid pneumonia on ?1st January, **William P. Boozer**, son of F. L. and E. P. Boozer, aged 16 years, 6 months and 15 days.

Died at his residence in Tipton Co., Tenn. on the 14th of March, 1859, **James A. McCain**, in the fiftieth year of his age. Disease--consumption--the deceased had been a consistent member of the church. First at Tirzah, Co., N. C., and for the last twenty three years at Salem. And for the last ten or twelve years he had served in the office of deacon and treasurer of the congregation.

April 15, 1859

Died, January 29, 1859 in Mecklenburg Co., N. C., Mrs. **Matilda P.**, widow of the late Stephen **M'Rum**, in the fifty sixth year of her age. ... member of Associate Reformed Presbyterian Church at Little Steel Creek. ... three surviving sons.

Departed this life, March 29, 1859, in Mecklenburg Co., N. C., Mrs. **Mary Grier**, wife of Maj. Zenas A. Grier and daughter of the late Maj. Saml. M'Comb of Charlotte, N. C., aged about 42 years. Member of A. Reform.

Presbyterian Church at Little Steel. ... left a husband and seven children.

Married on 31st March by Rev. H. Quigg, Mr. **James G.Harvey** to **Miss E. Stewart**, youngest daughter of James Stewart, Esq., Newton Co., Ga.

April 22, 1859

Died in Lincoln Co., Tenn. on the 3d of February, 1859, **John S. Foster**, in the 27th year of his age. ... a lone brother is all of the family that survives.

Departed this life on the 20th of March, Mrs. **Mathy Moore**, in the 84th year of her age. ... she was a grandmother to the lamented Parkinson.

Also, April 6th, little **Walker**, infant son of Samuel H. and Martha J. **Sloan**, of brain fever.

Departed this life in Oktibbeha Co., Miss. on the 22nd of March, Mrs. **Sarah Wray**, the wife of P. J. Wray and a daughter of Mr. James Hemphill Cooper, aged 21 years. ... Only a few months passed, we beheld her arrayed in white, surrounded by youthful associates, uniting her hand and her heart in the institution of marriage.

Died on the 21st March, 1859, ... **John T. Weir,** son of Samuel T. and Martha P. Weir, aged 5 months and 24 days-- of Sparta, Ill.

April 29, 1859

Died at the residence of her father, Lusk Davis, on the 11th of April, 1859, Mrs. **Sarah Jane Wylie** in her 25th year, member of Salem Church.

Died at his residence near Mercer, Pa. on the 8th inst., Rev. **Joseph Banks,** in the 53rd year of his age.

May 6, 1859

Died in Louisville, Ga. on the 24th of April of typhoid pneumonia, **John Smith**, about 14 years of age.

Died in Jefferson Co., Ga. on the 20th of April, **Robert Emmet Trimble**, son of James and Susan Trimble, aged 12 years.

Departed this life at his residence in Tippah Co., Miss., after a protracted illness, on the 9th day of April, Mr. **Thomas Bryson** , aged fifty two years and three days. Mr. Bryson was born in Laurens District, S. C., and most of his days were spent in the neighborhood where he was born. ... [member of] A. R. P. Church at Providence...[and elder] ... until he removed West. ... He has left five children, an aged mother, and several brothers and sisters.

Miss **Jane Sarvies** of Crowder's Creek, N. C., died March 8, 1859 ... member of A. R. Church at Tirzah, Gaston Co., N. C.

Died of pneumonia on the 17th February, 1859 at Cedar Springs, Spartanburg District, S. C., **Catherine D. Chalmers**, daughter of Dr. A. W. and F. Chalmers, nineteen years, nine months and ten days. ... [member of Church at] Head Spring, Newberry District, S. C.. . deprived of her eyesight about seven years ago.

In less than five weeks from the time she was consigned to the cold and silent tomb, her mother, **Francis Chalmers**... [died] aged fifty two years, two months and thirty seven days. ... leaves behind her an aged husband and large family.

[Married] on the 14th of April by the Rev. D. G. Phillips, Mr. **S. F. Boyd** of Muscogee Co. to **Miss G. M. Lowry** of Jefferson Co., Ga.

Married on the 21st of April, 1859 by Rev. A. S. Montgomery, Mr. **T. P. Wilson** of Winston Co., Miss, to **Miss R.L.Dysart** of Marshall Co., Tenn.

May 20, 1859

Died near Due West, S. C. on the 16th of May, 1859, **John E. Ellis, sr.** in the sixty fifth year of his age. He was born in the vicinity and spent his long life among the friends of his youth and childhood. For about eighteen years he had been a member of the A. R. Church at Due West, from which, we trust, he was taken to the upper and better sanctuary. For a considerable time he had been afflicted with convulsions... He leaves a widow and a large family.

Died of scarlet fever on the 4th of April, 1859, **David Pressly,** only child of W. H. and Mrs. Sarah M. **Wiseman**, aged 16 months. On the 21st of January, 1857, these parents were called, in the Providence of God, to give up their first born child, an infant daughter, only two weeks old.

Married on the 10th inst. by Rev. S. C. Millen, Rev. **R. Lathan** and Miss **Fannie R.**, daughter of Dr. A. I. **Barron,** all of Yorkville.

----- on the 4th inst. by Rev. E. E. Boyce, **Alexander Glass** and Miss **Margaret Barry**, all of York District.

Due West Telescope

Died on the 14th of May, **Alexander Patrick**, in the 34th year of his age. ....He had no family--but left two brothers and one sister[member of Mt. Olivet].

Died on the 13th of May, **Robert McCleane**, also in the prime of life.....[Rev. R. A. Ross wrote that] Mr. McCleane was not a professor of religion. He was an orderly citizen, an attentive hearer of the Gospel, and a liberal supporter of the church. He left a deeply bereaved wife and three children.

Died in Cabarrus Co., N. C. on the 26th of April, **Margaret Jennett Snell**, wife of Samuel K. W. Snell, in her 26th year, leaving a husband and one child. ... member of the Presbyterian Church at Rocky River for 5 years.

June 10, 1859

Died in Dallas Co., Ala. on the 17th of April, 1859, an **infant** daughter of James and Delilah **Chisolm**.

Died at the residence of her father, Dr. E. E. Pressly, near Due West, S. C., on the 4th inst., Mrs. **Lizzie J. Boyd**, wife of Rev. J. C. Boyd of Newberry, S. C. ... Mrs. Boyd was in the twenty fifth year of her age; had been married a little less than three years, and leaves one little daughter about fifteen months.

Married on the 26th of May by Rev. J. A. Sloan, Mr. **John J. McCaughan** of Fayette Co., Tenn. and Miss **Bettie R. J. Moffatt** of Marshall Co., Miss.

June 17, 1859

Died in Fayetteville, Tenn. on the 20th April, **Thomas W. Stewart** in the 33rd year of his age. ... member of church at Prosperity.

Died in Maury Co., Tenn. on the 13th of May, Mr. **John Harris** in the 79th year of his age. ... He was born in Mecklenburg Co., N. C., married to Miss Agnes Matthews on the 12th of August, 1806, and moved to Maury Co., Tenn. in 1822. . . . one third of the ministers of the church are related to him.

Died in Maury Co., Tenn. on the 1st of June, 1859, Mr. **John McCandless** in the 62nd year of his age.

June 24, 1859

Died on the 23d of May, **Sarah Patrick**, in the 85th year of her age. ... member of A. R. Church at Sardis, Union District, S. C.

Also, on the day previous in the same house, **Nancy Isabella**, daughter of Isaac and Sarah **Patrick**. She was 2 years and 18 days old.

July 1, 1859

[Died] on Saturday evening, 18th June, **Lavinia A. McClinton**, little daughter of S. B. and Margaret McClinton, aged 8 years, 4 months and 10 days.

Died in Nashville, Tenn, December 7, 1858, in the thirty fifth year of her age, Mrs. **Ann Sinclair**, wife of James Sinclair. The deceased was a native of Edinburg, Scotland, and had been in this country but three years.

Mrs. **Jane Young**, wife of George Young, died at the residence of her father, John Creswell, Sr., the 19th of June, aged 39 years, 8 months and 4 days.

Died on the 27th of May, **Ebenezer Gordon Wiseman**, son of Mr. Hugh Wiseman, in the 19th year of his age.

Died in Monroe Co., Va. on the 23d day of April last, Mr. **Andrew Miller,** aged 86 years, 5 months and 8 days. He was born in Perthshire, Scotland, and emigrated to this country in 1801. ... was ruling elder in New Lebanon Church [for] ... 58 years.

July 8, 1859

Departed this life in Holmes Co., Miss. on the 30th of May, 1859, **John Thomas Lindsay**, only son of Thomas N. and Caroline Lindsay, aged eight months and two days.

Died in Iredell Co., N. C., 24th of May last, Mrs. **Barbara Morrison,** wife of Hiram Morrison, in the fifty second year of her age. ... From a girl she has been a consistent member of the church [Sterling]... a husband and six children mourn.

Departed this life in Dallas Co., Ala. on the 17th of June, 1859, **William Johnston**, in his 71st year. Little more than one year has passed since the death of Thomas Craig, one of the fathers and founders of the A. R. Church in Ala. Prosperity is in mourning again.... He has left a wife and four children.

Died in Freestone Co., Texas after 21 days of suffering, **Samuel,** the youngest son of James and Eliza **Robinson**.

Died on the 28th of May, 1859 at his residence in Nashville, Tenn., Mr. **Robert Wilson**, in the thirty ninth year of his age. ... was native of

County Tyrone, Ireland. Soon after his marriage there with Miss Margaret Hamilton, he emigrated to the United States in 1840... settled in Maryland, thence he removed to Pittsburg, thence to Nashville. He left a wife and six children.... A little more than four years ago he made a public profession of religion. He was one of the little band gathered together by Rev. H. T. Sloan when in March, 1855, he organized the A. R. Presbyterian Church in Nashville.

Married in Freestone Co., Texas on the 11th of May, 1859, Mr. **Walker Y. Davidson** and Miss **Ann E.**, second daughter of James **Robinson**.

July 15, 1859

Died June 3rd in Iredell Co., N. C., Mr. **Joseph E. Davidson** in the 80th year of his age....[earlier] joined the O. S. Presbyterian church....connected with congregation of New Perth more than twenty years ago. ... efficient ruling elder until his death. .. he leaves a widow and a large family of interesting children.

[Died] in Iredell Co., N. C., June 12th, Mrs. **Mary Willis**, in the 65th year of her age. ... native of S. C. ... more than twenty years ago became member of New Perth... leaves an aged husband, one son, and six daughters, all members of the same church. ...[on deathbed] calling all the family to her bedside, she looked at each for the last time in this world, gave her parting advice, and requested her only son to sing a Psalm; the 23rd was selected, and while it was being sung, she closed her eyes.

July 22, 1859

Died in Abbeville village on Friday the 8th instant, Miss **Julia C. White**, daughter of Ezekiel White in the 18th year of her age.

Died in Mecklenburg Co., N. C., June 27th, **James H. Bell**, in the 47th year of his age.

Died at Troy, Obion Co., Tenn. on the first of July, 1859, 7 o'clock, a. m.., Mrs. **Martha Moffatt**, consort of J. S. Moffatt, aged 57 years and seven months. ... [She leaves] a husband, three sons and two daughters.

Died in the residence of her son in law, Mr. P. Chisolm, in Dallas Co., Ala. on the 2d of July, 1859, Mrs. **Jane Craig**, in the 77th year of her age. ... [member of] Prosperity [Church] in Alabama.

Died in Pope Co., Ark. on the 29th of June, 1859 of congestion of the lungs, **John Munroe**, eldest son of Eli K. and Catherine **McCullough**, aged ten years, ten months and twenty three days.

Married by Rev. R. W. Brice on the 12th inst., Mr. **W. J. McKinstry** of Monticello, Ark. to Miss **Sarah Strong** of Chester District, S. C.

July 29, 1859

Died in Pope Co., Ark. on Saturday night, 12 o'clock, May 21, 1859, Mr. **John Franklin Oats**, in the forty sixth year of his age. In his youth he was taught and instructed in the principles of the A. R. Church in the congregation of Pisgah, N. C., at that time under the care of Rev. Wm. Dickson. After his marriage, he settled in York District, S. C., where he served as a ruling elder in the congregation of Smyrna. In autumn, 1853, he removed to the West with his family and settled in the congregation of Pisgah, Ark., where he again served as ruling elder. In the spring of '56, his health failed.

Married on 21st inst. by Rev. George A. Duboror, **Robert C. S. Lind** to **Marcella Josephine**, daughter of the late Anthony **Groves**, Esq., all of Philadelphia.

August 5, 1859

Died, 27th July, **Susan Ann**, wife of Jas. R. **Wilson**, in the 44th year of her age. ... member of King's Creek Church. ... She has left a husband, five children.

Died in Bourbon Co., Ky. on the 3d of June, Mrs. **Mary A. McClintock**, in the 29th year of her age. ... the only daughter of Henry Thompson, deceased, who for many years was a ruling elder in the Kinkston congregation. ... she was united in marriage with Wm. McClintock, Jr.

Departed this life at his residence in Oktibbeha Co., Miss. on the 12th instant, Dr. **S. J. Williams** in the forty fourth year of his age. ... ruling elder in the Associate Reformed Church in Starkville.

Married Monday morning, July 18th, by Rev. J. E. Pressly, Mr. **John Davidson**, Esq. and Miss **Esther Scroggs**, both of Iredell Co., N. C.

Married on the 21st July by Rev. J. H. Bryson, Mr. **C. S. Scott** to Miss **Calvernia Ralston**, daughter of David Ralston, Esq.,all of Maury Co., Tenn.

August 19, 1859

Died near Portersville, Tenn. on the night of the 28th of July, **Rachel E.**, second daughter of Dr. Wm. and Eleanor **McQuiston**, in her 5th year.

Also, on the morning of the 4th of August of the same disease, **Wm. Scott [McQuiston]**, youngest son of the same parents in his 3d year.

Also, on Sabbath morning, July 31st at Bloomington, Tenn., **Nancy E.**, second daughter of Dr. J. F. and Elizabeth T. **Harper** in her 9th year.

On the 24th July, **Thomas Creswell**, that aged disciple, having just closed his seventy sixth year.

August 26, 1859

Died in Mecklenburg Co., N. C. on the 3rd of August, 1859, Mrs. **Isabella H.**, wife of Rev. John **Hunter** and daughter of Jane and Richard Peoples in the 39th year of her age. ... [Fatally ill of bronchitis] she lay at her father's house, in a room adjoining one in which her only sister lay with a disease very like her own, but more rapid in its progress. ... Three days before Mrs. Hunter departed, her sister died. ...[She left] a husband and four motherless children.

Died in Mecklenburg Co., N. C. on the 30th of July, 1859, Miss **Elizabeth J. Peoples**, daughter of Richard and Jane Peoples.

Married on the 27th ult. at the house of the bride's mother by Rev. H. L. Vannuys, Rev. **B. L. Baldridge** of Leavenworth City, K. T. and Miss **Maria Gilmore**, Goshen, Ind.

September 2, 1859

Departed this life in Pickens Co., Ala, on the 14th of August, **Ivey O.**, daughter of John and Nancy **Hawthorn**, aged 13 years.

September 9, 1859

Died on the 1st of July, of flux, an **infant** daughter of Rev. J. L. **McDaniel**, aged three months.

Died at Monroe, Butler Co., Ohio on the 10th June, Miss **Nancy Cunningham** in the 79th year of her age. The deceased was born in the State of South Carolina. In early life she united with the A. R. Church at Due West, in that state under the pastoral care of Rev. McMullen. After her removal to Ohio, she united with the Associate Reformed Church at Mt. Pleasant, Monroe Co., Ohio and continued a consistent member for more than forty years.

Died of consumption June 9th, 1859 at his residence near Bloomington, Monroe Co., Ind., **Samuel Weir**, in the fiftieth year of his age. The subject of this notice was born in Chester District, S. C., and moved to Monroe Co. in 1837. ... was a ruling elder in the Associate Reformed Church. ... He leaves a loving wife and five children.

Died, August 28th, 1859, in Mecklenburg Co., N. C., **Thomas Pringle Grier**, aged 39 years, 8 months and one day. Early in life he engaged in mercantile business, first in Charlotte, N. C., afterwards in Philadelphia, and then in the neighborhood in which he was raised. In 1848, he removed to Iowa, and after spending about one year in that state, and finding that his health was beginning to decline from the severity of the climate, he removed to California, where he spent about nine years--first in the mining, and afterwards in the mercantile business. In the winter of 1857, he visited his friends in North Carolina, returned again in the spring to California returned home again some time in last November, and about the first of April in the present year, re-commenced merchandising in the immediate neighborhood of his friends.

Married on Tuesday, the 6th by Rev. J. I. Bonner, Mr. **Edwin Cox** of Green Co. Ala.and Miss **E.Jannie**, daughter of Jno.**Pratt**, Esq. near Due West.

September 23, 1859

Died in Mecklenburg Co., N. C. on the 5th of September, **John Edwards**, son of Jane and A. L. **Dearmond**, aged 4 years and one month.

Died in Jefferson Co., Pine Bluff, Ark. on the 22nd of August, 1859, Mrs. **Sarah A. M.**, wife of Dr. J. H. **Matthews** and daughter of Samuel and Mary M. Allen, in the thirty eighth year of her age. ... [early in] A. R. Church in which she lived a consistent and devoted member until she removed from the State of Tennessee to Arkansas, where her[sic] and her husband connected themselves with the Presbyterian church... A husband and five children are left.

Married near Ninety Six by Rev. James M. Chiles on 1st inst., **William G. Gayer** of Charleston to Miss **Cora C. Carter** of Abbeville District.

Married by Rev. J. I. Bonner on Wednesday evening the 21st of September, **D. W. Hawthorn**, Esq. of Due West and Miss **Alcippe Eugenia Bigby** of Abbeville District.

September 30, 1859

Departed this life, Sept. 15, 1859, Mrs. **Nancy Livingston**, wife of John Livingston of Newberry, S. C., aged 39 years, 9 months and 14 days. ... In early life she united with A. R. Church at Cannon Creek. .. She has left a husband and four children well nigh grown.

Due West Telescope

Married on the 15th inst. by the Rev. R. Lathan, **William A. Barron** and Miss **Eliza Hammond**, all of York District.

Married on the 31st ult. by Rev. A. Ranson, Mr. **Isaiah D. Irvine** to Miss **Jane E.**, daughter of Mr. Ezekiel **Alexander**, all of Mecklenburg Co.

Married at Cokesbury on the 21st of September by the Rev. D. Wills, Mr. **J. W. Eppes** of Laurensville, S. C. to Miss **Sallie C.**, daughter of Chas. M. **Pelot**, Esq. of Abbeville District.

----- on the 13th instant by Rev. J. A. Davies, Mr. **J. Meek McElwee** and Miss **Margaret Ann**, second daughter of Mr. James **Caldwell**, all of York District.

Married on Thursday, 22nd September, by the Rev. J. C. Chalmers, Mr. **Robert M. Caldwell** of Mecklenburg Co., N. C. to Miss **Ellen J.**, daughter of the late Hugh **Harris** of York District, S. C.

October 7, 1859

Departed this life at the home of Dr. Walter Brice, Little River, Fairfield District, S. C. on the morning of Friday the 23rd of September, 1859, Mrs. **Margaret Jane Brice**, wife of Wade Brice and daughter of the late William and Jane Bell.. .. the 22nd of November next, she would have been twenty one years of age. Nine months before her death, she was married.

Died at the residence of her father, Lusk Davis, in Tipton Co., Tenn. on the 18th of September, **Eliza A.**, consort of Wm. **McKinstry** in the 22nd year of her age. ... member of the A. R. Church at Salem.

October 21, 1859

Died, August 14, 1859 in Monroe Co., Va., Mrs. **Mary Jane Gray**, consort of Andrew Gray and daughter of Mr. G. and Mrs. E. E. Patton. ... [leaves] a husband and four little children.

Married 24th of September by Rev. J. E. Pressly, Mr. **Stephen Frontis, Jr.**, son of Rev. Stephen Frontis and Miss **Julia C. Leazer**, both of Rowan Co., N. C.

October 28, 1859

Died in Attala Co., Miss. on the 6th October inst. of bilious fever, **Mildred Louisa Miller**, daughter of Jno. and Martha J.Miller. ... in her tenth year.

Married on the 28th of September by the Rev. Mr. Pinkerton, Mr. **James W. Houser** of Augusta Co. to Miss **Nannie H. Harris**, youngest daughter of Robert Harris of Rockbridge Co., Va.

November 4, 1859

Died, August 26, 1859 , near Brownsville, Linn or Lunn Co., Oregon, **Andrew Bonner Crawford**, second son of Dr. Robert H. Crawford in the seventh year of his age.

It is with feelings of unmingled regret that we record the death of **Henry Bryson Taylor** in the 22d year of his age. On the 26th of August, he finished a short, but useful life. ... he was acting father to the household of a widowed mother.

Died in Alexander Co., N. C., though she resided in Mecklenburg Co., on the 31st August, in the thirtieth year of her age, Mrs. **Crissida Hunter**, wife of Thos. J. Hunter and daughter of Col. W. Cochran. ... [left] husband and four little children.

Married on Tuesday evening, the 18th October, ult. at Viney Grove, Lincoln Co., Tenn. by Rev. R. B. McMullen, D. D., Rev. **E. L. Patton**, President of Erskine College, and Miss **Mary**, daughter of Rev. **Henry Bryson**, D. D.

November 11, 1859

Died in Maury Co., Tenn. on the 16th of October, Mr. **Jas. S. Davis** .... his age was 23 years.

Died on the morning of the first day of November, **Hugh Dickson**, son of John T. and Sarah A. **Miller**. He was seven years and twenty seven days old.

Married on the 24th ult. by Rev. A. Ranson, Mr. **Sam W. Knox** and Mrs. **Sallie C. Wallace**, all of Mecklenburg Co., N. C.

Married, October 12th, by Rev. W. B. Pressly in Iredell Co. at the residence of her father, **Levi Gibson**, **Martha E.** and **Hiram Harkness**.

November 18, 1859

Mrs. L. S. F. Devlin, wife of Dr. Robert Devlin of Cedar Spring. . . . died November 3rd, 1859. ... aged 51 years and four days.

Married on the 27th ult. by Rev. H. Quigg, Mr. **Wm. T. Stewart** to

Due West Telescope

Miss **Sarah M. Thompson** of Newton Co., Ga.

November 25, 1859

Died of dropsy in York District, on the 24th of October, Mrs. **Mary Whitesides** in the 59th year of her age. ... member of the A. R. church ... at Smyrna.

Died on the 4th October in Newberry District, S. C. of congestive chill, **E. L. Moore** in the 30th year of his age. ... After leaving Erskine College, Mr. Moore was engaged as Principal of St. Matthews Academy.

Departed this life, November 7th at the residence of Mrs. Seals in Lowndes Co., Miss., Miss **Astatin Jane**, eldest daughter of John and Nancy **Hawthorn** of Pickens Co., Ala.. . . . was born the 13th day of January, 1833 in Abbeville District, S. C., near Due West, but removed to Alabama in 185--?

Married November 3rd, 1859 by Rev. J. C. Chalmers, Mr. **J. M. Stitt** to Miss **M. E. Stitt**, both of Mecklenburg Co., N. C.

----- also, November 10th, 1859 by the same, Mr. **Wm. A. Hannon** to Miss **Sophronia Henry**, both of Mecklenburg Co., N. C.

Married September 29th by Rev. R. McLees, Mr. **Ben Neil** to Miss **Mattie J.**, daughter of Mr. J. J **Devlin**.

Married at Long Cane, the 15th inst., by Rev. H. T. Sloan, Mr. **Wm.** McNair to Miss **Sarah David**.

December 2, 1859

Died on the 23rd ult., Dr. **Elias Branson**, aged about fifty years. ... During his long confinement [about seven months], he became deeply concerned about his spiritual and eternal interests, and sent for the writer [Rev. H. T. Sloan], who conversed freely with him, and pointed him to the Lamb of God. He seemed to have correct views of the plan of salvation, being a man of considerable intelligence and a reader of the Bible, although he had greatly neglected the preaching of the Gospel under a delusion, and he confessed, that a man could live as well out of the church as in it. This was a source of deep regret and he now desired to confess the name, which he had so long neglected. This he would have done over two months before his death; but as he then seemed to be recovering, it was deferred, that he might profess Christ publicly at Cedar Spring; but again relapsing and being anxious to confess the faith which he now cherished; a congregation assembled at his house, a sermon was preached, he was received on personal examination, and baptized in the name of the Father, Son, and Holy Ghost, lying on his death bed. Eight days later he died. ... He has left an only daughter.

Departed this life on the 1st of November of typhoid fever, Miss **Eliza Martin**, daughter of William and Jane Martin in the twenty ninth year of her age.

Died in Lafayette Co., Miss. on the 9th ult., **James D. Craig**, in the 72nd year of his age. ...About two years hence, **Agnes Craig**, the aged companion of the deceased. ... fell asleep... also in the 72nd year of her age.

Departed this life on the 22nd of October last, Mrs. **Mary M. Nelson,** daughter of the above parents and the wife of D. M. Nelson, aged 40 years, 5 months and 3 days. The subject of this notice had long been a consistent member of the A. R. Church, first of Hopewell, Maury Co., Tenn., and for many years of Shiloh, Lafayette Co., Miss., the place of her death. ... she left a beloved husband and a large and interesting family of children.

Died on the 24th of October in Old Providence, **Elijah Alexander Carson**, son of John Haup Carson, in the sixth year of his age.

Died on the 7th ult. in Old Providence, Va., Mr. **Joseph Cooper**, in the 82nd year of his age. Mr. Cooper was one of our oldest and unwavering members of the Associate Reformed Church. ... He lived to see the present *Stone* Church built in 1792, occupied the same seat, used and used faithfully his old Pocket Bible and Psalm book and was contemporary with the construction of a new and beautiful brick church.

Married on the 17th inst. by Rev. H. T. Sloan, Mr. **James Martin** to **Miss Hinton**.

Married, September 8th by Rev. J. A. Dickson, Mr. **Mitchell Simpson** of Madison Co. to Miss **Mollie F. Mealy** of Holmes Co.

Married on the 10th inst. by Rev. A. Ranson at the residence of the bride's father, Mr. **John Wallace** and Miss **Sarah Elizabeth**, daughter of M. M. **Wallace**, all of Mecklenburg Co., N. C.

Married on the 10th ult. by the Rev. H. L. Murphy, Dr. **Thompson Wilson** to Miss **Lydia Johnson**, all of Newberry District.

----- on Tuesday, the 1st ult. by Rev. D. H. A. M'Lean, D. D., Rev. **Joseph C. Nevin**, missionary elect of the United Presbyterian Church to China to Miss **Amanda S. Beggs** of Coltsville, Ohio.

Due West Telescope

December 9, 1859

Married in Marshall Co., Tenn. on the 8th of November, 1859 by Rev. A. S. Montgomery, Mr. **James N. Forrest** to Miss **Elizabeth Glascock**.

December 16, 1859

Died in Beaufort, S. C. on the 30th November, Mrs. **Isabell Grayson**, in the 36th year of her age, wife of H. A. Jones, Esq. of Abbeville District, and daughter of Dr. J. R. Verdier of the former place.

Married on the 1st inst. by Rev. H. T. Sloan, Mr. **J. L. Drennon** to Miss **Sallie**, daughter of **Isaac Kennedy**, Esq.

Married on the 1st ult. by the Rev. Wm. Carlisle, **J. O. Long** to Miss **Caroline Hatten**, all of Anderson District.

Married on the 1st inst. by the Rev. J. C. Williams, **W. L. Hudgens**, Esq. of Laurens to Miss **Carrie Klugh** of Cokesbury, Abbeville District, S. C.

December 23, 1859

Mrs. **Maria Patterson** died of disease of the heart at the residence of her husband, Mr. James Patterson, in Jefferson Co., Ga. on the 25th of November, 1859, aged about 58 years. She was a member of Ebenezer A. R. Church.

Married on the 6th inst. by the Rev. John S. Pressly, Mr. **J. I. Manning** to Miss **Drusilla Ann Boyd**, all of Anderson District.

----- also, by the same on the 15th inst., Mr. **James N. Campbell** to Miss **Martha Ann Sherard**, all of Anderson District.

Married at the residence of the bride's father, York District, S. C. on Wednesday, 6 o'clock, p. m., November 30th, 1859 by Rev. Wade Hill of North Carolina, Rev. **Chas. F. Bechtler**, formerly of Spartanburg, S. C., late of York District, S. C. (eldest son of Christopher Bechtler of Spartanburg so widely known for his workmanship in gold and watches; also, the associate founder of "the Bechtler coin") to Miss **Jennie L.**, second daughter of James **Wylie**, Esq. of York District, S. C.

January 6, 1860

Died in Newberry District, S. C. on the 14th ult., **Robert Carmical**, in the 75th year of his age. ... [leaves] a wife bereaved, children rendered fatherless, and servants berefit of a kind and generous master. . . .[member of] A. R.Church at Prosperity. ...[and] elected ruling elder.

Also, on the 22nd ult., Dr. **J. L. Hall**, in the 27th year of his age. ...[also, member] at Prosperity, S. C.

Died near Monticello, Ark. on the 26th of September after a short illness, **Richard Wright**, in the 45th year of his age. For many years a member of the A. R. P. Church at Salem, under Father Wilson's pastoral care, about six years ago, with his family, he emigrated to Arkansas, and was one of the few who composed the first organization of Associate Reformed Presbyterians in Monticello.

Died in Mecklenburg Co., N. C. of typhoid fever on the 13th of October, **William Baxter Grier**, in the 19th year of his age. His death occurred during the short vacancy, called for, as he thought, by his youthfulness, between the time of leaving college [graduated from Erskine College, Class of 1859] and commencing the study of theology.

Married on the 22nd ult. by Rev. J. C. Boyd, **Spencer Neel** and Miss **Fannie Reid**, all of Newberry District, S. C.

----- on the 25th October by the Rev. T. S. Lee, Rev. **J. M. Brown** of Monticello, Ark. to Miss **Sallie E. Marshall** of Bath Co., Ky.

----- on the 21st December ult. in the Scotch Presbyterian church in New York by the Rev. Jos. McElroy, the Rev. **A. W. Leland**, Professor in the Theological Seminary in Columbia, S. C., and Miss **Clara A. Blight** of Dresden, Germany.

----- the 8th December, 1859 by Rev. A. Ranson, Mr. **R. C. Montgomery** and Miss **Mary C. Hutchison**, all of Mecklenburg Co., N. C.

----- also, by the same on the same inst., Mr. **D. B. Garrison** and **Miss M. H. Hunter**, daughter of H. G. Hunter.

----- by the same on the 22nd, Mr. **Joseph H. Beard**, and Miss **Rebecca C. Caldwell**.

---- -on the 26th December by Rev. J. I. Bonner, **F. R. Pinkerton** of Wilcox Co., Ala. and Miss **Armathine**, daughter of Elbert **Johnson**, Esq. of Abbeville District, S. C.

---- Thursday, 15th ult. by Rev. W. B. Pressly, Mr. **J. R. Davidson** and Miss **Sarah**, oldest daughter of Col. A. M. **Walker**, both of Statesville, N. C.

---- on the 15th December by Rev. H. L. Murphy, Mr. **J. B. Wilson** to Miss **Eusebie Wright**.

---- at the residence of the bride's father in Madison Co., Miss. on the evening of the 20th December by Rev. J. A. Dickson, Mr. **H. C. McCain** of Tipton Co., Tenn. to Miss **M. Clemmie Simpson**, second daughter of Thos. Simpson, Esq.

---- also, on 7th September by Rev .J. Wilson, Mr. **R. Calvin Simonton** of Obion Co., Tenn. to Miss **Martha E. Wilson** of Tipton Co., Tenn.

January 13, 1860

Departed this life on the 2nd October, Mrs. **Margaret Cain**, in the 70th year of her age. ... member of the A. R. Church at Sharon. ... leaves behind her in the same church two sons and one daughter.

Died in Marshall Co., Tenn. on the 23rd August, 1859, Mr. **Samuel Jobe**, aged 81 years, 11 months and 19 days. ..born in Guillford Co., N. C. and raised up in the G. A. Presbyterian church. After emigrating to Tennessee, he joined the A. R. Presbyterian Church at Head Springs, Marshall Co., Tenn. ... He has left three sons and one daughter.

Married in the City of Nashville on the 19th December, 1859 by Rev. A. S. Montgomery, Mr. **J. M. Sinclair** to **Mrs. Louisa Ferguson**.

Married by Rev. H. Quigg on the 20th December, 1859, Mr. **James T. Boyd** and Miss **Susannah E. Thompson** of Newton Co., Ga.

Married by the same on the 22nd December, 1859, Mr. **James S. Gardner** and Miss **Eliza M. Boyd** of Newton Co., Ga.

Married at Anderson on the 27th ult. by Rev. A. A. Morse, Mr. **T. J. Glover** of Orangeburg and Miss **E. Toccoa**, daughter of Judge J. N. **Whitner** of Anderson.

Married in the City of Nashville, Tenn. on the 27th December ult. by Rev. R. C. Grier, D. D., Rev. **J. G. Miller** and **Miss --- Williams** of that city.

January 20, 1860

Died in Mecklenburg Co., N. C., November 28th, 1859, **James Manson,** aged 3 years, 10 months and 16 days, son of William G. and Nancy E. **Garison**.

Married on January 4th by Judge Jas J. Brown, Capt. **W. H. Hall** to Miss **Mary Jane**, daughter of the late Benjamin **Perdew**, Esq., all of Jefferson Co., Ga.

January 27, 1860

Married on Tuesday evening, January 10th, at Col. John A. Calhoun by Rev. B. Johnston, Mr. **Andrew Simonds** to Miss **Sallie Calhoun**.

----- in Abbeville on Tuesday evening, January 17th, at the residence of William Hill, Esq. by Rev. J. C. Williams, Mr. **Nathaniel Knox** to Miss **Mary Jane Hill**.

Married by Rev. Mr. Smith on the 22nd November, Mr. **Abel N. W. Belk** of Lancaster District, S. C. to Miss **Sarah**, daughter of Robert and Dorcas **Walkup** of Union Co., N. C.

Married by Rev. D. P. Robinson on the 24th November, Col. **William J. McCain** and Miss **Jane**, daughter of John and Hannah **Walker**, all of Union Co., N. C.

February 3, 1860

Died, during accouchment, on the 3rd November, 1859, near Bloomington, Indiana, **Catherine B.**, wife of W. H. **Curry**, in the 40th year of her age. She was born in Chester District, S. C., March 24, 1820, and was the daughter of Widow A. Nelson. At the age of 16, she .... [joined the] Presbyterian church (O. S.) under the pastoral care of Rev. Leroy Davis, at the church--commonly known as "the Brick Church"--on the waters of Rocky Creek, and which was formerly occupied by Rev. H. McMillen of Cedarville, Ohio. She shortly afterwards, with her mother and brothers, connected with Rev. McDonald's congregation (A. R.) at Union. In the spring of 1842, she with her mother's family moved to Bloomington, Indiana, and connected with Rev. Turner's--(the A. P., now U. P.)--congregation, and was a consistent member until her death. She was married to the writer on the 7th February, 1856. ...[and] at her marriage, she took charge of a family of step children.

Married on the 5th January by Rev. David Pressly, Mr. **Henry P. Sanders** to Miss **Margaret Cochran**, all of Oktibbeha C., Miss.

February 10, 1860

Married on the 17th January by Rev. C. B. Betts, Mr. **John Sloan** and Miss **Elizabeth Balkhead,** all of Fairfield District, S. C.

Married on the 29th ult. at the residence of the bride's mother by Rev. B. F. Mauldin, Mr. **S. Newton Williams** of Anderson to Miss **M. Ann Archer** of Pickens.

February 24, 1860

Died at his residence in Pinckneyville, Illinois on the 18th November, Dr. **A. P. Baldridge**, in the 62nd year of age. Dr. Baldridge died suddenly. ... during the night following that which [he] died, his brother, **Wm. Baldridge**, who had been with the Dr. during his sickness, was prostrated by an violent attack of the pleurisy, and in just one week after the Doctor's death, he also died.

Died in Pope Co., Arkansas, December 29th, 1859, Mrs. **Jane McElwee**, daughter of William and Elizabeth McElwee and wife of James McElwee, in the 42nd year of her age. The deceased was a native of York District, S. C., and remained there until August last, at which time, she, in company with her husband and family, started to Arkansas. She was taken sick in Prairie County in this state. ...[had been a member] of A. R. Church at Bethany in York District. ... she left an affectionate husband, six children.

Died of consumption in Newberry District, S. C. on the 7th inst., Mr. **Jas. J. Sloan**, in the 62nd year of his age. Mr. Sloan had been afflicted for something over thirty years with the disease which terminated his life. ... In 1818 or 1819, he was elected a ruling elder in the Cannon's Creek Church, and subsequently acted in that capacity in Head Spring.

Died of pneumonia in Iredell Co., N. C., January 15th, Mrs. **Margaret Neel**, having a short time entered the 59th year of her age. She had been for many years a consistent member of the A. R. Church.

Married on the evening of the 16th February by Rev. H. H. Spann, **George Adolph Fink**, Esq., formerly of Salisbury, N. C., but now editor of the Lexington (S. C.) *Flag*, to Miss **Laura H.**, daughter of Rev. H. A. **Smith**, local minister of the Methodist church.

Married on the 3rd inst. by Rev. J. M. Brown, Mr. **A. J. Wilson** to **Miss S. I. Wright**, all of Drew Co., Ark.

Married in Maury Co., Tenn. on the 2d of February by Rev. J. H. Bryson, Mr. **J. C. McGaw** to Miss **Amanda Murphy**.

Married on the 14th December by Rev. J. M. Young, **J. S. Johnson** to Miss **Georgia Chesnut**, all of Dallas Co., Ala.

March 2, 1860

Mrs. **Cassandra A.**, wife of Hiram P. **Guy**, departed this life on the 30th November, 1859. She died at the residence of her husband in Fayette Co., Tenn. She was the daughter of Wm. C. Tomlinson, formerly of N. C. ... [member] A. R. Presbyterian Church at Sardis. ... leaves two children and a husband.

Married on the 9th inst. by Rev. D. F. Haddon, Mr. **William Bryson** and Miss **Isabella McCarley**, all of Laurens, S. C.

----- by the same on the 21st., Mr. **Milton   Milam** and **Miss F. Montgomery**, all of Laurens, S. C.

March 9, 1860

Mr. **Samuel Sloan, Senr**. died in Lincoln, Tenn. on the 13th October in the 79th year of his age. He was born in Chester District, S. C., and in early life connected himself with the A. R. Church at Hopewell. . . . He emigrated to Tennessee among the first families that formed the Prosperity congregation.

Died in Lincoln, Tenn., January 9th, **James H. Phagans**, in the 26th year of his age.

Also, on February 7th, **Mrs. Eliza Phagans**, of consumption, in the 45th year of her age. Not a month, after the death of her son, she was called to follow. ... She leaves a husband and four children.

[Also from Lincoln, Tenn.] February 9th, 1860, died of hemorage [sic] . . . . Mrs. **Lizzy McCown,** in the 25th year of her age. ... Having lost her parents at an early age, her moral and religious culture was devolved upon her staunch Christian grand-parents... A bereaved husband, a little son ....[survive].

Married in Orangeburg, S. C. on the 22nd of February by Rev. John Bachman, D. D., Mr. **Henry Bull** to Miss **Eusebia Bachman**, daughter of Rev. Edwin A. and Mrs. Harriet A. **Bolles**.

Married on the 28th February, by Rev. J. Hunter, Mr. **A. B. Hood** to Miss **Laura C. Hunter**, daughter of Lorenzo Hunter, all of Mecklenburg Co., N. C.

March 16, 1860

Departed this life on Sabbath evening, the 12th February, at the residence of Mr. David Stoddard in Laurens District, S. C., Miss **Margaret Taylor**, in the 61st year of her age. ... [member] of A. R. church at Bethel.

Married by the Rev. H. H. Robison on the 27th October last, Mr. **J. Y. Jernigan** to **Miss S. J. Stewart**, all of Tippah, Miss.

----- also by the same on the 18th January, Mr. **H. A. Hawthorn** of Pontotoc to **Miss A. B. Moore** of Tippah, Miss.

----- also by the same, February 16th, Mr. **H. J. Wiseman** to **Miss E. J. Barkly[?]**, all of Tippah, Miss.

March 23, 1860

William P. Rollins, only surviving son of John Rollins of Burke Co., Ga., died at his father's residence on the 13th February, 1860, aged about 21.

Married on the 8th of March by Rev. Bivins of, Mr. **Reuben H. Chapalier** of Columbia to Miss **Moselle A.Patterson** of Jefferson Co., Ga.

March 30, 1860

Died in Mecklenburg Co., N. C. on the 15th March, **James W. Henderson**, infant son of Col. Robert and Mary **Cochran**, in the seventeenth month of his age.

Married on the 20th inst. by Rev. C. B. Betts, Mr. **John A. Duncan** of Fairfield District to **Miss F. F. Williamson** of Winnsboro, S. C.

Married at the bride's father on the 15th by Rev. William Banks, **Thomas T. Long** of Fernandina, Fla. to Miss **Eliza J. Anderson** of Chester District.

April 6, 1860

Married in the city of Nashville on the 19th of March, 1860 by Rev. A. S. Montgomery, Mr. **George Moore** to Miss **Mary Tolmie**, both of that city.

Married at the residence of the bride's mother in Tipton Co., Tenn. on the 22d of March by the Rev. J. Wilson, Mr. **J. Calvin Nelson** (an alumnus of Erskine College) of Obion Co., Tenn. to **Miss Mat Kilpatrick.**

----- on the 10th of February, Mr. **R. M. Moore**, principal of the Male Academy at Somerville, Tenn. to Miss **Bettie McClelland**, assistant teacher in the celebrated "Model Female College" in the same village.

----- near Portersville, Tenn. on the 13th of February by the Rev. John Wilson, Mr. **Abner Glass** to Miss **Mattie**, daughter of Davis **Irwin,** of

Tipton Co., Tenn.

----- on the 6th of March by the Rev. Mr. Lee, Mr. **T. B. Adkins** of the firm of McClennan & Adkins, Portersville, Tenn. to Miss **Bettie McClennan** of that vicinity.

April 13, 1860

Died, March 23d of pneumonia at the house of the late Robt. Millen, **Mrs. Lynn**, mother in law of Mr. Millen, being over seventy years of age. She proposed spending a few days with her daughter, Mrs. Millen, after the funeral of her husband, and while there, was taken sick and died. ... consistent member of Union Church.

Died at his residence in Anderson District, March 12th, Mr. **Saml. Buchanan**, Sr., aged eighty years. He had been a member of the Associate Reformed Church at Shiloh for about 50 years, and for a number of years a ruling elder. He was one of the members of the organization of Shiloh Church, donated the land on which the church was built, saw it grow up, and enjoy the regular ministrations of word and ordinances, and by death and emigration decline, until for years before his death, he was left (with perhaps one exception) the only remaining member of that church.

Departed this life at Monticello, Ark. about Christmas last. ...Miss **Melissa A. Cherry**, daughter of John and Mary Cherry, Chester District, S. C. in the fifteenth year of his age. She left home last fall to visit her sister, and spend this year at school at this place [father is a ruling elder at Union].

Died of pneumonia at his residence in Chester District, S. C. on the 10th March, Mr. **Robt. Millen,** in the sixty first year of his age. He had been for many years a ruling elder in Union A. R. P. Church where he had been raised.

Married on the 4th of November, 1859 in Beaufort by the Rev. Mr. Coburn of the Fourth S. C. Conference, Mr. **James V. Johnson** of Beaufort to Miss **Sallie F.**, daughter of Maj. H. A. **Jones** of Abbeville.

April 20, 1860

Departed this life on Wednesday the 4th April, **John Kennedy**, in the 71st year of his age. The deceased at some point long ago connected with the Associate Church at Sharon, York District. After that church had disorganized and it was proposed to re-organize in connection with the A. R. Church, Mr. Kennedy with three others were elected by the congregation, or that part of it which was favorable to union, to the office of ruling elder.

Departed this life on Saturday, 31st of March, **Robt. N. Kennedy,** son of John and Naomi Kennedy of York District. The deceased was near the close of his 20th year.

Rarely have we been called to announce a sadder thing than the death of Mr. **J. W. Hanks**, a member of the Junior Class at Erskine College, which occurred on Tuesday morning the 17th inst. Mr. Hanks was from Wilcox Co., Ala. and entered college last November, leaving behind a widowed mother and brothers and sisters younger than himself.

Died in Old Providence, Augusta Co., Va. on the 26th of March, 1860, Mr. **Elijah Carson**, in the 72d year of his age. The deceased has been from his youth a member of Old Providence Church. ... He never would accept the eldership though elected, saying "he had two brothers in the Session, which was too many for one family."

Married by Rev. D. G. Phillips, Mr. **P. M. Causey** to **Miss L. E. J. Alexander** at the residence of the bride's father, Maj. J. W. Alexander, in Jefferson Co., Ga.

Married on the 10th inst. at the residence of the bride's father, Mr. **James W. Fowler** of Abbeville to Miss **Celia Chalmers** of Newberry, S. C.

<u>May 4, 1860</u>

Died on the 27th ult., **Leila Rosalie**, youngest child of Dr. E. E. and Mrs. Mary **Pressly**. It was little over a year old.

Died in Pontotoc, Miss., September 13th, 1858, **Oswald Elijah**, first born of William J. and Ellen J. **Wilbanks**, aged not quite 7 months.

Died in Micanopy, Fla. on Thursday morning, the 22nd of March, of congestion of the brain, Mrs. **Angeline Stewart**, wife of Dr. James A. Stewart. The deceased was the daughter of Wm. and Isabella Rankin of DeSoto Co., Miss. Mrs. Stewart was born 2nd April, 1830 in Purdy Co., Tenn., where her parents then resided.

Departed this life at the residence of her son, Dr. James A. Stewart, Mrs. **Mary Cooper Stewart**, the 25th March. The deceased was born in Abbeville District, S. C. on the 14th April, 1788. She united herself early in life to the Associate Reformed Presbyterian Church under the ministry of Rev. Mr. Blackstock at Cedar Spring (This should be Rev. Porter, we presume--Editor).

Married at the residence of Mr. R. P. Little in Jefferson Co., Ga. on the morning of the 24th of April by the Rev. D. G. Phillips, Mr. **A. J. Lockhart** to Miss **Annie E. Little**.

Married on Tuesday evening the 1st of May by Rev. J. I. Bonner, **Jas. Lipford**, Esq. of Williamston, S. C. and Miss **Lou**, daughter of Maj. Wm. **Dickson** of Abbeville District, S. C.

May 11, 1860

Mrs. **Nancy Wiseman**, wife of John Wiseman, died at the residence of her husband in Marshall Co., Miss. on the morning of the 6th of April, 1860. Mrs. Wiseman was in the fifty third year of her age, she was born in Laurens District, S. C., from which place she removed with her father at an early age to Alabama; there she grew up, there she married, and in the 22nd year of her age she made a public profession of religion in the O. S. Presbyterian Church under the ministry of Dr. J. H. Gray. ... she with her first husband removed to Mississippi; near Starkville; there she remained in connection with the O. S. Church until the organization of the A. R. Church which she and her husband connected themselves with. For the last 7 or 8 years of her life she was a member of the A. R. Church at Mt. Carmel, Miss.

Mr. **E. White** died at his residence at Marshall Co., Miss. of inflammation of the lungs on the morning of the 27th of April, 1860. He leaves a widow to mourn his loss. From the nature of his disease he was deranged to a certain extent most of the time. The attending physician said he was getting well, until a short time before he died, very few supposed him dangerous on this account. ...He made a public profession of Christ some 10 or 12 years since, but had been overtaken by intemperate habits and excluded from the communion of the church and we hope that this had a salutary effect on his soul. He came to his right mind before he died, and expressed resignation to the will of God.

Married on Tuesday morning, 9 o'clock, April 24, 1860, by W. R. Dickey, preacher of the M. E. church, South, Mr. **James Wiseman** to Miss **Adaline S. Kirk** of Marshall Co., Miss. at the residence of Mr. Wm. Harrell.

May 18, 1860

Died in Maury Co., Tenn on the 2nd of April, Mrs. **Sallie E. Kerr**, second daughter of Andrew Scott, Esq.

Died of puerperal fever in York District, S. C. on the 7th of March, Mrs. **Sarah C. Caldwell**, aged 24 years. The deceased early connected herself with the church at New Hope, Fairfield District, under the pastoral care of Dr. Boyce, where she remained until she married, at which time she removed to the residence of her husband in York District, being in the bounds of Sharon congregation.

Due West Telescope

Died of disease of the heart on the 25th April, Mr. **James Corry,** aged 74 years. The deceased was a member of the A. R. Church, holding his membership at Sardis, Union District, S. C. of which he was also an elder.

Died in Obion Co., Tenn., April 25th, **Eliza**, wife of S. A. **Baker**, in the 37th year of her age. The deceased was born in Chester District, S. C. Her father, Nathan McDonald, emigrated to Tennessee where she married. In 1844, she connected herself with the A. R. Presbyterian Church at Troy.

Departed this life in Dallas Co., Ala. on the 30th April, 1860, Mrs. **Jane Moore**, in the 74th year of her age. ... from early life a member of the A. R. Church. In 1846, she was robbed of her husband by the hand of death. Since then of a beloved daughter, and later still, of a son, Rev. **J. N. Moore**.

Died in Newton, N. C., March 17th, 1860, **J. P. Pendergrass**, aged 17 years, 3 months and 24 days. The above was the last surviving child of eight to a widowed mother. His disease was hereditary consumption, and similar to that of which nearly all of the others have died.

In Iredell Co., N. C., April 4th, at the house of Mr. J. E. Stephenson, Dr. **A. McSwain Wilkinson**, aged 30 years, 6 months and 17 days. Dr. Wilkinson was a cousin of the youth whose death is recorded above. He was raised in the Sterling congregation, made a public profession of faith at Shiloh [O. S. Presbyterian].

[Died] in Statesville, N. C., April 16th, Mrs. **Jane E.**, wife of R. Q. **Davidson**, aged 23 years, 8 months and 3 days. She was the daughter of Mr. Samuel Bell of Statesville, ruling elder in the Presbyterian church. ... [She was a member of] the New Sterling congregation.

Married at the house of Mr. Jno. Kerr by Rev. W. B. Pressly, March 6, 1860, Mr. **James W. Sumpter** and Miss **Sarah E. Patterson**, both of Iredell, N. C.

Married on Thursday the 3rd inst. by Rev. J. O. Lindsay, **Mr. -- Cater** and **Miss S. C. Giles** of Lowndesville, S. C.

May 25, 1860

Died near Pisgah, Gaston Co., N. C., Miss **Salena Faris,** on the 1st of May, in her forty eighth year. She was a member of a large family and has left but one of that family behind her--a sister --Mrs. Beattie, at whose home she was living, and who stood at her dying bed. Miss Faris was a native of York District, and raised near the Nation Ford; made a profession early in the Methodist and afterward in the A. R. Church, Pisgah, N. C.

Died of spasms, **Thos. Henry**, youngest son of Col. S. C. M. and L. **Brown**, near Mt. Bethel, April 15th, aged about 15 months. This is three out of four dear ones these parents have committed to the earth, and may the Author of the bereavement give grace to endure it.

Died at his residence near Charlotte, N. C. on 30th April of typhoid pneumonia, Mr. **Eli Griffith**, aged 63 years, the deceased was a member of Sardis A. R. P. Church, and has been an elder for many years.

Died on the 2nd inst. of typhoid fever after an illness of two days, Mrs. **Margaret**, consort of Eli **Griffith**, aged 62 years. Mrs. Griffith was a member at Sardis, to which she had united herself at the age of 16 or 17 years.

Died in Mecklenburg Co., N. C. on the morning of the 10th of May of asthma, Mr. **Jonathan Reid**, in the 60th year of his age. Early in life, the deceased made a profession of religion and connected with the G. A. Presbyterian Church, and was for several years a ruling elder in connection with that body at Big Steel Church; but for the last ten or eleven years, had been a consistent member and also a member of the session in the Associate Reformed Presbyterian Church at Little Steel Church. ... He has left a widow, one son and his family, a stepson, and two little daughters.

Married on the 10th of May by Rev. J. C. Chalmers, Mr. **Wm. E. Walker** and **Miss --- Davis**, both of Mecklenburg Co., N. C.

June 1, 1860

Died, April 16th, 1860 at the residence of her son, John Young, Esq. in Iredell Co., N. C., Mrs. **Ann Young**, in the 93rd year of her age.

Married at La Grange, Tenn. on Thursday the 10th May by Rev. Porter McMullen, Capt. **James S. Boyd** of Knoxville, Tenn. and Miss **Iva McMullen** of the former place.

June 8, 1860

Mr. **John Wiseman** died at his residence in Marshall Co., Miss. on the 4th of May, 1860. Mr. Wiseman was in the 53rd year of his age; he was born in S. C., removed to Ala., where he married and made a profession of his faith in Christ by connecting himself with the O. S. Presbyterian Church. ... Mr. Wiseman and his family removed at an early day to Miss., near Starkville, where he continued in the O. S. Presbyterian Church until the organization of the A. R. Church, when he with his wife cast in their lot with that branch of the church. ... For the last six or seven years, his membership was with the Mt.

Carmel Church, Miss. ... leaves five children. ... his wife has gone on before him.

Died on the 9th of April in Mecklenburg Co., N. C., **Charles H. Cochran,** in the 21st year of his age. ...He leaves a wife and one child.

Died near Monticello, Ark. of scarlet fever on the 4th of May, **Andrew Dickson,** aged three years and seven months....son of S. D. and Sarah Dickson.

Mrs. **Mary Weed**, wife of Andrew Weed and mother of Rev. J. P. Weed, departed this life at the residence of her husband in Marshall Co., Miss. on the 18th of May, 1860. ... Mr. Wiseman, her brother, died just four days before. ... Mrs. Weed was born in Newberry District, S. C. on the 22nd April, 1800, and was a little over three score years old at her death; she was baptized in her infancy by Rev. McClintock, was married to Nathaniel Weed in her 19th year, settled with her husband in Cedar Spring, Abbeville District, S. C., made a public profession of her attachment to Christ in 1819 under the ministry of Dr. John T. Pressly; in 1828 she removed to Alabama and there being no A. R. Church in that portion of the state they connected themselves with the O. S. Presbyterian Church .... In 1833, the family removed to Miss., and became a part of those who united in the organization of the A. R. Presbyterian Church at Starkville, Miss. In 1856, the family came to Marshall Co., Miss. where they united with the A. R. church of Mt. Carmel.

June 15, 1860

Mr. **Andrew B. L. Fleming** died of dysentery at the residence of his mother in Jefferson Co., Ga. on the 3d May, 1860, aged 27 years.

Departed this life, March 29, 1860, **Margaret Ann**, second daughter of Charles A. and Margaret **Lancaster**, all of Obion Co., Tenn. ... she was shut out, measurably from the world, being born deaf and dumb. ... She died at the age of 11 years.

Died of pneumonia at his residence in Chester District, S. C. on the 12th April, Mr. **John Cherry**, in the 56th year of his age. For many years he had been a ruling elder in Union Associate Reformed Presbyterian Church, in which he had been born and raised. ... leaves a wife and several children.

Died at his residence, Chester District, S. C., on the 14th of April, 1860, Mr. **Wm. A. Burns,** aged about 38 years. He was taken with pneumonia on the 12th, and died on the morning of the 14th.... leaves a wife and three children.

Died on the 12th March, 1860, **James H. Simpson,** infant son of Thos.

E. and Margaret Simpson, aged 9 months and 20 days.

Departed this life at his residence in Yell Co., Ark., August 19th, 1859, Mr. **D. M. Walkup**, in the 63rd year of his age. His disease was pneumonia. Mr. Walkup was born and raised in Mecklenburg (now Union) Co., N. C. He was for many years a member and ruling elder in the Associate Reformed Church at Tirzah. He left his native state in the fall of 1855, and arrived in Arkansas about the 1st of January, 1856. He first stopped a year or two in Philips Co.--thence he removed to Columbia, and thence to Yell where he died.

June 22, 1860

Died in Mecklenburg Co., N. C., June 4th, of disease of the heart, Mr. **Thos. H. Grier**, in the 47th year of his age. ... He had been, about 15 years, a consistent member of the A. R. Church at Little Steel Creek, N. C. ... left a widow, three sisters.

June 29, 1860

Died, May 13th of consumption, at the residence of her uncle, Wm. Oats, of York District, S. C.; **Mary Jane**, eldest daughter of J. F. (deceased) and Eliza E. **Oats** in the 20th year of her age. ... On 12th of January, she left her home in Pope Co., Ark. in company with a friend to seek health among her friends in York District (her nativity) ... She left a bereaved mother, brothers and sisters.

Married at Robert S. Ketchin on 12th by Rev. C. B. Betts, Mr. **J. G. Wilkinson** of Charlotte and Mrs. **Nannie J. Commings** of Winnsboro.

Married on the 26th June by Rev. J. C. Boyd, Mr. **W. A. Pratt** and Miss **Zenobia Sharp**, all of Abbeville District, S. C.

July 13, 1860

Died, Mr. **S. R. Underwood**, a worthy citizen of this place [in Miss.] departed this life on Wednesday the 11th inst. of typhoid fever.

Died of dropsy in Tippah Co., Miss. on the 5th of May, 1860, Mrs. **Margaret Moore**, consort of Thomas Moore, in the 54th year of her age. ... member of the A. R. Church for a number of years, first at Prosperity, Lincoln Co., Tenn, and then at Ebenezer, Miss.

Dr. **A. A. Tate** died on the 27th of May at his residence in Lincoln Co., Tenn., aged 42 years. ... he connected himself with the A. R. Church at Bethel about 12 years ago. ... He left a wife and a large family of children.

(from the *Florida Dispatch*) Departed this life at Senatobia, Miss. at the residence of William and Isabella Rankin, its grandparents, on Saturday, the 26th of May, **Isabella Perry Stewart**, infant daughter of Dr. James A. Stewart of Micanopy, Fla., aged one year, one month and thirteen days.

Married on the 3d inst. by Rev. H. T. Sloan, Mr. **John Gray** to Miss **Lizzie**, daughter of Maj. H. A. **Jones**.

Married at the residence of the bride's father in Holmes Co., Miss. by Rev. J. A. Dickson, Mr. **John M. Simpson** of Bolivar Co. to Miss **Mary C. Shine** of Holmes Co., Miss. on the 17th of May.

July 20, 1860

Died in Madison Co., Miss., June 20, **Joseph Jerome**, second son of Mr. J. M. and Mrs. Louisa **Flemming**, aged 3 years, 5 months and 25 days.

Died on the 2nd inst. in Mecklenburg Co., N. C. of congestive fever, Mrs. **Martha L. Grier**, wife of Mr. James H. Grier, in the 38th year of her age. ... member of A. R. Church at Little Steel Creek. She has left an affectionate husband and four little children.

July 27, 1860

Died in Tippah Co., Miss on the 8th of June, 1860, **Martha Glendora**, daughter of L. D. and Mrs. Caroline **Gibson.** Aged about nine months.

Departed this life at Senatobia, DeSoto Co., Miss. at the residence of William and Isabella Rankin, its grandparents, **Mary Elizabeth Stewart**, infant daughter of Dr. James A. Stewart of Micanopy, Fla., aged one year, two months and 28 days. Thus in little over a month has this little one followed her twin sister.

Mrs. **Nancy M. McBryde**, wife of E. P. McBryde, died at her husband's residence in Drew Co., Ark. on the 28th February, 1860, after an illness of twenty days, aged 21 years, 4 months and 17 days. Disease, puerperal fever.

Died of bronchial affliction on the 14th of June, 1860, **D. M. Nelson**, in the 49th year of his age. He was born in Lancaster District, S. C., Dec. 10th, 1811, but the greater portion of his life was spent in Lafayette Co., Miss. ...[member] of Shiloh Church in the latter place. ... ruling elder. ... Last fall with his family of motherless children, he removed to Hopkins Co., Texas.

Departed this life in Dallas Co., Ala. on the 26th of June, 1860, Mrs. **Elizabeth Chesnut**, in the 45th year of her age. ...She survived her husband, John Chesnut, a ruling elder in the A. R. church, only a few years. ... She has left six children.

Died in Maury Co., Tenn. on the 10th of June, Mr. **William J. Davis** ... He married in September, 1858, and moved to St. Francis Co., Ark. Being in bad health, he came home to his father's.

Died in Marshall Co., Tenn. on the 3d of February, 1860, **John Blair**, Esq., in the 46th year of his age. ... [reared a Covenanter] joined the Associate Reformed Presbyterian Church. ... He left a wife and seven children, five by a former wife and two by the surviving one.

August 10, 1860

Departed this life in Dallas Co., Ala. on the 23rd of July, 1860 in the fourth year of his age, **James Thomas**, son of J. J. and Elizabeth **Moore**.

Died on the 16th of June, Mrs. **Sarah S. Cochran,** in Mecklenburg Co., N. C. in the 29th year of her age. ... leaves a husband and two small children.

Also, the melancholy task is imposed on us to record the death by the same disease [typhoid fever], of Mrs. **Margery Cochran**, on the 8th of July in the twenty first year of her age. This lady, a sister in law of the one whose death has just been recorded, leaves a husband and one little child.

Married July 19th by Rev. J. C. Chalmers, Mr. **James Smith** and Mrs. **Maggie L. Porter**, both of Mecklenburg Co., N. C.

----- also, on the 26th by the same, Mr. **H. B. McAlister** and Miss **Lucinda Dixon**, of Mecklenburg Co., N. C.

Married at 5 o'clock on Thursday morning, August 6, 1860 by Rev. J. I. Bonner, **Thos. N. Polhill**, Editor of the *Louisville* (Ga.) *Gazette* and Miss **Josephine V. Hawthorn**, daughter of A. C. Hawthorn of Due West, S. C.

August 17, 1860

Died in Iredell Co., N. C., July 5th, Mrs. **Louisa**, wife of A. M. **Walker**, Jr. and daughter of Wm. Miller, Sr., aged 25 years. ... She leaves a husband and two children, the youngest an infant of 7 days.
Also, in the same county, July 12th, Mrs. **Betsy Tays**, in her 88th year. ... member of Amity Church.

Died near Pisgah, Gaston Co., N. C., July 15th, 1860, **James Andrew Wilson**, only child of William and Nancy Wilson. ... Little Jimmie was near two years old.

Died at his residence in Lancaster District, S. C. on the 22nd of July, Mr. **Robert Nelson**, in the 80th year of his age. He was an orderly and consistent member of the Associate Reformed Church for about 50 years, having connected himself with the congregation under the pastoral care of Rev. William Blackstock in the year 1810, and worshipped at Tirzah, Union Co., N. C. ... Mr. Nelson married Miss Nancy Nisbet, who, together with seven children survive.

Died at house of Francis Beattie near Pisgah, Gaston, N. C., January 26th, 1860, Mrs. **Esther Beattie**. Mrs. Beattie had been a widow for many years. Her husband, **James Beattie**, a native of Carlisle, Pa., was near the spot and heard the roar of battle, that memorable day, when Col. Campbell and his faithful mountain boys routed the Tories on King's Mountain. He was some time clerk in Long Creek. ... filled for many years the office of ruling elder in Pisgah A. R. Church. In 1824, he and his family moved to Macon Co., N. C. and built a house of worship there, and perhaps organized a church, which was occasionally visited by Dr. McElwee and others. Then in 1828, James Beattie died. His widow returned to Crowder's Creek and resided with her little children.

Married in Marshall Co., Tenn. on the 24th July by Rev. A. S. Montgomery, Mr. **James H. Glenn** to Miss **Margaret E. Leonard**.

Married on Thursday the 2d of August by Rev. J. O. Lindsay, Rev. **J. A. R. Lowry** of the A. R. Presbytery of Ga. and Miss **M. Jannie McCaslan**, daughter of M. O. McCaslan of Abbeville District, S. C.

<u>August 24, 1860</u>

Less than a month ago it was our painful duty to record the death of Dr. E. E. Pressly; now we have to state that his widow, Mrs. **Mary Pressly**, is also dead. She was called away on the morning of the 20th inst. ... In the last six months four members of this family--the father, the mother and two children, one an infant-- have been buried. In the last seven years nine members of the family have died. Altogether, about fourteen children, the most of them infants, two were married daughters, have entered into rest.

Mrs. Mary Pressly was the second wife of Dr. P., to whom he was married about seven years ago. She was the daughter of Mrs. Taylor of Bethel, in Laurens, and sister of the wife of Rev. D. F. Haddon. ... mother of three children.

James F. Harper, Esq. departed this life at his residence on Kerr's Creek, Va. on Sabbath the 19th of August. ... Capt. Harper was born on the 16th of August, 1798... in his own county he was very extensively known and universally respected. ... was called to represent his county in the State Legislature. At the time of his death... he was a justice of the peace. .... for many years he had been a ruling elder in Ebenezer congregation; and at the same time clerk of Session and treasurer of the congregation. ... He left six children, all of whom but the youngest, a little boy of ten years, are members of the church.

September 14, 1860

Died at the home of her brother, Col. W. M. Walkup, in Union Co., N. C. on the 27th ult. of chronic bronchitis, after several months of illness, Mrs. **Ann J. Belk**, wife of Mr. D. A. Belk of Lancaster District, S. C. and daughter of the late Robert Walkup of Union Co., N. C., aged 34 years. ... she left a husband, two children and two brothers.

William Stone, infant and only child of George and Mary **Cain**, died at their residence in Jefferson Co., Ga. on the 10th of July, 1860, aged 7 months.

Married by Rev. W. M. McElwee on the 6th inst., Rev. **Monroe Oats** of First Presbytery to Miss **Amanda S. Harper**, daughter of James F. Harper, deceased, late of Rockbridge Co., Va.

Married on the 22nd ult. by Rev. J. C. Porter, Mr. **Josiah Thompson** and Miss **Nancy E. McCrery**, both of Warren Co., Illinois.

September 21, 1860

Died in Pontotoc Co., Miss., June 27th, 1860, Miss **Ann Caldwell**, daughter of William Caldwell, Sr. Miss Caldwell was born June 16, 1830 in Anderson District, S. C. She united herself with the Associate Reformed Church at Hopewell in 1852.

Died, July 11, 1860, in Pontotoc Co., Miss., Mrs. **Jane Haynie**, wife of the late Elijah Haynie and daughter of Wm. Caldwell, Sr. Mrs. Haynie was born October 29th, 1816. She was a member of the Associate Reformed Church previous to her removal to Mississippi, but when she came to this county, she with her husband, joined the O. S. Presbyterian Church at New Albany, Miss., ...[survived by] two children, an aged father, brother and sisters.

Died in Mecklenburg Co., N. C., July the 16th, Mrs. **Mary M. Bigham**, in her 52nd year. The deceased was the wife of Jas. Bigham, an elder of Prosperity; and, also by birth, was one of the Hunter family so numerous in Mecklenburg. ...[leaves] a husband and six children.

The mortal remains of Mrs. **Peggy McKeown** were conveyed to their last resting place in Hopewell graveyard on the 14th inst. She died on the evening previous, at her home, the residence of Robert Nixon Hemphill. ... She was probably about eighty five years of age, being the first born of John Nixon and Mary Adair who were married in 1774.

History relates that her father, Capt. John Nixon, was among the foremost of "the fighting men" at the outbreak of the war. When the British had possession of the country in 1780, he raised a company, having much influence in his neighborhood, and the unbounded confidence of his men, and in every action acquitted himself with distinction.

A party of loyalists had collected a great deal of plunder from the Whigs of Chester. Nixon got on their trail and pursued them to the line of Newberry and Union Districts. They took refuge in a house, from which, as it was strongly fortified, they could not be dislodged. Nixon was in the act of firing the house when he received the shot which terminated his career not long afterwards. He had been a terror to the loyalists, and they were bent on vengeance to his family. Consequently Mrs. Nixon took her children, and Negroes, and such articles as she could in a wagon, and fled to North Carolina for protection. In the winter of 1781, she returned to South Carolina, and afterwards married David McCalla, who had been in camp with and fought side by side with her former husband.

She was the mother of eight children--six by the last husband and two by the former--Mrs. McKeown, the subject of this notice, and the widow of the late Dr. John Hemphill, who died the 1st of Feb., 1854. They were much together in life and their remains now rest by each other in the churchyard. The scenes and events of the war made a lasting impression on Mrs. McKeown's mind, and appeared to be ever fresh in her memory.

At Huck's defeat, Col. Floyd, an English officer, escaped on horseback, but his boy, Sam, was captured and sold as a part of the booty. He was purchased by Capt. Nixon, and remained with the family during life. He attended McCalla's Mill some forty years, until, by reason of age, he felt unable to perform the labor. Everyone in this section knew "Miller Sam," and he maintained a character beyond suspicion. He spent the remainder of his days, after leaving the mill, at Mrs. Hemphill's, with her and Mrs. McKeown, and took great pleasure with occasionally going up to the big house to carry his "young mistresses" through the war. Sam made a profession of religion at a time when it was almost regarded as a matter of curiosity to see a colored person at the communion table; quite a change, however, has taken place, and nearly one-fourth of the present communicants at Hopewell are blacks.

Married by Rev. V. Young on Wednesday the 12th inst., Dr. **G. W. Tribble** and Miss **Manie Barmore**, all of Abbeville District.

Due West Telescope

Died in Mecklenburg Co., N. C. on the 3d of April, 1860, **R. Deborah Boyce**, wife of Hugh Boyce and daughter of Lorenzo and Ann Hunter, aged 22 years, 7 months and 7 days. She leaves two small children and her husband.

Married on the 30th August by Rev. J. H. Bryson, Mr. **Felix Matthews** to Miss **Mary Agnes**, eldest daughter of A. H. **Davis**, of Maury Co., Tenn.

October 5, 1860

Mr. **Isaac Lackey**, an esteemed member of Ebenezer congregation, Rockbridge Co., Va., departed this life on Sabbath, the 16th of Sept., in the 40th year of his life. ... a large family consisting of his desolate consort and thirteen youg children are left.

Departed this life at the home of John Douglass, sr., Fairfield District, S. C. on the 6th of Sept., 1860, Miss **Mary Jane Erwin**, sister of Rev. T. W. Erwin and daughter of Caleb Erwin, decd. of Mecklenburg Co., N. C. She was well educated, having been two years in the Carolina College at Wadesborough, N. C., and afterwards graduating in the Female College at Yorkville..

October 12, 1860

Died of croup in Tippah Co., Miss. on the 11th July, **John Edward**, eldest son of Rev. J. L. **McDaniel**, aged 5 years and 4 days.

Died at the residence of her husband David Wilson in Tipton Co., Tenn. on the 20th of September in the sixty sixth year of her age, **Mary Wilson**... born in Fairfield District, S. C. ...[member of Presbyterian church] until her removal to Tennessee with her husband and family in fall of '49. In the spring of 1850, they united with the A. R. Church at Salem. ... [leaves] aged companion and affectionate children [all grown and members of the church].

October 19, 1860

Died of typhoid fever on the 9th of August, Mr. **S. McKeown**, in the 22nd year of his age. ...[member of] A. R. Church at Smyrna, York District.

Died of flux on the 3d of August, **Elizabeth Jane**, daughter of Abram and Margaret S. **Neelands**, aged 2 years.

Died of sore throat on the 23d of September, **Jane Carlisle**, daughter of Thomas and Eliza **McDill**, She was 7 years and 11 months old.

Due West Telescope

Died at his residence in Chester District, S. C. on the 6th inst., Dr. **Stirling Blain**, a graduate of Erskine College of the Class of 1847.

Died in Gaston Co., N. C., Sept. 23, 1860, **John McElwee**, September 28th, 1860, **Gardiner Spring**; sons of Rev. E. E. and R. E. **Boyce**, Spring was 5 years old and died 5 days after his brother, who was 3 years and 5 months old. Putrid sore throat was their disease.

Mrs. **Maria R. Boyd**, wife of James Boyd, Sr. of Chester District, died on the 13th in her 37th year. ... her maiden name was McDowell, and .... she was raised in Fairfield District in connection with the Presbyterian church of Lebanon known as "the Stone Church." Since her marriage, she has been a member of the A. R. Church at Hopewell. Some five or six weeks since, Mrs. Boyd was severely burned by her clothes taking fire, while she was attending to her domestic duties; the flames, catching from behind, she did not discover them until she was in imminent danger. It occurred providentially that Mr. Boyd was in the house at an unusual hour, and came to her relief. With great difficulty, and after having his hands badly burned, he succeeded in tearing the clothes from her and quenching the fire. But she was left in a pitiful condition, and parched from her feet to her head.

Died on the 29th ult. of congestive chill in Crittendon Co., Ark., **Robert Grier**, son of Wm. M. and Mary **Bigham** in the third year of his age.

Married on the 27th Sept. by Rev. C. B. Betts, **Jno. S. Robinson** and **Miss -- Gladney** of Fairfield, S. C.

Died on Friday, October 12th, at the residence of Mr. John Douglass, Fairfield District, S. C. of typhoid dysentery, **Lorenna Caroline**, infant daughter of William and Emeline **Boyce** of York District, S. C., aged about 13 months. ... interred at the family burying place at Lower Steel Creek Church.

Died at Bethel Church, Ala. on the 27th ult., **Felix**, infant son of J. C. and Julia **Jones**, aged about 2 years.

Died at her father, James Montgomery, in Fulton Co., Ark. on the 22nd of August, **Elizabeth Hannah Montgomery**, aged 29 years, 6 months. The deceased connected herself with the A. R.Church at Prosperity, Fulton Co., Ark.

Married at the residence of James H. Haddon near Due West, S. C. on the 1st Nov., inst. by Rev. J. I. Bonner, **Mr. Wise** of Mississippi and **Miss Martin**, daughter of Jno. Martin of California.

Married on the 16th Oct. by Rev. John T. Pressly at the bride's father, Abbeville, **James D. Neel**, M. D. of Newberry, S. C. to Miss **Margaret Savannah Elizabeth**, youngest daughter of Dr. George W. **Pressly**.

----- on the 25th ult. by Rev. John S. Pressly, Capt. **Abel Robins** of Pickens to Mrs. **Eliza Felton** of Anderson.

November 16, 1860

Departed this life near Starkville, Miss. on the 20th of October, **John C. Watt**, aged 8 years and 12 days...."Little Johnny" came to his death by a fall from a tree. He and his elder brother had accompanied to the forest a couple of Negroes, who were hauling wood with a wagon. While the Negroes were engaged in loading their wagon, the little brothers ascended a hickory nut tree, and were delighting themselves by gathering the fruit. Johnny had ascended some forty or fifty feet, when suddenly he fell. His skull and shoulders were fractured....

Died at the residence of his father, Dr. E. Agnew, in Tippah Co., Miss. on Monday, October 8, 1860, **James Rutherford Agnew**. Rutherford was born near Due West in Abbeville District, January 1, 1838. ... [member of] Associate Reformed Church at Bethany.

Married by Rev. J. E. Pressly, October 16th, Mr. **Elam Neel** and Miss **Jane Frazier** of Iredell Co., N. C.

----- by the same, October 30th, Mr. **Cyrus Johnston** and Miss **Mary M. Neel** of Iredell Co., N. C.

Married on the 6th inst. by Rev. V. Young, Mr. **John N. McKeown**, formerly of Chester District, to Miss **Emma C. Pratt**, Abbeville District.

November 23, 1860

Died in Marshall Co., Tenn. on the 2nd of October, 1860, Mrs. **Rachel McDaniel**, wife of Mr. Allen McDaniel, in the 41st year of her age. ... member of the A. R. Church of Headsprings. Her husband lived out of the pale of the visible church for several years after their marriage, but was eventually won, no doubt, by the chaste conversation of his wife. ... She has left a kind and affectionate husband and five children

Died in Bedford Co., Tenn. on the 28th of July, 1860, Mr. **Samuel Thompson**, in the 77th year of his age. ... member of the A. R. Church for nearly two years. The writer [A. S. Montgomery] received him into the church and baptized him, when 75 years old.... he left an aged companion.

Died in Madison Co., Ky. on the 14th of October, 1860 in the 34th year of her age, Mrs. **Isabell J. Gwyn**, wife of Andrew Gwyn. In '42 she became a member of the A. R. Church... she leaves her husband and four lovely children.

Died in Williamson Co., Tenn. on the 2nd October, 1860, Mrs. **Elizabeth McGahey**, in the 67th year of her age. ... member of the A. R. Church at Headsprings, Tenn. for many years. A few years ago, she with her husband moved to Williamson Co. to reside with their son and only surviving child.

Married on Tuesday, October 16th by Rev. Jas. McHatton, Rev. **J. B. Foster** of Dayton to Miss **N. Maria Brown** of Morning Sun, Ohio.

<u>November 30, 1860</u>

Died in Maury Co., Tenn. on the 2nd of November, **Mrs. E. Barker**, eldest daughter of Hugh McCain.

Died on the 20th October, 1860 of typhoid fever, Miss **Barbara Isabella Millen**, daughter of John Millen, sr. of Chester District, S. C. in the 22nd year of her age. ... graduated at Yorkville Female College ...[member] of A. R. P. church at Union, of which her father had long been a ruling elder.

Married by Rev. J. E. Pressly, November 8th, Mr. **W. C. Clark** of Mecklenburg and Miss **Jane Bradley** of Iredell Co., N. C.

<u>December 7, 1860</u>

Died in Mecklenburg Co., N. C. on the 7th of November, **Maggie**, infant daughter of Wm. T. and Margery F. **Alexander**, one year, eight months.

Died in Yorkville, Saturday night, October 27th, Mrs. **Nancy Blair**, having a few days before closed her 84th year. Mrs. Blair was the widow of that excellent man, John Blair, Esq., who had gone before her some twelve years. She was a native of Ireland; her father, Mr. John Erwin, having come to America when she was about twelve years old, and settled in Iredell Co., N. C., a few miles north of Statesville.

Died in Phillips Co., Ark. on the 15th of August, Mr. **Samuel Barron**, in the 64th year of his age. Mr. Barron emigrated from York District, S. C. to

Arkansas in 1845. At that time he was a member of the A. R. Church, but finding none of his own church in that portion of Arkansas in which he settled, he connected himself with the Old School Presbyterians.

Departed this life on the 22nd September at the house of her brother in law, A. Forbes, in Obion Co., Tenn., **Elizabeth Buchanan**, aged about 54 years. The subject of this notice was baptized in the Associate Church, and in early life made a public profession of faith in Christ in that church in York District, S. C. About twenty years ago, she connected herself with the A. R. Church at Troy, Tenn.

Married November 21st by Rev. J. E. Pressly, Mr. **W. W. Witherspoon** and Miss **Mary C. McNeely** of Iredell Co., N. C.

Married November 26th, 1860 at the house of A. P. Connor by Rev. H. T. Sloan, Miss **Kitty Billard** to Mr. **John L. Devlin,** all of Abbeville, S. C.

December 21, 1860

Died at the residence of her father in Tipton Co., Tenn. on the 1st of Nov., 1860, Miss **Sarah Baird** in the 24th year of her age. Disease, typhoid pneumonia.... for several years a consistent member of the A. R. Church at Salem.

Died at his residence in Tipton Co., Tenn. on the 10th of Nov., **Wm. Ross McCain**, aged fifty three years. Disease, chronic bronchitis. The deceased had been from early life an exemplary member of the A. R. Church; first at Tirzah, N. C. and afterwards in Tenn. For the last twenty four years he has been an efficient ruling elder. He was elected and ordained to the office in the summer of 1836 when Bro. Bryson organized the congregation at Salem....
He has left a widow and nine children. ... The two oldest are married and are now living in Arkansas. The other seven are still with their mother; five of them the children of his former companion. ... In compliance with a wish previously expressed, the 23rd Psalm was sung by his friends while he was dying. He was buried on Sabbath morning before public worship commenced.

Married on the 27th of Sept., 1860 at the residence of Rev. W. A. Pollock by the same, Mr. **J. M. Cooper** to Miss **Mary Hamilton**, of Sparta, Ill.

Married on the 28th ult. by the Rev. T. D. Gwin, Mr. **John G. Williams** of Laurens to Miss **Theresa O.**, daughter of Mr. John Hopkins **Williams** of Newberry.

----- on Thursday morning, the 6th ult. by Rev. A. O. Darby, **S. A. Douglass**, Esq., Editor of the Spartanburg *Express* to Miss **Mary F. Byers** of Union District.

Married at Stoney Point, Abbeville District, S. C. on the evening of the 27th ult. by the Rev. John McLees, Mr. **A. M. Aiken** of Winnsboro to Miss **Emma F.**, daughter of the late Joel **Smith** of the former place.

Married by the Rev. H. Quigg on the evening of the 6th inst., Mr. **William G. Lowry** and Miss **Margaret R. Boyd** of Newton Co., Ga.

Married on the 18th inst. by Rev. Henry Jacobs, Pastor of the Thearith Israel congregation, Charleston, Mr. **G. A. Visanska** to Miss **Anna R.**, daughter of Moses I. and **Leath Winstock**, both of Due West, Abbeville District.

January 4, 1861

Died in Lincoln Co., Tenn., October 20th, in the 34th year of his age, Mr. **John Henry Drennan**. ... member of Prosperity and New Hope congregation. ... He has left a wife and four children.

Died in Marshall Co., Tenn. on the 13th of December, 1860, **Wiley**, infant son of Daniel and Louisa **Davis**, aged one year, 5 months and 12 days.

Died in Marshall Co., Tenn. on the 28th November, 1860, Mrs. **Mary Thompson**, in the 75th year of her age. ... Mrs. Thompson lived to bury two husbands. The first, **John Davis**, died February 29th, 1835, and the second, Mr. **Samuel Thompson**, died only a few months before herself.

Died in Franklin Co., Ala., December 13th, 1860, 5 minutes after 9 o'clock, p. m., **E. L. Hamilton**, second son of Reece and Margaret Hamilton, aged 33 years, 7 months and 28 days. ... member of A. R. Church. ... He left a wife and five children.

Married in Marshall Co., Tenn. on the 6th of December, 1860, by Rev. A. S. Montgomery, Mr. **Samuel Orr** to **Miss M. Catherine Davis**.

Married December 20th, 1860, on Long Cane by Rev. H. T. Sloan, Mr. **Franklin Young** to Miss **Martha Langley**.

Married on the 8th December by Rev. J. H. Strong, Mr. **R. S. Strong** of Tipton Co., Tenn. to Mrs. **Martha J. Nelson** of Lafayette, Miss.

Married by Rev. J. C. Boyd on December 19th, Mr. **George A. Young** of Miss. and **Miss E. E. Spence** of Frog Level, S. C.

----- also, by the same, on December 20th, Mr. **Maxwell Reid** of Miss.

and **Miss M. E. Reid** of Newberry District, S. C.

----- also, by the same, on November 20th, Mr. **John Drennon** of Abbeville and **Mrs. S. Davis** of Newberry District, S. C.

Married on the 20th December at 6 1/2 o'clock, p. m. by Rev. R. W. Brice, assisted by Rev. L. McDonald, Mr. **James A. Brice** of Fairfield District to Miss **M. Josephine**, daughter of Rev. L. **McDonald** of Chester District.

----- also, on the same evening, at 8 o'clock, p. m., at the residence of Dr. Wm. Wylie by Rev. L. McDonald, assisted by Rev. R. W. Brice, Mr. **W. L. Roddey** to Miss **Anna C. Baskin**, all of Chester District, S. C.

Married on 20th December, 1860, at the residence of the bride's mother, Mrs. Blain, in Fayette Co., Tenn. by Rev. J. A. Sloan, Mr. **John P. Wiseman** of Marshall Co., Miss. to Miss **Mariah Blain** of the former county and state.

Married in Franklin Co., Ala., December 4th, 1860, by Rev. Mr. Spraggans, Mr. **C. M. Hamilton** to Miss **Permelia Rea**.

Married on the 17th ult. by the Rev. Wm. Martin, Major **H. A. Jones** of Abbeville to Miss **Nellie Hutchison** of Columbia.

January 11, 1861

Died in Tipton Co., Tenn. on the 18th November, 1860, Mr. **Samuel Henderson**, in the 20th year of his age.

Married December 4th at the home of the bride by Rev. C. B. Betts, Mr. **Thos. Gladney** and Miss **Martha Harvey**, all of Fairfield District, S. C.

Married on the 3rd inst. by Rev. J. C. Boyd, Mr. **I. C. Swirgard** and Miss **Mary H. McNinch**, all of Frog Level, Newberry District, S. C.

Married at the residence of the bride's father in Tipton Co., Tenn. by Rev. J. Wilson, and on the 20th of March, Mr. **Alexander S. Hyndman** to **Miss Mat McClerkin**, all of Tipton Co., Tenn.

----- on the 25th September by Rev. J. H. Strong, Mr. **Charles Strong** to Miss **Sallie Simonton**, all of Tipton Co., Tenn.

----- near Bloomington, Tipton Co., Tenn. on the 19th December by Rev. D. H. Cummins, Mr. **Richard Templeton** to **Mrs. Eliza Cherry**, all of the above county.

----- on the evening of the 4th December by Robt. Bonds, Esq., Mr. **Osborn H. McCreight** to **Miss --- Merrill**, all of Tipton Co., Tenn.

----- on the morning of the 12th of December by Rev. D. H. Cummins, Mr. **John McClaughlin** to **Mrs. M. A. Strong**, consort of the late Wm. J. Strong, all of Tipton Co., Tenn.

January 18, 1861

It grieves me to record the death of **Joseph Lindsay**, in the 29th year of his age, on the 12th of December. He was killed by the collision of railroad trains near Chattanooga as he returned from Due West, where he had been superintending the business of his uncle, (the late Dr. Pressly). While the passenger train was "wooding," as he was stepping into another car for water, it was struck by another train coming up as he was on the platform, and both of his legs were broken. They returned with him to Chattanooga immediately, where physicians and strangers rendered every assistance in their power, but with the coldness of the night, together with the loss of so much blood, so chilled his manly frame, that nothing could rally his vital powers, and he soon died.

Died in Lincoln, Tenn. on the 24th December, Mr. **Archy Kidd**, in a good old age, about four score. He was born in Nova Scotia, and at an early age moved with his parents to Long Cane, Abbeville District, S. C. There he remained until he had a family, and when the tide of emigration from that section commenced pouring into middle Tennessee, he was carried upon one of the waves to these mountain fastnesses. He settled in the bounds of Bethel, was among the original members comprising that congregation, and was probably the first ruling elder ever ordained over that congregation if he was not before an elder in Long Cane. ... He left an aged partner, several children, and many grandchildren.

Died at his home in Lincoln Co., Tenn., December 30th, Mr. **James A. Willson**, in the 35th year of his age. ... A few months ago, he buried his fourth and last child--a little while before his widowed mother and a while before that, his father.

February 1, 1861

Died of pneumonia in Neely's Creek congregation, York District, S. C. on 15th December, Mrs. **Ellen Abernathy**, in the 34th year of her age. ...[early a member] of Presbyterian church. .. after her marriage some years ago she transferred her connection to the A. R. Presbyterian Church at Neely's Creek. ..[left] husband and children.

Married on the 24th ult. by Rev. J. C. Boyd, Mr. **Leavy Coon** and Miss **Nannie Jones**, all of Newberry, S. C.

February 15, 1861

It was Sabbath morning about 8 o'clock, February 3d, 1861, when **Mrs. A. L. Kennedy**, wife of Isaac Kennedy, Esq., departed this life in the 52d year of her life. ... member of A. R. Church at Cedar Spring. ... She has left a bereaved husband and stepchildren.

Married in Wilcox Co., Ala., January 17th, 1861, by Rev. J. M. Young, Mr. **T. J. Craig** and **Miss M. J. Cooper**.

February 22, 1861

Died in Tipton Co., Tenn. on the 22nd of January, Mrs. **Martha McCain**, in the 75th year of her age. Disease, typhoid pneumonia. The deceased had long been a member of the A. R. church, first at Tirzah in North Carolina, and afterwards for about twenty five years at Salem, Tenn. ... She lived to see her large family all members of the church of her choice, one of them a minister, two of them ruling elders, two of them deacons. Three of her sons had preceded her to the house appointed for all living. The last (W. R.) only being a few months in advance of her.

Died in Tipton Co., Tenn. on the 30th of January, **David Wilson,** in the 73rd year of his age. [Reared in O. S. Presbyterian church in Fairfield District, S. C.] in 1849, he removed to Tennessee, and preferring the principles and usuages of the A. R. church, he connected himself, together with his family, with Salem in the year 1850. ... He has left one son and three daughters.

Married on the evening of the 7th inst. by Rev. C. B. Betts, Mr. **Samuel Cathcart** to Miss **Anna Elder**, all of Winnsboro, S. C.

--------- by Rev. J. E. Pressly, January 29th, Mr. **G. G. McKnight** to Miss **Nancy E. Atwell** of Rowan Co., N. C.

Married on the 13th of December last by Rev. J. M. Brown, Mr. **Robert Knox** to **Miss E. D. McCain**.

--------- on the 10th of January, 1861, by the same, Mr. **James Hogue** to Miss **Nannie Harper**.

-------- also, on the 24th by the same, Mr. **G. N. Jenning** to **Miss E. H. Wilson**, all of Drew Co., Ark.

Married on the evening of the 4th Feb. at the residence of the bride's father by Rev. W. S. Moffatt, Mr. **Robt. A. Ross** and Miss **Mary Cochran**.

---- by the same on the 5th, Mr. **Wm. Cochran** and Miss **Mattie Ross**, all of Fulton Co., Ark.

March 8, 1861

Departed this life on the 1st of February in his own house in Fairfield District, S. C., **William Stevenson, Sr.** ... born June 24, 1782. ... i n Ireland, but was brought to this country in early life by his parents; the last 75 years of his life were spent in the area of a few miles within the limits of New Hope congregation. ... He raised a large family, nine children surviving him, three sons and six daughters.

Married on the 26th of February by Rev. J. C. Chalmers, **E. P. Chalmers** to Miss **E. Virginia Spearman** of Newberry District, S. C.

Married near Covington, Tipton Co., Tenn. on the 7th of February by the Rev. James Holmes, D. D., Dr. **John L. Payne** of the vicinity of Portersville to Miss **M. Fannie McGregor**.

---- on the 24th of January by Esq. Boswell, Mr. **John Kelly** to **Miss Baskins**, all of Tipton Co., Tenn.

---- near Shelby Depot, Shelby Co., Tenn. on the 23rd of January by the Rev. Mr. Ewing, Mr. **J. L. Bolton** to Miss **Henrietta Polk**, both of the above named county.

---- on Feb. 25th at the house of Dr. Jos. Marshall by Rev. H. T. Sloan, **Mrs. M. L. Cochran** of Abbeville to Dr. **T. C. Griffin** of Fla.

March 15, 1861

Died in Obion Co., Tenn. on the 15th of February, Mr. **Robt. B. Brown**, aged 39 years. Disease, pneumonia. ... He leaves a wife and four small children. Mr. Brown connected himself with the A. R. Church in the fall communion. His Christian race was but short, but we trust real.

Mr. **John Bradley**, whose remarkable sudden death was announced last week [March 8th issue reported that he had died on March 2nd "when in the act of shaving to prepare for the coming Sabbath"] was in the seventy sixth year of his age. ... He connected himself with the A. R. Church at Long Cane under Father Porter after the fifth day's examination as the custom then was, when only sixteen years of age. Consequently, he had been a consistent member for about sixty years, and a ruling elder for more than twenty years. He was the last of those baptized in infancy by Dr. Clark. ... Having lost his companion a few years ago, he lived alone with his servants, although in sight of some of his children, and spent much time in reading. He lived to see his children, five in number, all prosperously settled around him, members of the same church and walking in his footsteps.

Mrs. **Jane Lindsay**, sister of Mr. Bradley, who rode from home that day, a distance of five or six miles, in perfect health, and had walked the last mile after hearing of her brother's death, was only permitted to see the corpse until she also dropped into eternity without a struggle or lingering breath. ... Mrs. Lindsay was about sixty five years of age. ... She left seven children, three sons and four daughters.

Married on the 31st of Jan., 1861 by the Rev. H. H. Robison, Mr. **J. W. Sanders** to Miss **Lethe Wiseman**, all of Tippah Co., Miss.

Married on the evening of the 20th of Feb. by Rev. R. L. Grier, Mr. **T. B. Moffatt** and Miss **Nannie Hamilton**, all of Obion Co., Tenn.

Married at Gaston Co., N. C. on the 27th ultimo. by Rev. E. E. Boyce, Mr. **William A. Pearson** and Miss **Nancy E. Weir**.

March 22, 1861

Died in Wilcox Co., Ala. on the 7th of March, **Joseph Jones** in the eighty first year of his age. ... The deceased filled a large place in our Zion. He was indeed a pillar in the church. His descendants compose the larger part of the membership of Bethel. ... He was born and raised in Abbeville District, S. C. From there he removed to the State of Missouri, and after a few years stay he emigrated to Alabama and settled the spot where he closed his earthly pilgrimage. He and his brother, Robert Jones, were the first A. R. Presbyterian settlers in the County of Wilcox where now exist two flourishing churches. He was ordained an elder in Lebanon church, the original organization in 1828....

Died in Xenia, Ohio on the evening of February 28th, the Rev. **James Patterson Smart**, pastor of the United Presbyterian congregation of Massie Creek.

Died on the 15th of February, **Elizabeth Jane**, daughter of John R. and Martha **McDaniel**, in the eighth year of her age.

Due West Telescope

Died at his residence in Fulton Co., Ark. on the 11th ultimo., Mr. **John Wiley**, of bronchial affection or consumption, in the 51st year of his age. He was a member of the A. R. P. Church.

[Died] at the residence of his father on the 5th inst., **William B. Cochran**, in the 25th year of his age. He was married but about a month since.

---- on the 19th of December, 1860, **Silas Hemphill**, aged 11 months and 18 days, infant son of John C. and Margaret L. **Cooper**.

---- also on the 3rd ult., **William Wilson**, infant son of R. C. and Martha E. **Simonton**, aged 5 months and 18 days.

Married on the 15th of February by the Rev. J. M. Brown, Mr. **Wm. McKinstry** and Miss **Margaret Wright**, all of Drew Co., Ark.

Died March 21st in Mecklenburg Co., N. C., Miss **Martha H. Grier**, daughter of Col. Thomas J. and Mary Grier, aged about 44 years. ... consistent member of Associate Church and after the union of the Associate and Associate Reformed Church, of the latter at Little Steel Creek.

Died on the 8th of February, 1860 in Chester District, **Mary**, daughter of J. A. and I. H. **Roseborough**, aged 18 months. Also, on the 27th January last, **James**, and on the 28th of March, **William**, twin sons of the same parents, aged about five months. They were the grandchildren of Mrs. Moffatt of Chester.

Married on the 28th by Rev. Jno. Miller at the residence of the bride's father, Mr. **Wm. Crawford** to Miss **Minnie Griffith**, all of Wilcox Co., Ala.

Married on the 9th inst. by Rev. John S. Pressly, Mr. **Benjamin F. Hutchison** of Anderson District to Miss **Rebekah Pressly** of Lowndesville, Abbeville District.

Died on Kerr's Creek, Rockbridge Co., Va., on the 17th April, Mrs. **Margaret Miller**, wife of Andrew Miller, in the -- year of her age. ... She leaves a venerable mother, a husband, and four chidren.

Married on Tuesday evening, May 7th by Rev. J. I. Bonner, Dr. **O. Perry Hawthorn** of Due West and Miss **Jane**, daughter of Captain Benjamin **Smith** of Abbeville.

May 17, 1861

Mr. **Robert Patterson** died at his residence in Jefferson Co., Ga. on the 21st of April, 1861, aged about 50 years.

Died in Chester District, S. C. on the 4th of May, Miss **Jenny**, wife of Garner **White**, in the 64th year of her age. ... Mrs. White was one of the oldest members of the A. R. Church at Hopewell. ... She leaves an afflicted husband, one daughter and three sons.

May 31, 1861

Died in Obion Co., Tenn. on the 22nd of March, little **Mary Rosannah**, the daughter of David W. and Mrs. Louisa **Stewart**, aged about 8 years.

Departed this life after a long illness, April 19th, **Agnes M.**, daughter of Mr. Oliver and Mrs. Susannah **McCaslin**, aged 21 years and two days.

Married on the 15th inst. by Rev. Wm. Banks, Rev. **R. Z. Johnston** of North Carolina to **Miss C. M. Caldwell** of Chester District, S. C.

Married at the residence of the bride's father on the 10th inst. by Rev. D. McNeil Turner, Mr. **F. A. Harrison** of Anderson to Miss **Mary E. Perrin** of Abbeville village.

June 7, 1861

Died near Due West on Tuesday morning, 28th ult., Mrs. **Jane Ellis**, wife of Robert Ellis.

Married by Rev. J. E. Pressly, May 21st, Mr. **John R. Smith** and Miss **Margaret Goodnight** of Cabarrus Co., N. C.

---- by the same, May 23rd, Mr. **James Young** of Iredell and Miss **Mary Corkle** of Rowan Co., N. C.

Married 28th May by Rev. D. F. Haddon, Rev. **J. C. Boyd** of Newberry and **Miss M. F. McClintock**, daughter of John McClintock of Laurens.

Due West Telescope

Died in Hopkins Co., Texas, **J. C. G. Nelson**, on the 23rd March in the twentieth year of his age.

Departed this life May 5th, **John Wilson**, infant son of Joel and Margaret Jane **Butler**.

Died in Wilcox Co., Ala., May 1, 1861, Mrs. **Jane P. Young**, wife of John Young, Esq., in the 33d year of her age.

Married on the 13th of May by Rev. W. B. Pressly, Mr. **W. W. White** to Miss **Esther Kistler**, both of Iredell.

---- on the 5th June by the same, Mr. **James Morrison** to Miss **Mary A. Hall** of Iredell.

Died in Wilcox Co., Ala., on the 29th of May, 1861, Mrs. **Missouri C. Pressly**, wife of Dr. Joseph Pressly, in the 25th year of her age.

Died in San Jose City, California, on the 19th of March, **Lawrence**, only child of Mr. and Mrs. L. **Archer**, aged 6 years.

Died on the 14th inst., Mrs. **Mary Ann Martin**, aged 78 years, 5 months and 13 days. The deceased was a native of Newberry District, and connected herself, in early life, with the A. R. Presbyterian Church at King's Creek. ... many years ago, her husband and family moved to Abbeville, and were transferred to Cedar Spring. ... The deceased left three sons, and a goodly number of grandchildren.

Married at the parsonage, June 12th by Rev. J. E. Pressly, Mr. **Wm. C. Moore** and Miss **Sarah J. Hamilton**, all of Cabarrus Co., N. C.

Died, June 5th, in Mecklenburg Co., N. C., Mrs. **Mary McGinnis**, in the sixty eighth year of her age. ... leaves two children, a son and a daughter who have families and homes of their own, an aged husband.

Died at Newberry C. H., S. C., 16th of June, 1861, of diarrhea, **William Arthur**, only child of Dr. R. S. and M. A. **Whaley**, aged one year, six months and twenty eight days.

Died in Pontotoc Co., Miss on Saturday, May 25, 1861, **William Caldwell, Sr.**, in the 75th year of his age. The deceased was born in Newberry District, S. C., December 8th, 1786. In his early manhood he united himself with the Church at Gilder's Creek, under the ministry of Rev. John Renwick. In 1819, he removed himself to Anderson District, and was a member of Shiloh Church from its organization until his removal from the state. In 1845, he removed to Mississippi, and settled in Pontotoc County, where he resided until his death. ...[member of] Hopewell church. ... He leaves five sons, two daughters.

July 12, 1861

Drowned on the 5th of June, 1861, **Silas Arthur Cooper**, aged 21 years and 8 months. ... He leaves behind an aged mother, a brother, a sister. ... He had been harvesting for Mr. James Quinn, and after the day's work was over, he went with some young men to take a bathe. Mr. Cooper could not swim and did not intend to go very far into the water, and it is supposed that he slipped off the gradually sloping bank into the lake where the water is some ten or twelve feet deep. There were two boys on the bank at the time. ... Oh, what a warning to all. ...[D. K.]

Married at the parsonage by Rev. J. E. Pressly, Mr. **Wilson H. Mock** and Miss **Mary A. Cashion** of Mecklenburg Co., N. C.

July 19, 1861

Died in this district on the 28th ult., Dr. **William H. Allen**, in the 23rd year of his age. The deceased something more than a year ago graduated from the Dental College of Surgery, Philadelphia, and started upon his professional career with the most flattering prospects; but consumption seized upon him.

Died in Chester District, S. C. on the 29th of June, Mrs. **Sarah,** wife of David **Wilson**, Esq., in the 67th year of her age. ... from early youth she had been a member of the A. R. Church at Hopewell.

July 26, 1861

Died in Due West, July 17th, **Cosmor Dent** , infant son of J. Y. and H. D. **Sitton**, aged 13 months. ... husband is in the army in Virginia, and knew nothing of the illness of his little boy.

Also, at the same place, on the 19th July, of typhoid dysentery, **Elizabeth Emma**, infant daughter of M. and J. **Bell**, aged near 15 months. ... As in the former one, the father of the little child has gone to fight the battles of his country, and was consequently absent from home.

Died, June 23rd, Miss **Peggy Frazier** of Iredell Co., N. C. ...[member of] A. R. Church at New Sterling.

Died, June 22nd, 1861, **Wm. Pressly**, first born of H. L. and I. **Clodfelter**, aged three years and two months. Disease, flux.

August 2, 1861

Died, July 18th, 1861, in York District, S. C., Miss **Nancy Selina Harris**, in the 42nd year of her age.

Departed this life in Madison, Miss. on the 15th of June, Mrs. **Jane Cochran**, aged 55 years. ... She has left two daughters and a son.

Drowned in Gaston Co., N. C., July 15th, two brothers, **Samuel L.** and **Robert L. Whitesides**, sons of William Whitesides, the former 23, and the latter 22 years.
The circumstances of this most melancholy casualty are as follows: the two young men, in company with another relative, were bathing in William Crawford's mill pond--that part of the pond was not above their depth, except a ditch which had formerly been cut to dry the field when under cultivation. Samuel got into the ditch, and not being an expert waterman, sank. Robert went to his relief, and the two locked arms in a death embrace, and went down. ... Samuel was a communing member of Pisgah.

Married on the 20th June by Rev. David Pressly, Mr. **H. P. Reese** to Miss **Josephine S. P. Shepherd**, all of Oktibbeha Co., Miss.

August 9, 1861

Died at Due West, Thursday evening, the 1st inst., Mr. **Robert Drennen**, in the 57th year of his age. ... Mr. Drennen was trained up under the ministry of Dr. John I. Pressly during the pastorate of Long Cane and Cedar Spring. ... he was elected a ruling elder during the pastorate of Rev. W. R. Hemphill, Dr. Pressly's successor. About six years since, he came to Due West, and acted as a member of the Session in the congregation here, until his death.

Departed this life near Due West on August 4th, Mrs. **Sarah A. Miller**, consort of John T. Miller. ... she leaves a husband and five children.

Died at her residence, Laurens District, S. C., July 25th, Mrs. **Elizabeth Taylor**, in the 66th year of her age. ... For more than forty years. ... member of Bethel Church, Laurens District.

August 16, 1861

Died, August 2nd, 1861, **Robert H. Ranson**, in the 34th year of his age. The deceased was one of the gallant corps who nobly jeopardized their lives in vindicating the rights of the South from the aggressions of a ruthless foe. He was attached to Capt. Dean's Company of the 4th Regiment of South Carolina Volunteers, Anderson District. He sustained the rank of First Corporal. At the memorable battle of Bull Run, he received a ball in his left arm, between the elbow and the shoulder, by which it was shattered to pieces. Amputation ensued. He was kindly transported to the residence of a Dr. Lutch, some 40 miles from the scene of action. .. of Baptist communion.

Married on the 11th ult. of Wacahoota, Fla. by Rev. F. C. Johnson, Dr. **G. B. Hunter** to Miss **Sallie W.**, daughter of John **Fleming**.

Married on the 8th inst. at the parsonage by Rev. A. Ranson, Mr. **Wm. A. Brown** and Mrs. **Sarah H. Johnson**.

---- also, at the house of the bride's father, Mr. **Jno. C. McAulay** and Miss **Jane E.**, daughter of James and Margaret **Reid**. All of Mecklenburg Co., N. C.

Married on the 24th ult. by Rev. J. E. Pressly, Mr. **Samuel A. Brown** to Miss **Jane Barringer** of Iredell Co., N. C.

August 23, 1861

Departed this life at the residence of her son, R. G. Davis, in Drew Co., Ark., Mrs. **Sarah Davis**, at the advanced age of 77 years. ... She was born in Lancaster District, S. C. ... She raised a goodly number of children in "the nurture and admonition of the Lord," one a minister in the A. R. Church.

August 30, 1861

Died in York District, S. C., August 16th, 1861, **Franklin McElwee**, son of Newman McElwee, in his 19th year. ... He was a rising junior in Erskine College, and had been home with his people but a few weeks till fever laid him low.

Died, July 30th, 1861, **Artemissa M. I. Frazier**, third daughter of Wm.

and Mary Frazier, aged 14 years.

Died, July 17th, **Alexander Mathison**, also on the 6th of August, **Angus Mathison**, son of Alexander Mathison, both of typhoid fever. The son leaves a family of his own, a wife and three small children. Being the only child, he lived with his father and mother.

Died on the 12th of August, **Daniel Frazier**, youngest son of Daniel Frazier, Senr., aged 27 years.

September 6, 1861

Died in Newton Co., Ga., on the 16th of August, 1861, **Susannah**, beloved wife of Mr. James Y. **Thompson**, in the 58th year of her age. ... Was born and raised in Fairfield District, S. C. When early in life, she connected herself with Lebanon church under the pastorate of the Rev. Mr. Young. Her father, Mr. Aiken, with his family, having afterwards moved to this state, she connected herself in 1834 with the Bethany Presbyterian Church of this place. ... she leaves a sorrowing husband, four sons and a daughter.

Married--Pope Co., Ark., on 28th of May, by Rev. John Patrick, Mr. **John F. Falls, Jr.** to **Mrs. S. A. Alexander**, daughter of Silas R. Parker.

October 4, 1861

Died in Iredell Co., N. C., August 18th, 1861, **Mary Matilda,** daughter of Hiram **Morrison**, Sr., aged 16 years, 8 months and 19 days

[Died] September 8th, 1861, **Decatur**, only son of Hiram and Adline **Scroggs.**

[Died] on the night of the same Sabbath evening, Mr. **Thomas Morrison,** the oldest member of the Session at New Sterling. ... He had passed his fourscore.

[Died] August 31st, Martha, youngest child of **John Walker**. Disease, flux.

[Died] September 11th, **William Quincy,** infant of Archy and Louisa **Barkley**.

October 11, 1861

Departed this life at the residence of Dr. C. P. Montgomery, Starkville,

Miss. on the 9th of August, Dr. **Wm. H. Merinar**, aged 39 years and 10 months. ... member of Baptist church . ... Although having no fondness for the changing scenes of political life, yet a few years ago he had been chosen the representative of this county in the State Legislature. This relation he sustained at the time of his death. ... He was among the first who volunteered their services in defence of the South. He was a member of that noble company, the "Oktibbeha Rescue"--who went forth to repel an invading foe. When the company arrived at Corinth, he was constituted Surgeon General of the State of Mississippi. ... While engaged in attending to the sick and dying he was attacked with diarrhea. ... conveyed back to Starkville. .. [he died] in the house of a relative.

Died in Iredell Co., N. C., September 23rd, **Mary C.**, wife of Milos **Bready**, aged 24 years. ... member of New Sterling. ... leaves a husband and two little daughters.

[Died] in Alexander Co., N. C., September 27th, the youngest **child** of Milton and -- **Alexander**, aged three years.

Died of measles on the 10th ult. at her residence near Middlebrook, Augusta Co., Va., Mrs. **Elizabeth Carson**, wife of John Carson, Esq., in the 55th year of her age. ... member of Old Providence Church.

Died near Hillsboro, Ark. on the 9th of September, 1861, **Ebenezer E. McMillen**, son of Andrew and Mary J. McMillen, aged one year and two months.

Died in Wilcox Co., Ala., on the 6th of August, 1861, Mrs. **Sarah Hines**, in the 34th year of her age.

Died at Viney Grove, Tenn. on the 28th of August, Mrs. **Sarah McMullin**, in the 63d year of her age. Her disease was chronic bronchitis. She was a native of Abbeville District, S. C. In early life she connected herself with the Presbyterian church at Rocky River, then under the care of Dr. Moses Waddle. On her removal with her husband to this country, she identified herself with the A. R. Church at Bethel, then under the care of her brother in law.

Married on the 13th of August near Starkville, Miss. by Rev. David Pressly, Rev. **W. J. Lowry** of Camden, Ala. to Miss **Maggie Bell**.

October 18, 1861

Departed this life in Jefferson Co., Ga., September 30, 1861, **Agness Lowry**, daughter of Joseph L. and Lydia **Trimble**, aged two years.

Died on the night of the 8th of September at Fort Pillow, Lauderdale Co., Tenn., Mr. **Thomas T. M. McCoy**, of typhoid dysentery, aged about 35 years. ... Member of the A. R. P. Church at Greensboro, Ark. He was a volunteer and had gone to defend his country.

Died of pulmonary consumption at the residence of his mother in Abbeville District on the 31st of July last, **James Dawson**, in the 45th year of his age. ...[member of] the A. R. Church at Little Generostee in Anderson District.

November 8, 1861

Died near Centreville, in Virginia, on the 15th October, Mr. **Henry Manley Darlington**, in the 18th year of his age. The deceased was a member of the 4th Regiment, S. C. V. Being engaged in business at Anderson C. H. when the call was made for volunteers, he promptly enrolled himself. ... He was in the battle of Manassas Plains [and emerged] uninjured. About the 1st September, he was attacked with typhoid fever. ... and this disease claimed its victim.

Died on the 18th ult. at his residence in Rock Hill, York District, S. C., **Thomas E. Roddy**, in the 29th year of his age. He was the son of John Roddy, Esq. who preceded him to the grave fourteen months, and Mary Wylie Roddy of the congregation of Neely's Creek. ...[At the outset of war] when the "Indian Land Guards" were organized, he accepted a subordinate, but arduous and responsible office, which he discharged with great fidelity, and to the entire satisfaction of the Adjutant of the 12th Regiment. At the late communion at Neely's Creek, he and several of his companions in arms, obtained a furlough, and came home to renew their vows to their covenant-keeping God. ...[on his return to service] to Camp Johnson, at Lightwood Knot Springs, where he was attacked with measles, succeeded by typhoid fever, which after a period of two weeks, put an end to his promising life. ... He leaves a young wife.

Died at the residence of its grandmother in Dallas Co., Ala., on the 27th of September, 1861, little **Mary Eliza Hines**, infant daughter of Mr. Robert Hines of Wilcox Co., Ala., aged two months.

November 15, 1861

Died in Fairfield District the 27th October, **Nannie**, infant daughter of John S. and M. B. **Douglass**, aged 15 months.

Married by Rev. H. Quigg on the 17th of October, 1861, Mr. **L. F. Stephenson** and Miss **Janet Thompson**, daughter of David Thompson, Esq. of Newton Co., Ga.

Married, September 12th at the parsonage by Rev. J. C. Chalmers, Mr. **Wm. M. Prather [?]** and **Miss H. M. Haynes**, both of Mecklenburg Co., N. C.

---- also, October 29th at the residence of the bride's father by the same, Mr. **J. W. Dixon** and Miss **Larina Brown**, both of Mecklenburg.

November 22, 1861

Departed this life in Pontotoc, Miss., after an illness of two weeks from fever, on the 22nd October, 1861, Mrs. **Margaret I.**, wife of Rev. J. L. **Young**, in the 48th year of her age. She was born in the County Monaghan, Ireland, but her parents while she was small removed to America and settled in Laurens District, S. C. where the greater part of her life was spent.

Died on the 3rd October at the residence of her son in law, Rev. E. E. Boyce, Mrs. **Rebekah McElwee**, on the 69th year of her age. The deceased was the daughter of the late William McElwee, Esq. of York District, S. C. and a relict of John R. McElwee, who preceded her to the grave a little upwards of 14 years. She was born and reared up in Bethany congregation.

Died of typhoid or brain fever on the 7th of October after an illness of about four weeks, **William Miller**, son of Thos. L. Miller of Broad Creek congregation, Rockbridge Co., Va.

Married on the 5th inst. by Rev. D. F. Haddon, Mr. **E. E. Lindsay** of Tenn. and **Miss N. L. Taylor** of Laurens, S. C.

November 29, 1861

Death of **Samuel Andrew McBryde**... [member] 2nd Mississippi Regiment ...[killed] Manassas (Va.) 21st of July... member of Ebenezer, Miss. ... son of James T. McBryde, a ruling elder in Ebenezer. ... was in the 21st year of his age.

Married on the 19th instant by the Rev. David Wills, Professor **Robert Garlington** of Newberry to Miss **Mary E.**, daughter of Col. John D. **Williams** of Laurens District.

December 6, 1861

John Meek McElwee, son of J. N. McElwee, died at his home, Clark's Fork, York District, S. C., Sabbath night, 11 o'clock, August 25, 1861 in the 27th year of his age. ... leaves a bereaved wife and little daughter.

[Died] **Rachel N. McElwee**, sister of the above, an only sister, died October 16th, 1861 ... member of A. R. Church at Bethany.

Died in Rockbridge Co., Va. on the 16th of September, **Joseph P. Kinnear**, Esq. ...[member of] Timber Ridge Church . ... active and efficient member of "Second Rockbridge Dragoons" ...[died of typhoid fever].

Died in Rockbridge, Va. on the 8th ult., **Martha Virginia**, daughter of Mr. and Mrs. Lieutenant **Lusk**, aged about 21 months.

Married on the 21st ult. by Rev. J. E. Pressly, Mr. **A. A. Davidson** to Miss **Celia M. Brown** of Iredell Co., N. C.

Married on the 7th ult. by Rev. R. W. Brice, Mr. **Thomas Sterling** to Miss **Caroline**, daughter of R. **Boyd**, Senr., all of Chester, S. C.

<u>December 13, 1861</u>

[Died] in camp in Va. on the 23d of November, John Louis **Donald**, son of Col. Saml. Donald of Abbeville District, S. C. ... in 22nd year of his age. ... a member of the 7th Regiment, S. C. V., he was called to Va., where, after having passed safely through many perils and dangers from the enemy. ... he fell by the hands of a drunken assassin--who made upon him an unprovoked, murderous attack... [member of] Greenville Presbyterian congregation.

Died at the residence of her father, near Waterloo, Laurens District, on the 31st of October, Miss **Naomi A. McCrady**, daughter of Robert and Jane McCrady in the 27th year of her age. ... member of the A. R. Church at Head Spring, Laurens District.

Died in Bethel Church, Wilcox Co., Ala., **John Clarke**, infant son of Mr. T. C. and Eliza **McBride**.

Died in Wilcox Co., Ala. on the 7th ult., Mr. **Green Dunham**, im the thirty seventh year of his age. ... He leaves an affectionate wife and two little orphans. ... member of Methodist church.

Died in Alexander County on the 11th ult., **Preston Lafayette**, aged 7 years, 6 months. Also, on the 19th, **Laura Josephine**, only surviving child of Mr. and Mrs. J. F. **Miller**. Disease, diphteria. The father, a cavalier in Capt. Andrew's Squadron, arrived at home in time to witness the death of his last child.

Departed his life Wednesday the 6th ultimo., **James Brice**, son of Samuel and Dorcas Brice of New Hope, Fairfield District, S. C. He was about 19 years and 4 months old. It was his lot to die far away from his father's house, in the Hampton's Legion in Virginia. ... He fought manfully on the memorable 21st of July, at Manassas, and escaped the dangers of that battle field to fall a victim to typhoid fever on the 6th of November.

Died, Sabbath morning, December 1st, 1861, **Robert Samuel McClinton**, son of Samuel B. McClinton, Esq., in the 19th year of his age. ... He had well nigh completed his sophomore year at Erskine College, when the exercises of that institution were suspended on account of the war excitement. For a short period he remained at home, but about the month of June enrolled his name on the muster roll of Capt. James M. Perrin's Company. ... He died on Sullivan's Island, after only six days' sickness.

Died on the 4th ult. in Rockbridge Co., Va., **James Nevins**, of typhoid fever, in the 21st year of his age. ...He was a member of "Rockbridge 2nd Dragoons."

Died suddenly in Rockbridge Co., Va. on the 27th May, 1861, **Hugh Brownlee**, in the 61st year of his age. Mr. Brownlee was a ruling elder in the A. R. congregation at Old Providence, Augusta Co., Va.

Died at his residence in Marshall Co., Tenn. on the 19th ult. in the 78th year of his age, Mr. **Irwin McAdams**. The subject of this notice had been a ruling elder of the A. R. Presbyterian Church of Head Springs, since its organization some thirty odd years ago.

Married in Alexander Co., N. C. by Rev. W. B. Pressly on the 28th November, Mr. **John W. Sherrill** to Miss **Martha A. Morrison**.

Married on the 3rd inst. in Chester District by Rev. R. W. Brice, Mr. **Charles B. Boyce** to Miss **A. Jane Mills**, daughter of J. Y. Mills, Esq.

Married on the 3rd instant by Rev. E. E. Boyce, **Joseph Wistar Allison**, M. D. to Miss **Rachel Newman Kennedy**, all of York District, S. C.

January 3, 1862

Departed this life at his residence in Fulton Co., Ark. on the --- ult. of typhoid pneumonia, Mr. **Wm. Paden**. The subject of this notice was born and reared in Greenville District, S. C. in connection with the Greenville Presbyterian Church, which he sustained until his late removal to this place when he cast in his lot with the A. R. P. Church. ...He was taken away in the midst of his days, being about 45 years of age and leaves a weakly [sic] wife and large family behind.

Departed this life September 20th in Fulton Co., Ark. of whooping cough, **Mary Susan Elizabeth,** infant daughter of W. I. and Jane **Chesnut,** aged 9 months and 20 days.

---- in Craighead Co., on the 8th of March, 1861, **James Daniel,** infant son of Robert H. and Margaret A. **McKay,** aged 2 years, 7 months and 11 days.

Died on the plains of Manassas the 21st of July, Mr. **George B. Carmical.** ... son of Mr. William T. Carmical, elder in the White Oak Church, Coweta Co., Ga. ... belonged to the 7th Regiment, Georgia Volunteers.

Died suddenly of strangulated hernia, November, 1861, **Jonathan B. Adamson,** in the 67th year of his age. ... member of Cedar Spring ...[leaves] a widowed mother and seven children.

Married on Tuesday, the 10th of December by Dr. Boyce at the residence of the bride, the Rev. **John Hunter** of N. C. to Mrs. **Martha Bell** of Little River, Fairfield District, S. C.

Married at the parsonage, December 10th by Rev. J. E. Pressly, Mr. **Wm. D. Tevepaugh** and Miss **Mary E. Atwell** of Cabarrus Co., N. C.

January 17, 1862

Died on the 21st inst., **Mary Robinson,** in the 62nd year of her age. .. [member] Cedar Spring. ... She was never married but resided under the parental roof with a younger sister and her husband.

Died in Chester District on the 18th of December last, Mr. **Alexander Jamison** in the 53rd year of his age. ... member of A. R. Church at Hopewell.

Killed in the battle of Drainesville on the 20th of December, **Thornwell Brownlee,** son of G. H. and M. Brownlee of Calhoun Co., Ala. ... only 17 years old at time of death. He was a member of the O. S. Presbyterian Church.

Among the slain in the "Battle of Drainesville, Va." on the 20th of December last was Mr. **William S. McDill,** a son of Thomas McDill of Chester District, S. C. and a member of Company G of the Sixth Regiment, S. C. V. [member of Hopewell].

Mr. **James McKeown,** son of Samuel and Jenny McKeown of Chester District, S. C., was also killed at Drainesville, on the 20th ultimo., as is supposed by the same 1st Kentucky Regiment which made the mistake of firing into the South Carolina Regiment, supposing them to be the enemy [member of Hopewell].

Married at the parsonage of the Rev. J. E. Pressly, Mr. **F. F. Dewese** of Mecklenburg, N. C. to Miss **Ann Atwell** of Cabarrus Co.

<u>January 24, 1862</u>

Died of chronic diarrhea, June 16, 1860, **Agnes**, wife of John **Pickens**, elder of Mount Nebo Church, Bradley Co., Tenn., aged 67 years, 9 months and 16 days.

---- **Josiah Alexander Denton**, son of Cornelius C. and Elizabeth Denton of Bradley Co., Tenn., aged one year, ten months and twelve days.

---- **John McClerkin Weir**, August 9, 1861, in M'Minn Co., Tenn., elder in the Mt. Nebo Church, in the 75th year of his age.

---- **Josiah Johnston** of Cleveland, Tenn., October 2, 1861, an elder in the A. R. Church at Mt. Nebo, aged 75 years, 9 months and 10 days.

Died about the first of October, 1861 in Nashville, **Rebecca Hume**, widow of Rev. Wm. Hume, in the 73d year of her age.

Died, October 30th, 1861, **Margaret Woodcock**, aged about 74 years and 9 months. ... member of A. R. Church in south Nashville.

<u>February 7, 1862</u>

Died in Rockbridge, Va. on the 27th ult., **Wm. Lusk**, Esq., in the 77th year of his life. ... He was one of the oldest magistrates in the County [Augusta] ... and member of the A. R. Church of Old Providence.

Joseph Dickson Wylie, son of J. B. Wylie of Chester District, S. C., died in the hospital at Huguenot Springs, Va. on the 17th January last, in the 25th year of his age. He was a member of the 6th S. C. Regiment. He took sick at the camp near Centreville, Va. early in December [Rev. John H. Simpson who wrote this notice also noted that he arrived at the hospital the day following Wylie's death and then carried the body to Chester].

Died of croup on the 19th January, **Jane**, daughter of Andrew and Elizabeth **Strong**, in the 5th year of her age.

Died in Mecklenburg Co., N. C. on the 4th of December, Mr. **Thomas Hunter, Jr.** in the 52nd year of his age. ... member of the Sardis Church for 25 years or more.

Due West Telescope

Died in Old Providence, Augusta Co., Va. on the 11th day of February, of typhoid fever, **John I. Lotts**, in the 32d year of his age.

Died the 17th inst. on Sullivan's Island, Mr. **W. Lafayette Haddon**. He was a member of "Marshall Rifles," Capt. Miller's Company in Orr's Regiment. Attacked with measles early in November and having partially recovered, he visited his home in December. . . . He returned to camp too soon, as on his arrival he was taken immediately to the hospital, typhoid fever ensued.

March 7, 1862

Mr. **Peter Hamilton** of Swan Creek, Lincoln Co., Tenn., died on the 28th of December from an abscess upon his liver. He was an old man (near four score), much loved and honored for his piety and worth. He was born in Ireland, emigrated to Fairfield District, S. C., in early youth--where he remained a long time-- thence he moved to this county at an early period in its settlement. He was a consistent member of the A. R. Church for more than half a century.

Also, Mr. **James Wiley, Sr.**, on the 30th of January, 1862 of chronic consumption in the 70th year of his age. He was a native of Cedar Spring, but emigrated to this country more than thirty years ago. He was an unpretending Christian . . . . and a very useful man in the church and in the world. These both have left families and a large circle of relatives mourn their loss.

And, my [the writer was Rev. A. S. Sloan] next door neighbor, Mrs. **Susan Askins**, in the 50th year of her age, very suddenly of typhoid fever.

Married in Fulton Co., Ark. by Rev. W. S. Moffatt, Mr. **John H. Peden** and Miss **Elizabeth Cochran** on the 11th of July, 1861.

--- on the 28th of January, 1862, by Rev. W. S. Moffatt, Mr. **J. C. Nisbett** and Miss **Fannie C. Cooper**, all of Fulton Co., Ark.

March 21, 1862

Died near Due West on the 19th instant, Mr. **James H. Haddon**, in the 54th year of his age. Mr. Haddon contracted this disease, typhoid fever, from nursing his son, lately deceased, on Sullivan's Island. ...For several years he had been a ruling elder in the A. R. congregation at Due West.

Married by Rev. D. F. Haddon on the 11th of March inst., Mr. **R. F. Bryson** and Miss **Josephine Haddon** of Due West.

<u>April 11, 1862</u>

Died of consumption at his residence in Lancaster District, March 11th, Mr. **James Faulkner**, in the 52nd year of his age. ... In his vocation he was a husbandman; but possessed a very considerable degree of mechanical ingenuity.

Died in Bowling Green, Ky., on the 3rd of February, Mr. **John Goins**, in the 27th year of his age. He was a member of Mount Zion congregation, Drew Co., Ark. ... A volunteer, he died in the service of his country.

Also, in Drew Co., Ark., March 2nd, Mrs. **Martha Lyles**, wife of Thomas Lyles; and then on the next day their son, **Franklin Lyles**. Mrs. Lyles was in her 42nd year; a member of Mount Zion. ... She leaves a mourning husband and a large family of children, many. ... Franklin was in his 19th year. A volunteer, he had just returned from the Potomac, having enlisted for the war. ... Thus two of our young men, elders' sons, have fallen in this unnatural war.

Died in great peace on the 12th ult., **Jane Bicket**, aged 77 years. ... [member of] Cedar Spring congregation.

Died of consumption in the hospital at Camp Pemberton on the 6th of January, **Robert G. McCrady**, son of Robert and Jane McCrady, in the 23rd year of his age. He was born and raised in Laurens District, S. C., and though of feeble constitution, he responded to his country's call, by volunteering in September last, in Company A, 13th Regiment.

<u>April 18, 1862</u>

Died at her residence in York District, S. C., Miss **Nancy Cathcart**, on the 28th of March, aged 40 years and 11 days. ...[since] 1845 a member of the A. R. Church of Tirzah, York District, S. C.

Died on the 6th of January, **James Franklin Barron**, infant son of J. L., and V. A. Barron. ... was about three months and 25 days old.

Married in Pope Co., Ark. on the 5th of March, 1862, by Rev. J. Patrick, Rev. **D. Kerr** and Miss **Nancy R. Oats**.

----also, by the same on the 11th of March, Mr. **Wm. A. Bell** and Miss **Margaret E. Dickey**.

<u>May 2, 1862</u>

Died in camp in Centreville, Va., February 23rd, of pneumonia, **David**

Hopkins, aged 33 years. He was born and raised in Pickens District, S. C....
He was a member of Company I, 4th Regiment, S. C. V., and was in the
memorable battle of Manassas Plains.

Died near Relf's Bluff, Drew Co., Ark. on the 15th of March, 1862, Mrs.
Sarah E. Brown, wife of Rev. J. M. Brown; disease, something like typhoid
pneumonia. She was just entering her 22nd year and the third of her marriage.

Married on the morning of Thursday the 24th of April by Dr. Boyce at the
house of Alexander Douglass, Fairfield District, Rev. **James H. Peoples** and
Miss **Margaret Douglass**.

May 9, 1862

Died at Savannah, Ga. on the 26th of February, 1862, **Andrew Gardner**,
son of William and Mary Gardner, in the 23rd year of his age. ... He was one of
the most exemplary members of Hopewell [Church]. He volunteered in the
"Henderson Company" to defend the coast. ... and fell victim to camp disease.

May 16, 1862

Died, April 22d, 1862, of typhoid fever, Mr. **James Faulkner**, aged about
70 years. The deceased had been for many years a member of the A. R. Church,
formerly at Bethany, York District, S. C. and lately at Little Steel Creek,
Mecklenburg, N. C. He has left an afflicted wife, two sons and three daughters.

Died in Crittendon Co., Ark. on the 15th of February, Mr. **William M.
Bigham**, in the 46th year of his age; he died of congestive chill.

Married, April 29, 1862, by Rev. J. C. Chalmers, Mr. **J. E. Caldwell** of
Mecklenburg Co. and **Miss E. J. Harris** of York District.

May 30, 1862

Died in Mecklenburg Co., N. C., March 31st, Mrs. **Martha**, wife of
Samuel **Black**, aged seventy five years and twenty days. She was a native of
eastern Va., but came a young orphan into North Carolina. ...[member of]
Gilead. ... She had lived with her husband for more than fifty six years.. ... Her
only child, a daughter, died in the bloom of her youth. Her place was, in part,
supplied by orphan children of others, to whom she proved to be a mother.

Died in Chimborizo Hospital, Richmond, Va., April 27th, 1862, **Hugh
Toland Renwick**, son of Col. J. S. and Mary Renwick, in the 19th year of
his age. His disease was pneumonia, in conjunction with measles.

June 6, 1862

Departed this life on the 14th of April near Starkville, Miss., Mr. **Joseph Valentine**, in the 35th year of his age. His disease was consumption. The subject of this notice was a worthy member of the Baptist church, and was united in marriage with a member of the Associate Reformed Presbyterian church.

On the 16th of April, Oktibbeha Co., Miss., Mr. **James Cooper**, aged about 20 years. His disease was contracted in the camp. ...was a member of a company known as "the Confederates." This company was first sent to Marion, Miss.; then to Savannah, Ga. and subsequently to Fernandina, Fla. At this station ...[he] lost his health.

June 13, 1862

Died at her residence in York District, S. C. on the 28th of April, Mrs. **Jane E. Miller**, wife of B. R. Miller, aged 31 years and 25 days. The subject of this notice was a consistent member of the A. R. church, her place of worship, Tirzah, York District, S. C. ...[She leaves] six small children. The youngest a babe five weeks old.

John, son of Wm. W. and Jane **McMorries** of Newberry, S. C. died in Confederate service near Richmond, Va., leaving a devoted wife and a motherless boy. ...It was four in the evening of the memorable first of June, that Johnny died with the roar of battle near by in his ear.

June 20, 1862

Died on the 7th of June, inst., an **infant** daughter of Robt. H. and Mary E. **Harris**, aged 4 months.

Mr. **William D. Stone** died on the 4th of June at his residence in Jefferson Co., Ga. He had been for about 20 years a ruling elder in Ebenezer Church, and will be remembered by many, who formed his acquaintance at Presbyteries and Synods, which he often attended as a delegate. ... he was a good son, husband, father, master, citizen, neighbor, church member, and elder. . . . He died from the effect of measles at the early age of about 51 years.

Died at Camp Mangum near Raleigh, 7th inst., Mr. **Wm. Cochran** , from the effect of measles. The deceased was a consistent member of the A. R. Church at Coddle Creek, Cabarrus Co., N. C., and having volunteered his services for the present struggle, he, in a few weeks, fell victim to disease at the camp of instruction. Another widow, and the fatherless children are thus added to the bereaved heartbroken throng.

Due West Telescope

Died in Mecklenburg Co., N. C. on the 12th of April, Mrs. **Margaret B. McLaughlin** in the seventy fourth year of her age. The deceased was connected in her early life with the G. A. P. church, but the principal number of her days were spent in the communion of the A. R. P. Church at Sardis. ... She leaves three sons, the Rev. I. G. , one of the number, all of whom have gathered around them families of their own.

In Mecklenburg Co., N. C. on the 8th of May, Mr. **Isaac Grier**, aged between forty five and fifty years. ... He died in connection with the A. R. P. Church at Back Creek. Mr. Grier leaves a widow and four sons--one, Rev. R. L., within the military lines of the enemy in Tennessee, and another in the army on the coast of his native state.

A mournful event has elicited our feelings. ... for the memory of Mrs. **Polly Clinkscales**, who departed this life the 13th of June, after a painful illness of some 10 weeks, at her son in law's--C. Ellis, in the upper part of Abbeville District. For more than thirty years, a consistent member of the Baptist church at Little River. ...[she died] at the advanced age of 74 years one month.

Died at the hospital in Yalabusha Co., Miss., May 21st, **William Hawthorn,** son of John and Nancy Hawthorn of Pickens Co., Ala. His disease was pneumonia. He had passed through the bloody scenes of the battle of Shiloh and escaped unhurt, but being naturally of delicate constitution, his health soon failed.

Died of typhoid pneumonia on the first of June in Richmond, Va., **F. M. McKee**, son of Wm. and Nancy McKee of Abbeville, S. C. He was just entering the twenty ninth year of his age. ... member of Methodist church. ... left a devoted wife and little daughter. ...He died in the Confederate service.

Died on the 5th inst., **Fannie I. Hinkley**, daughter of Charles and Josephine Hinkley of Frog Level, Newberry, S. C., aged 5 years.

Died in the Kent Paine & Co.'s Hospital, Richmond, June 6th, 1862, **E. A. Morrison**, aged 21 years and 3 months. Mr. Morrison was a soldier in the 4th N. C. Regiment, Company E. He died from a wound received by a grape shot in the hip in the battle on the 31st of May. He leaves an aged father, Mr. Hiram Morrison, Sr., and three brothers and a sister.

Died in Iredell Co., N. C., June 12th, 1862, **John P.**, infant son of Mr. and Mrs. Wm. **Fleming**, aged 1 year, 6 months and 22 days.

<u>July 11, 1862</u>

Another of the noble martyrs who has fallen in defence of his country's honor is the lamented **William H. Thompson,** son of Dr. Thomas H. Thompson of Newberry, S. C. "Willie"-- graduated very young at Erskine College. Soon after, he chose Physic as his profession and had been prosecuting its study for some time under his father, intending to make himself master of his profession by attending the best medical schools which his own country and France could command--but when the war broke out, he early enrolled himself as a private in the Quitman Rifles under Capt. Jas. Nance in the 3rd Regiment, S. C. V. Very soon he was connected with the medical department of the regiment where he continued at the post of duty to the very hour when he was struck by the fatal shell on the evening of the 18th of June, 1862 in a skirmish on the Chickahominey before Richmond. ... died the next morning having barely passed his twentieth birthday.

Died at Richmond, Va. on the 5th inst., **J. P. P. Barron** of York District, S. C., aged 18 years, 8 months and 25 days. ... on first volunteering, he connected himself with the Catawba Light Infantry, 5th Regiment, S. C. V. When the period for which his regiment entered the service expired, he re-volunteered and connected himself with the Jasper Light Infantry, Palmetto Sharp Shooters, Col. Jenkins the former col. of the 5th Regiment, S. C. V. Our young friend fought through the memorable battle of Manassas; he was in action on the bloody field of Williamsburg [where he suffered his fatal wound] ... member of the A. R. Church at Tirzah, York District, S. C.

Died in Bethel Church, Wilcox Co., Ala. on the evening of the 21st June ultimo., **Elizabeth Lorraine Miller**, daughter of Rev. John and Sarah Miller, in the 14th year of her age.

Clara, daughter of B. M. and Jenny **Blease**, died in Newberry, June 23d, after a short illness.

<u>July 25, 1862</u>

Killed on the battlefield, Richmond, Va. on the first of July, 1862, private **J. Willis** of Company C, 7th Regiment. He was in his 21st year at the time of his death. ... He went with the company to Charleston the 15th April, and . . . .he transferred his service to the Confederate States, and on the 4th of June, 1861, marched to Virginia where he remained up to the time of his death.

One of the most promising young men of the vicinity of Due West was **Willie Ellis**, son of Joseph Ellis. He was a smart boy, took a high stand in his class at Erskine College, where he had been a student for several years. But

160

answering to the call of his country, he volunteered in Orr's Regiment about a year ago. As a soldier he behaved himself nobly, but he sickened and died in Richmond on Monday the 14th inst. His father was with him in his last illness, which was no doubt a great comfort to him. Willis was buried in the soldiers' burying ground near Richmond, in the same grave as his friend and neighbor, Lieut. Latimer, it being found impossible to bring their bodies home at present.

Died at Richmond, Va., on Sabbath, the 13th July, inst., Lieut. **B. Milton Latimer**, of Company G, 1st Regiment Rifles, S. C. V. Lieut. Latimer was slightly wounded in the battle on Friday the 27th June, but died of fever. ... He has left a wife with one little child.

Killed in the battle of Gaines' Mill near Richmond, Va., June 27th, 1862, **Stephen J. McReum,** aged about 25 years. The deceased had been for several years a consistent member of the A. R. Church at Little Steel Creek, Mecklenburg Co., N. C. ...[He had] joined the 3rd, now known as the 13th Regiment, N. C. V.

Also, killed in the battle of Gaines' Mill near Richmond, Va., June 27th, 1862, **Samuel McCombs Grier**, oldest son of Maj. Z. A. Grier and member of 13th Regiment, N. C. V., in the 19th year of his age.

Died on the 27th of May, **James Meek**, son of Wm. and Rebecca **Wylie**, in the 12th year of his age.

On the evening of July 13th inst., (the Sabbath) at 4 o'clock, p. m., the remains of **Jabez P. Robinson**, 3rd Sergeant, Company C, 7th Regiment, S. C. V., was buried in the cemetery of his fathers. In the battle of 29th June (Sabbath) before Richmond, Sergeant Robinson fell mortally wounded, and died in a short time. ... [member of] church at Horeb (Baptist0.

On Tuesday, the 1st July, 1862, on the battle field near Richmond fell private **Samuel Knox** of Company C, 7th S. C. Regiment. He was shot through the head and died almost instantly. He was 24 years of age at the time of his death. Private Knox was a native of Ireland and emigrated to this country when quite young. ... He was among the first to rally to her [S. C.] standards. Together with the rest of his company, he transferred his services to the Confederate States the 4th of June, 1861, and was immediately sent to Virginia, where he remained at his post up to his death.

Died in the hospital at Richmond on the 9th inst., **Robt. M. Ellis** of the vicinity of Due West, and a member of Capt. Miller's company, 1st Regiment Rifles, S. C. V. Robert joined the regiment last spring and was made a member of the regimental band. He was a son of John E. Ellis, Esq., dec'd., was raised up in the A. R. church.

Died in Charlotte, N. C., July 15th, 1862 of congestion of the brain, **Willie Walkup**, son and only child of Dr. Jas. M. and Mrs. Eugenia A. **Miller**, aged two years, two months and four days.

August 15, 1862

Albert Ker Boyce, son of Mrs. Catherine Boyce and gandson of the late Chancellor Johnstone of Newberry, S. C., died in Richmond on the 10th July, in the 20th year of his age of a wound received in the bloody battle near Gaines' farm, on the 27th June.

Jas. D. McConnel, son of S. F. McConnel, Anderson District, S. C. died in the Winder Hospital Hospital, Richmond, on the 22nd of July. He was slightly wounded in the battle of Gaines' Mill, but had measurably recovered from the wound, and had obtained a furlough to return to the home for a few weeks when he was attacked with erysipelas from the effects of which he died. ... He was a member of Orr's Regiment. He joined the A. R. Church at Concord, Anderson District in his youth. He was about twenty three years old.

Died in Newton Co., Ga. on the 25th of June, 1862, Mrs. **Eliza Nesbit**, wife of Mr. Robert Nesbit, having recently entered her 63rd year.

Died at Meridian, Miss. on the 9th of June, 1862 of typhoid fever, Capt. **Joseph H. Cunningham** in the 37th year of his age. Capt. Cunningham was a native of Abbeville District, S. C. and died a member of the 19th Regt.

August 29, 1862

Died at his residence in Mecklenburg Co., N. C., August 9, 1862 of typhoid fever, Lieut. **C. B. Boyce**, eldest son of Rev. James Boyce and the late Mrs. Mary Ann Boyce of Fairfield District, S. C. in the 26th year of his age. The deceased was born September 13, 1836, graduated at Erskine College, Due West, S. C., August, 1858, and settled in Mecklenburg Co., N. C. in the spring of 1861, and in the ensuing fall was married to Miss Jane Mills, daughter of Maj. J. Y. Mills of Chester District, S. C. ... After serving his term of enlistment in Virginia as a private in the 1st Regt., S. C. V., he took an active part in raising a company for the 11th (known as Bethel) Regiment, N. C. V. in which he served as a Lieutenant until he contracted the fever which resulted in his death.

On Monday, July 14, 1862, Mrs. **Mary Jordan**, wife of Samuel Jordan, Esq., departed this life after four days sickness, aged 54 years, 5 months and 14 days. ... member ... Cedar Spring.

162

Departed this life on the 24th July, **John Pressly Brice**, aged 24 years and 7 months. ... He graduated in Erskine College about the year 1856, studied law, and settled in Washington, Ark., where he pursued his profession. He joined the army in March last, and served in the Artillery Department as 2nd Lieutenant in Fort Pillow. After a time he was ordered to Corinth, but falling sick, he returned to his father, William Brice, Fairfield District on the 4th June where he died on the 24th of July, of an affection of the lungs.

[Under the title]"Some of the Dead of Cedar Spring and Long Cane" by H. T. Sloan. In the great battle before Richmond, June 27th, **Hamilton Young** of Long Cane, Abbeville, S. C. was killed. ... though a wife and seven children were dependent on his exertions, he cheerfully offered himself with four brothers and joined Capt. Taggart's Company, 14th Regiment, S. C. V. Enjoying good health, he was ever at the post of duty and of danger, and fell while fighting with great bravery [Rev. Sloan was present at his funeral when he was buried by his four brothers].

But 'ere I left the scene, I looked across the vault, and there lay another, the body of **John A. Goodwin** (with two others, **Clark** and **Basset**), son of Samuel Goodwin, also of Long Cane. John was a nice young man of 18 summers, the last surviving son of his parents.

About the middle of July, **Thomas Fell**, the son of William Fell of Cedar Spring, Abbeville, S. C., died of fever at Lanterville Springs, Miss. ... He volunteered in Capt. Lites' Company, 19th Regiment, S. C. V. and went to Corinth. ... died in 28th year of his age. ... he has left a wife and two children.

September 5, 1862

Samuel R. Patterson, son of James Patterson and member of the A. R. Church at Ebenezer, Jefferson Co., Ga., was mortally wounded, died and was buried on the battle field before Richmond, Va. on the 1st July, 1862.

Samuel F. Boyd of Muscogee Co., Ga., son in law of Mrs. Mary Lowry of Jefferson County, died of fever at Savannah, Ga. on the 29th July, 1862. He belonged to the army at Savannah. ... left a wife and two little children.

Thomas B. Jordan, son of B. Jordan of Cedar Spring, Abbeville, S. C., died of typhoid fever in the hospital near Richmond, July 20th in the 35th year of his age. He volunteered in Capt. James M. Perrin's Company, Orr's Rifles.

September 12, 1862

Among the patriot martyrs. ... deserves to be recorded the name of Capt. **W.**

L. Hudgins, who died in the city of Charleston, July 2, 1862 in the 26th year of his age. When Port Royal fell and our state was menaced, he left his quiet home. ... at the time of the reorganization of Col. James' Battalion, to which he belonged, [he was] ... promoted to the rank of captain in Company C, in which he had enlisted as a private. Capt. Hudgins graduated at Erskine College in 1856, was admitted to the bar in 1858, and was married to Miss Eliza C. Klugh of Cokesbury, S. C. in 1859

Died at New Madrid, Mo. the 15th of April, **Harris Jones** in the 17th year of his age. ... one of the promising young men of the Bethel Church, Wilcox Co., Ala. He belonged to the 1st Regiment of Alabama, and was taken prisoner at Island No. 10 on the 8th of April. On the following day, he was violently attacked with pneumonia, and died in the hands of the enemy.

Died in the Army of Virginia near the Petersburg & Richmond Railroad, **Charles Fox**, in the 19th year of his age. Another one of the noble youth whom Bethel Church, Ala. has given to the cause of Southern Independence.

Died in Mecklenburg Co., N. C., March 28th, 1862 of erysipelas, Gen. **Wm. Allen**, aged 77 years, 8 months and 7 days. ...[member and] ruling elder of Prosperity Church.

Also, at the residence of the above, April 18th, **Sarah Allen**, aged 79 years, 2 months and 8 days. The decease of her brother was the occasion for her being in his house, little thinking that when going, she was going there to die. ... member of Back Creek.

Died at Lynchburg, Va. of disease unknown, May 23d, private **Hugh E. McAuley** of Company --, 37th Regiment, N. C. Troops; aged 24 years, 3 months and 4 days. ... He was in the battle near Newbern. After going to Virginia, his health, still affected by measles, failed. .. in him, Gilead has lost a promising member.

When the history of this war is written, many noble names will be recorded as its victims. Among these will be that of **Jos. H. Chalmers** of Newberry, S. C. He fell June 27th in a charge on the enemy's battery near Gaines' Mill, pierced through the breast by a ball. ... He was a member of Company B, 1st Regiment, S. C. V.

Died on the 12th of August, **Nancy Bell Miller**, daughter of B. R. and E. J. Miller, aged 2 years, 3 months and 12 days.

Also, on the 16th of June ult., **Martha Adelaide Eugenia Barron**, daughter of J. L. and Amanda Barron, aged nine years, one month and two days.

Due West Telescope

Died of a wound received in his breast in the late battle of Manassas, **James Monroe McCaslan**, son of James and Margaret McCaslan of Abbeville District, S. C. Near fifteen months ago, he volunteered in Capt. Perrin's Company, Col. Orr's 1st Rifle Regiment. . . . Monroe was a graduate of Davidson College, a pious and consistent member of the Presbyterian Church at Hopewell. ... he has fallen at the early age of 22 years.

Died at the house of his father, Chester District, S. C. on the 28th of June last, **John S. Hamilton**, in the 19th year of his age. In obedience to the call of his country, he volunteered in her defence, and repaired to camp in the vicinity of Charleston, where he served with fidelity and zeal, till stricken down by camp fever. . . . member of the church at Union.

Also, at College Hospital at Columbia, S. C. on the 27th August, **James H. Hamilton**, only brother of the above, and with the same disease, in the 29th year of his age. ... consistent member of Union Church.

David Pressly Wilbanks departed this life on the 27th March, 1862 at Corinth, Miss., aged thirty four years, nine months and five days. ... left an affectionate wife and three loving children. Though he died not on the battle field by the deadly missile of the enemy, yet his death was nonetheless glorious.

Killed in the battle of Sharpsburg, Maryland on the 17th September, 1862, Adjutant **Thomas M. Chiles** in the 24th year of his age. Adjt. Chiles was a graduate of Erskine College in the Class of '58. After graduation, he taught school a year, and then commenced the study of medicine; he was attending his first course of lectures in Nashville, Tenn., when South Carolina seceded, he immediately came home and joined a company of minutemen then organized in the neighborhood. ... He was a sergeant in Company C. ...[and] at the organization of the 7th Regt. he was appointed Adjutant. ... He received a wound in the mouth in storming the Maryland Heights on the 13th September, early on the morning of the 17th, and fought till about noon, when he was struck on the forehead and immediately expired.

Departed this life in the hospital at Warrenton, Va. on the 14th of September, Lieut. **J. Hemphill Bigham**, in the 26th year of his age. The deceased was wounded in the battle of Manassas on 30th of August. His wound was not thought to be mortal; but after being removed to the hospital he was attacked with erysipelas. ... After receiving his wound, by some means, he fell into the hands of the enemy, who kept him a day or two. He was then retaken by the Confederates and placed in a hospital. He said his wound was dressed, and he was otherwise tenderly cared for while in the hands of the enemy. ... member of the A. R. P. Church at Sharon, York District, S. C.

Died in Spartanburg District, August 27th, of putrid sore throat, **Laura Antoinette**, daughter of Elbert D. and Sarah A. **Anderson**, aged 2 years, 4 months and 7 days.

October 17, 1862

Rev. H. T. Sloan, "More of Cedar Spring and Long Cane's Dead"- **Abner P. Young**, a member of Capt. Taggart's company, 14th Regiment, S. C. V., was killed on Friday evening, August 29th in the battle of Manassas in the 33d year of his age, leaving a young wife and one child, a sister, three brothers in the army [with one already killed] ... consistent member of Long Cane Church.

John Bradley, son of Archibald Bradley, also fell on Monday evening following near Centreville on the 1st of September, a member of the same company and regiment. ..[also] a member of Long Cane Church. He died at the age of 36 years, leaving an interesting wife and four daughters.

James Kennedy, the son of Mrs. Sarah Kennedy, also deserves notice. ... though "Jimmy" had scarcely attained to 17 years when his country called, he nobly volunteered with the first, a member of Capt. P. H. Bradley's company. ...[served] until the memorable 17th of September, near Sharpsburg, Maryland where he fell mortally wounded and expired by the next day.

Francis Marion Beattie died in Scottsville, Va., 5th August, 1862. He was a volunteer from N. C., and with his regiment was in the battles of Williamsburg and Seven Pines and escapted unhurt, but fell at last by disease. ... Mr. Beattie was decently buried in Scottsville, Va.

Died in Richmond, Va., **Thomas O. Crawford**, on the 26th July, 1862, in the 38th year of his age. He was a volunteer and was wounded in the battle near Richmond. ... He was a member of Pisgah A. R. Church, Gaston, N. C.

About the same time and in the same hospital, **Wilson Love**, a promising young man, died of wounds received in the Richmond battle. He was elected to the office of ruling elder in Pisgah. ... leaves a wife and two children.

Died at home in bed and surrounded by her friends, Mrs. **Margaret Montgomery Carson**. Born near Landsford in Chester, daughter of James Montgomery, elder in Neely's Creek, who with his family moved to Crowder's Mt. in the latter part of the last century. She was married to James Carson who died thirty years ago. ... She was confined at home near 20 years before her death, which took place August 10, 1862.

Robert G. White, son of Gardiner White of Chester District, S. C., fell in the late battle of Manassas Plains in the 24th year of his age. He was a member of the "Chester Greys," 23d S. C. Regiment. ...[member] of A. R. Church at Hopewell.

October 24, 1862

J. Adolphus White, son of Col. White, Alexander, N. C., after passing through the battle of Manassas, was shot Monday evening, September 2d in the battle of Germantown, and died the next morning. Adolphus volunteered for the war in Capt. Peoples' Company and assisted in forming it in the Spring of '61. Was in the battles of Newbern, Hanover, and Richmond. In the latter he was slightly wounded. ... he had just passed his twentieth year.

Died in Alexander Co., N. C. of diptheria, Wednesday evening, September 3rd, **Margaret E. F.**, oldest child of Mr. Junius **Morrison**; Thursday morning after, **John Sidney A.**, youngest child of the same.

Died near Richmond, July 7th, 1862, **A. D. Campbell**, aged 19 years, three weeks and 2 days. He was a native of Anderson District, S. C. He was a member of Company D., Capt. Harrison, Orr's 1st Regiment Rifles, S. C. V., and was one of the many sons of the South who fell on the 27th June. He was pierced by no less than three well sent missles.

October 31, 1862

Died at the Belmont Hospital near Livingston, Va. on the 11th August, Mr. **John Anderson, Jr.**, in the 44th year of his age. Mr. Anderson died of fever contracted in the military service of his country. ... elder in Church at Ebenezer.

Among the many worthy sons of the South who have falled ....[was] **W. Oliver Moore**, son of J. J. and Elizabeth Moore of Dallas Co., Ala. He fell at the battle of Seven Pines on the 31st May in the 29th year of his age.

William Patterson, Senr..died in Burke Co., Ga. on the 21st of September, 1862. Born in May, 1776, he saw the beginning and the division of the great American Republic. ...[member] of Bethel.

November 7, 1862

Died in York District, S. C., October 3, 1862 of typhoid fever, **Emma Rose**, eldest daughter of H. C. and Jane **Harris**, aged 18 years and seven days. She was taken sick at High Point, N. C. . . . . consistent member of the A. R. Church at Lower Steel Creek, York District. S. C.

Due West Telescope

Died in Camp Butler, Chicago, Illinois, the 28th August, **William T. Newbury**, aged 18 years and six month, another one of that noble band of youth, whom Bethel church, Oak Hill, Ala. has sent out in defence of our invaded country, "Willie," volunteered in the Wilcox "True Blues," Company B, 1st Regiment, about the commencement of the year. The regiment had been in defence of Penscola, but last spring were ordered to Isle No. 10 where, they fell into the hands of the enemy.

Also, at home, Oak Hill, Ala., on the 26th October, **James N. Dale** in the 24th year of his age. This is the fifth young man Bethel Church has lost . . . like his comrade in arms, whose death is recorded above, he was taken prisoner on Isle No. 10, and for seven weary months was confined at Chicago, Camp Butler. Under the confinement, his health gave way, and when exchanged at Vicksburg, he was ordered to the hospital at Lauderdale Springs, Miss.

Died near Hillsboro, Union Co., Ark. on the 27th September, 1862, **Elenor Anna Evangeline,** daughter of Andrew and Mary J. **McMillen** in the sixth year of her age.

Departed this life, June 24th, 1862, at the Chimborozo Hospital, Richmond, Va. in the triumph of Christian faith, Private **William Thomas Miller**, son of M. T. and L. E. Miller and member of Company K, 17th Mississippi Volunteers. He was a member of the M. E. Church, South at Pine Grove Society, Coffeeville Circuit, Memphis Conference. He volunteered about the 1st of May, 1861

Died at Warrenton, Va., October 5th, Lieut. **John W. Baird** in the 32nd year of his age. He was born and partly raised in Chester District, S. C. His parents moved to Tipton Co., Tenn. where he received his academic education, after which he repaired to Erskine College where he graduated in 1855. He then repaired to Miami University, Ohio, where he prosecuted his studies further, particularly the mathematics, for which he had a great aptitude and taste.
Having selected teaching as his profession, he travelled through the North, examining their system with a view of perfecting himself in the theory and practice of profession.
On his return South, he taught for some time in Alabama. When elected to take charge of the Male Academy of Chesterville, he returned to his native state, where he had been successfully employed as principal of the above academy until the breaking out of the war.
Having married Miss Sarah Simpson of Chesterville, in the meantime, he

engaged in his calling with fair prospect of usefulness in that location. But when the young men of our country were summoned to the tented field, he volunteered, and during last spring and summer was in the battle of Manassas, where he was severely wounded in the ankle. Hopes were entertained of his recovery, but typhoid fever supervening, he died on the 5th of October. ... Ruling elder of Union congregation. .. he leaves a wife and two children.

S. T. H. Williams was born August 11, 1822, and died at his residence near Laurensville, S. C., October 19, 1862.... After receiving a preparatory training in the Laurensville Academy, he entered Erskine College, Abbeville District. ... he graduated in 1848 [and] .... soon after leaving college, he engaged in the study of law, which he successfully prosecuted, after admission to the bar. He commenced the practice of his profession at Laurensville... In 1857, he married Miss Williams of Newberry.

Another son of Cedar Spring Church has fallen a victim to this cruel and relentless war. **James M. Purdy** died at Danville, Ky. of typhoid pneumonia in the 23d year of his age. He was a member of Capt. White's Company, 19th Regiment, S. C. V. (Col. Lythgoe), had encountered the trials and hardships of the Western campaign and borne up under the long and wasting march of Bragg's army into Kentucky, but was taken sick and sent back to Danville, where he died among strangers, but with only about ten days of sickness, on the 30th of September, 1862. He has left a young and most affectionate wife and tender babe.

Died at Germantown, near Memphis, on the 10th of May, **Robert Bryson**, in the 39th year of his age. The deceased was born and raised in Laurens District, S. C., and emigrated with his little family several years ago to Arkansas, [former member of] A. R. Church at Providence, Laurens, S. C. ... leaves a bereaved widow, an aged father and mother, five brothers and five sisters.

December 5, 1862

"Many soldiers are daily going to their final resting place...." Such was the fate of **Joseph D. Oates**, a native of North Carolina. He moved in 1850 to Pope Co., Ark., where he has ever since resided, until the breaking out of the present war. ... He volunteered his services in March, 1862 to the Confederate States, and in April was ordered to Corinth. He was in the memorable retreat of the Western army from Corinth to Tupelo, Miss., and in the retreat he contracted the malignant typhoid fever, which finally carried him to the grave. ... member of A. R. Church. ... He leaves a wife and two small children.

Mrs. **Agnes Gordon** died at the house of her son in law in Jefferson Co., Ga. on the 4th of September, 1862... She had been a member of the Church at Ebenezer, seventy two years.

Miss **Margaret Burke** of Jefferson Co., Ga., an exemplary mother of the Church at Ebenezer, Ga., died at the residence of a friend in Twiggs Co. on the 31st October, 1862.

Departed this life on 22d November, **Samuel Mitchel**, in the 61st year of his age. The disease of which he died was pneumonia of which he was sick about one week. The deceased was a native of Abbeville District, born in the heart of that section known as the "Flatwoods," near which spot he spent the larger portion of his life. About the year 1843, for the more successful prosecution of the mercantile business, in which he was engaged, he located at Lowndesville, where he spent his remaining days. ... He leaves a wife to mourn him.

Died, November 11, 1862 in Mecklenburg Co., N. C. of chronic dysentery, **Samuel C. Youngblood**, in the 31st year of his age, leaving a wife and two little children. He was among the first in his neighborhood who volunteered in the Confederate service; was a member of the Randalsburg Company in the 3d, formerly, but now the 13th N. C. Volunteers. He was on "the sick list" at the time of the evacuation of Yorktown, and the fight at Williamsburg last summer, and in making his escape from the latter place was lost for nearly a week, during which time he suffered many hardships, from hunger, exposure and fatigue. Whilst yet feeble, he rejoined his company and participated in battles near Richmond, but soon afterwards fell a victim to the disease which terminated in his death.

December 19, 1862

Hannah Elizabeth Nelson, after a brief illness, died on the 13th of November at the residence of her uncle, Col. John McKenny, Rockbridge Co., Va. She was in her 18th year.

Departed this life in the Banner Hospital, Richmond, Va. on the 24th of July, **James H. Young**. ... The subject of this obituary was born in Abbeville District, and with his parents, emigrated to the West about the year 1843. From Mississippi, the state of their adoption, he returned to his native district and completed his academic and collegiate education. He graduated in Erskine College in the Class of 1856. Having returned to his adopted state, and resumed his place in the midst of friends, he was quietly and usefully employed in pursuits congenial to his taste, until the commencement of the war in 1861. He was among those who responded to the first call for volunteers made for the Confederate Government. ... As a private, in the 14th Miss. Regt., he went to the State of Virginia. ... He was in Gen Joseph E. Johnston's army at Harper's Ferry, Winchester and Manassas--in the memorable retreat from Manassas and Yorktown--in the detachment sent to re-inforce Gen. Jackson's army at Gordonsville previous to the great battle of Richmond--and under Gen. Jackson in the flank movement upon McClellan's army on the ever memorable 27th of June. It fell to his lot to participate in one of the first charges upon the enemy, in which he fell. Although not apparently mortally wounded, yet for want of necessary surgical attention, his life was added to the costly sacrifice for our country's independence.

It becomes my painful duty to record the death of **William Gibson**, ruling elder in Cedar Spring and Long Cane congregation. Mr. Gibson, at his country's call, buckled on his armor and repaired to the Coast--member of Dr. J. W. Hearst's Company. In one week he was attacked with pneumonia, and returned home on furlough, and in four days after closed his eyes on all things terrestial. .. He leaves a bereaved widow and aged mother.

February 13, 1863

Died in York District, S. C. on the 23rd of January, **Thomas L. Castles**, in the 31st year of his age. He entered the service of his country last spring, and was a member of the 13th Regiment, S. C. V. He was in the battles before Richmond and Manassas, and though escaped unhurt, yet he was seized with diarrhea and was furloughed home.... member of Smyrna Church.

Louisa Emily, oldest daughter of Thomas and Frances C. **McConnell**, departed this life in Franklin Co., Ga. in January 12, 1863, aged seventeen years and one months.

On the 2d of December, 1862, **Alex Evans McConnell**, brother of Louisa, died of the same disease (diptheria), aged 2 years, nine months and twenty days.

Departed this life on the 8th of January, **infant** daughter of J. G. and E. **Lowry.**

May 15, 1863

Samuel P. McGaw died of chronic diarrhea, Lynchburg, Va., December 10, 1862, in the 21st year of his age. He was a member of Company B, Capt. Jas. M. Perrin's, Orr's Rifle Regiment.

James Wilson, a member of the 7th S. C. Regiment, died of pneumonia, Chimborozo Hospital, Richmond, Va., after a short illness. He joined the Church at Cedar Spring a number of years ago, but for a time did not walk as becometh the Gospel, but camp life seems to have been greatly sanctified to his soul. ... he wished to have his children baptized. ... His wife now mourns in solitude with five children.

Robert Samuel and **William**, children of Walter **Richey**, died of scarlet fever, April 25th and 28th.

Died of on the 26th of March, **Fannie E. Jolly**, aged fifteen years, five months and sixteen days. She was the youngest child of James and Nancy Jolly.

Died of apoplexy on the 27th of April, 1863, **James Jolly**, aged fifty seven years, ten months and fourteen days. ... left a sickly companion, two sons and three daughters.

Died of congestion of the brain in Decatur, Ga., on April 20, 1863, **Willie**, son of Dr. D. W. **Reid**. ... aged six years and seven months.

Died of diptheria in Elbert Co., Ga. on the 12th April, 1863, **Luther Mason**, son of L. W. H. and M. J. **McAlister**, aged 3 years, 7 months and 15 days.

June 19, 1863

James S. Wilson, son of Capt. John R. and Mrs. Mary Wilson, was killed at the battle of Chancellorsville, Va. on the morning of the 3d of May, 1863. James was born on the 6th of September, 1841 in Abbeville District, near the village of Due West. . . .Whilst he was a member of the Junior Class in Erskine College. . . he volunteered in January and entered the service on the 15th April, 1861 as a private in Company B, 7th Regt., S. C. V. He was with this regiment in its camps of instruction near Charleston and Aiken, S. C., in its passage to Virginia, in its march to Fairfax C. H., in its perilous retreat in the face of an overwhelming army back to the plains of Manassas. After the bloody battle and rout of the 21st of July, he was with the regiment in its advance to Vienna far ahead of the main army. . .[illness brought discharge in April or May, 1862, but after regaining his health], In February, 1863, he attached himself to Company G, 1st Regiment Rifles, S. C. V., then lying near Fredericksburg, Va. In this regiment, he faithfully discharged the duties of a soldier until the recent bloody battle of Chancellorsville on the morning of the 3d of May (the day of the battle), he was on the roster for detached or rear duty; but being anxious to meet the foes of his country, by permission of his gallant captain, he exchanged place with another, and with his Bible in his bosom plunged into the thickest of the strife. About 8 o'clock, a. m., he received a ball in his left breast. He fell and expired in a moment.

Of those who fell on the late bloody field of Chancellorsville, Va., the name of Capt. **William Jennings Kerr** deserves honorable mention. He was the eldest son of J. B. and A. J. Kerr of Charlotte, N. C. A young lawyer of much promise and noble aspirations, and the subject of many fond hopes and fervent prayers. Having graduated at Erskine College in the Class of 1854, for a time, he seriously contemplated devoting himself to the work of the holy ministry; but fearing he might not be called to that sacred office, selected the legal profession, believing that it was not incompatible with a life of Christian integrity and a holy walk with God. ...[studied law with Judge Pearson and entered practice until the outbreak of war when] He and two others raised the first Company "for the war" in old Mecklenburg. His regiment served on the Coast, repaired in the spring of '62 for Virginia, and shared in the battle before Richmond, where he was severely wounded--recovering, he hastened to his command at Winchester, was twice struck in the first battle of Fredericksburg, but was reserved to share in the thickest of the fight at Chancellorsville, where he received the fatal shot Sabbath morning, while standing on the enemies' breast works, cheering his men on to victory.

Among the many who fell on the battlefield of Chancellorsville was **James Meredith** (ordinarily known as "Mitty") **Witherspoon**. His thigh was broken by a musket ball, as his regiment was charging a battery on Sabbath, the 3d of May. His remains were brought on by Rev. J. H. Simpson and committed to the care of friends, who had them interred at New Hope, Fairfield District, on Sabbath, 24th of May. "Mitty" was the son of the late Rev. John G. Witherspoon and the stepson of the Rev. J. Boyce. He joined the N. C. T. in May of last year, was engaged in the conflicts before Richmond, marched to Maryland, fought at Boonesboro' and Sharpsburg, was at the Fredericksburg engagement last winter, but fell at last at Chancellorsville, having been in seven battles, aged 19 years and about 3 weeks. A brother, a sister, a mother [survive].

Died in the field hospital near Chancellorsville, Va. on the 7th of May, Orderly Sergeant **Robert Morrison Caldwell** of the 7th Regiment, N. C. Troops, aged 27 years. He had participated in nearly every battle in Virginia since the battles before Richmond. . . .following his heroic leader, Jackson, in all his famed marches and thoughout the memorable Maryland campaign, and had escaped unhurt until the sanguinary battle of the 3d of May near Chancellorsville, where he received a mortal wound. . . . member of the G. A. Presbyterian Church at Rocky River, Cabarrus Co., N. C.

Mrs. **Margaret Smith** of Little River, Fairfield District, is now among the dead. She departed this life on the morning of Friday the 5th of June, 1863 in the house of her son in law Henry Steele near Monticello. She was rising her 77th year, having attained to her 76th on the 26th of May last. She was raised up in connection with the "Brick Church" (Associate Reformed) and continued a member until 1844 when she joined Jackson's Creek. She was a half-sister to John A. Martin.

Died at Newberry, S. C., May 2d, 1863, Mrs. **Mary Graham**, daughter of William and Elizabeth Fair.

Died of Cholera infantum, May 28th, 1863, **Mattie McClure**, a daughter of Rev. M. and Mrs. A. S. **Oates**, aged 1 year and 11 months.

Married at Greenwood, Abbeville District, on the 10th instant by Rev. Mr. Lawton, Mr. **Thos. W. Coogler** of Columbia, S. C. to Miss **Fannie D. Wilson** of the former place.

June 26, 1863

Died at the residence of her son in law, Rev. R. W. Brice on --ult., Mrs. **Jane Cunnigham Steel**, relict of Rev. John Steel, late of Ohio, in the 79th year of her age. She was born in Augusta Co., Va. on the 19th of February, 1785 and married Rev. John Steel at Jessamine Co., Ky., April 22, 1807. A few years since she came to Chester District, S. C. to reside with her daughter and son in law. She has left three sons, two of whom are in the ministry, and a daughter.

The subject of this memoir, Private **John N. Wright** of Capt. J. K. G. Nance's Company E of the 3d S. C. Regiment, and son of Robert C. and Margaret Ann Wright, was born on the 27th day of September, 1843, and mortally wounded in the bloody battle of Sharpsburg, Md. on the 17th of September, 1862.

Died at Camp Winder, Richmond, Va. on the 20th of May, 1863, **William Bradley** in the 28th year of his age. On the 11th of January, 1861, he voluntered as a private in Company C, 7th S. C. Regiment. . . . He passed through nearly all the important battles in Virginia without injury, until the battle of Chancellorsville; early in the day on Sabbath, the 3d of May, he was shot though the right breast. He was removed from the battlefield to Richmond, where he lingered on until the 20th . . . His remains were brought home by his faithful servant Andy, and were buried in the churchyard at Long Cane.

Died, 5th inst., Miss **P. P. Haddon**, daughter of Mr. Z. and Mrs. P. A. Haddon, in the 20th year of her age.

September 11, 1863

Died 9th of July of a wound received in the battle of Gettysburg, Pa., Lieut. **Wm. A. Brownlee** of Company H, 16th Ala. Regiment. He was gallantly discharging his duty in command of his company when he fell. Being left upon the field, he fell into the hands of the enemy by whom he was kindly treated. . . . He entered the service at the early part of the war, dropping his studies in College. . . . son of G. H. and M. Brownlee of Calhoun C., Ala., was 23 years old.

Death has claimed another victim, **W. C. Butler** of 3d S. C. Regiment was killed near Gettysburg, Pa, July 2d in his 22nd year of age.

Died August 11, 1863, **James Robert**, son of J. M. and Margaret **Whitesides**, aged about two years.

Also, died August 12, 1863, **John Thomas**, son of Moses and Martha S. **White**, aged 11 months and 12 days.

Married on the 3d inst. by Rev. J. E. Pressly at the parsonage in Cabarrus Co., N. C., Mr. **H. P. Helper** of Davidson College and Miss **Mattie McGaw** of Abbeville District, S. C.

-- on the 2d by the same, Mr. **Samuel A. Sims** and Miss **Sarah E. Andrew** of Cabarrus Co., N. C.

October 23, 1863

John C. Martin, Company C, 7th S. C. V., died at Petersburg, Va. on Sabbath, October 4, 1863 of wounds received at Gettysburg, Pa. and chronic diarrhea, being 26 years old. . . . He fell into the hands of the enemy and was carried to Devil's Island, N. Y. After a time he was sent back, reached Petersburg, lingered for a time and died. . . . He was a member of the A. R. Church at Cedar Spring.

Died in Winston Co., Miss. of congestion of the stomach and bowels, **Joseph D. Reid**, son of Dr. D. H. and Mary Q. Reid, on the 5th of August, aged 5 years, 8 months and 2 days.

November 20, 1863

T. M. McElwee, after completing his studies at Erskine College, set out for the far West in quest of some new and open field of usefulness in the latter part of 1859. The following year and till 18th July, 1861, he spent in teaching in Texas and Arkansas, at which date he volunteered in the C. S. army--marched to Memphis, and then New Madrid, and Island No. 10. When that place fell into the hands of the enemy in the spring of 1862, he was sick and made a captive when he was too far spent to know his unhappy lot. He was moved to New Madrid, Missouri, where he died in the hands of the enemy, 22nd April, 1862, and was buried by a fellow captive.

Index

Laura, 36
Berry, Dr. John, 57
  Dr. Joseph, 43
Betts, Rev. C. B., 71, 75, 78, 90,
  114, 117, 124, 131, 136, 138
Bicket, Jane, 156
Bigby, Alcippe Eugenia, 106
Bigham infant, 11
  J. Hemphill, 165-166
  James, 14
  Jane, 11
  Jas., 129
  Mary, 128, 131
  Robert Grier, 131
  Sarah L., 20
  Thos. G., 11
  William M., 20, 131, 157
Billard, Kitty, 134
Bishop, Rev. R. H., 36
Bivins, Rev. Dr., 117
Black, James H., 39
  Joseph, 39
  Judith F., 91
  Martha, 39, 157
  Samuel, 157
Blackstock, Rev., 3, 38, 70, 119, 127
Blackwood, Elmina Jane, 77
Blain, Mrs., 136
  Mariah, 136
  Narcissa, 72
  Stirling (Sterling) W., 88, 131
Blair, Hamilton, 57
  John, Esq., 27, 57, 126, 133
  Margaret, 57
  Nancy, 133
Blakely, David, 50
  Judith, 50
Blease, Basil M., 56, 160
  Clara, 160
  Elizabeth V., 56
  Harriet Bethany, 56
  Jenny, 160
Blight, Clara A., 112
Boggs, Rev. D. C., 76
Bolles, Rev. E. A., 116

Eusebia Bachman, 116
  Harriet A., 116
Bolton, J. L., 139
Bonds, Miss, 92
  Robt., Esq., 137
Bonner, Florence C., 54
  Rev. J. I., 75, 92, 106, 112,
    120, 126, 132, 142
  James, 82
  Dr. Joseph H., 54
  Margaret, 82
  Mary P., 82
  Sarah, 54
  William, 17
Boozer, E. P., 98
  F. L., 98
  William P., 98
Boswell, Esq., 139
Bothwell, Rev., 23
Bouchillon, J. L., 48
  Susan J., 48
Bowen, Mr., 51
Boyce, Albert Ker, 162
  Catherine, 162
  Charles B., 152, 162
  Clementia, 1
  Deborah, 8
  Rev. E. E., 44, 59, 66, 100,
    131, 140, 150, 152
  Elam B., 4
  Emeline, 73, 131
  Gardiner Springs, 131
  Hugh, 130
  Rev. J. K., 55
  Rev. James, 23, 31, 51, 59, 88,
    152, 157, 162, 173
  John, 14
  John McElwee, 131
  Laura Jane, 73
  Lorenna Caroline, 131
  Margaret Jane, 44
  Mary Ann, 23, 162
  Mary G., 4
  R. Deborah, 130
  R. E., 131

Index

Index

Index

Index

Index

Index

Index

Index

Index

Index

Index

Henry, 10
Kilpatrick, Isabella, 4
  Mat, 117
  Thomas, 4, 24
  Thomas D., 80
King, Martha, 89
Kinnear, Andrew, Esq., 89
  Joseph, Esq., 89
Kirk, Adaline S., 120
  Wm. A., 85, 90
Kistler, Esther, 143
Klugh, Carrie, 111
  Eliza C., 164
Knox, James, 21
  Nathaniel, 114
  Robert, 138
  Sam W., 108
  Samuel, 161
  Sarah, 88
  Wm., 88
Kown, Thomas, 9
Lacey, Rev. Drury, 66
Lackey, Hannah E., 44
  Isaac, 130
  Thomas, 39
Lama, Elizabeth, 33
  James, 33
Lancaster, Charles A., 123
  Margaret, 123
  Margaret Ann, 123
Land, Elizabeth, 35
  Francis, 33
Langely, Martha, 135
Lanneau, Rev. Basel, 98
Lathan, David, Esq., 3
  J. P., Esq., 67
  Jane, 97
  John, 30
  Rev. R., 100, 107
  Samuel, 97
  William B., 67-68
Latimer, B. Milton, 97, 161
Lawton, Rev., 173
Leazar, Julia C., 107
Lee, Rev. Mr., 118

Rev. T. S., 51, 112
Leland, Rev. A. W., 112
Lemon, David, 68
  Letitia Jane, 68
  Martha J., 68
  Mary Ann, 68
Leonard, Margaret E., 127
Leslie, Jane, 97
  Mary Martha Alice, 97
  N. M., 97
Lessly, A. P., 11
Lester, A. H., 65
  Margaret C., 65
Letcher, M. E., 52
Lewis, Eleanor J. G., 26
  Sarah Elizabeth, 26
  Wade W., 70
  William A., 26
Lind, Robert C. S., 104
Lindsay, Caroline, 102
  Cornelius E., 17
  E. E., 150
  Henry L., 17
  Rev. J. O., 121, 127
  James, 17
  James, Esq., 71
  Jane, 140
  John Lafayette, 9
  John Thomas, 102
  Joseph, 57, 137
  Joseph C., 9
  Polly Ann, 17
  Sarah, 9
  Thomas N., 102
  William, 71
Linn, John, 78
  Sarah, 78
Lipford, Jas., Esq., 120
  M. F., 73
Little, Annie E., 120
  Archibald, 8
  George, Esq., 89
  Jane, 8
  R. P., 119
Livingston, J. Fraser, 76

Index

Index

Index

Index

Index

197

Index

Index

Index

Index

Index

Index

www.ingramcontent.com/pod-product-compliance
Lightning Source LLC
Chambersburg PA
CBHW070910270326
41927CB00011B/2520